tear here

The Complete Idiot's Reference Card

Mysterious Artifacts and

Garden of Eden. Location unknown.

Tower of Babel. Source of the many languages sp have been located in Iraq.

Noah's Ark. Undiscovered, on Mt. Ararat or elsewhere.

The Ark of the Covenant. Location unknown.

The Holy Grail. Cup Jesus used during the Last Supper; location unknown.

Mt. Sinai. Site where Moses received the Ten Commandments; location in question.

Ten Lost Tribes of Israel. Whereabouts unknown.

Temple in Jerusalem. Temple destroyed, exact location disputed.

The Shroud of Turin. Actual burial shroud of Jesus?

Dead Sea Scrolls. Texts found this century that throw light on the religious world during the time of Jesus; monopoly controlling access to them has been busted, and the documents continue to be scrutinized.

Armageddon. Site of Megiddo in Israel, where the apocalyptic war between good and evil is supposed to take place. Battle yet to occur.

The Ten Plagues of the Exodus

1. The Nile turned to blood
2. Frogs
3. Gnats
4. Flies
5. Livestock affliction
6. Boils
7. Hail
8. Locusts
9. Darkness
10. Death of the firstborn

The Miracles of Jesus

The New Testament describes many miracles performed by Jesus. Check these out.

Healing

Matthew 8:1–4
Matthew 8:5–13
Matthew 8:14–15
Matthew 9:1–8
Matthew 9:20–22
Matthew 9:27–30
Matthew 12:10–13
Matthew 15:30–31
Matthew 20:30–34
Matthew 21:14
Mark 7:31–35
Mark 8:22–26
Luke 13:11–13
Luke 14:1–4
Luke 17:11–19
Luke 22:50–51
John 4:46–54
John 5:2–9
John 9:1–7

Driving out Demons

Matthew 8:16
Matthew 8:28–34
Matthew 9:32–33
Matthew 12:22
Matthew 15:22–28
Matthew 17:14–18
Luke 4:33–36

Raising from the Dead

Matthew 9:23–25
Luke 7:11–15
John 11:41–44

Food

Matthew 14:15–21
Matthew 15:32–39
Matthew 17:24–27
Luke 5:4–11
John 21:3–11

Water and Weather

Matthew 8:23–27
Matthew 14:25
Matthew 14:28–31

Others

Matthew 21:19. A tree is cursed and withers.
Luke 4:29–30. Jesus breezes through a crowd.
John 2:1–11. Jesus turns water into wine.

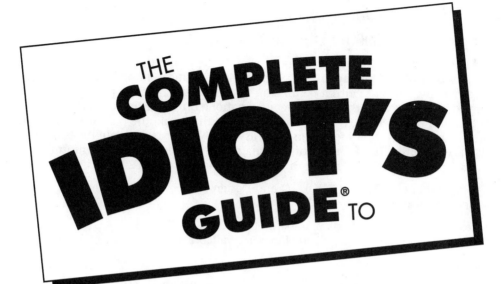

THE COMPLETE IDIOT'S GUIDE® TO

Biblical Mysteries

by Donald P. Ryan, Ph.D.

ALPHA
A Pearson Education Company

In memory of Maurice D. Schwartz

International Standard Book Number: 0-02-863831-X
Library of Congress Catalog Card Number: Available upon request.

02 01 8 7 6 5 4 3 2

Interpretation of the printing code: The rightmost number of the first series of numbers is the year of the book's printing; the rightmost number of the second series of numbers is the number of the book's printing. For example, a printing code of 00-1 shows that the first printing occurred in 2000.

Printed in the United States of America

Note: This publication contains the opinions and ideas of its author. It is intended to provide helpful and informative material on the subject matter covered. It is sold with the understanding that the author and publisher are not engaged in rendering professional services in the book. If the reader requires personal assistance or advice, a competent professional should be consulted.

The author and publisher specifically disclaim any responsibility for any liability, loss, or risk, personal or otherwise, which is incurred as a consequence, directly or indirectly, of the use and application of any of the contents of this book.

Publisher
Marie Butler-Knight

Product Manager
Phil Kitchel

Managing Editor
Cari Luna

Acquisitions Editor
Amy Zavatto

Development Editor
Mary H. Russell

Production Editor
Christy Wagner

Illustrator
Jody P. Schaeffer

Cover Designers
Mike Freeland
Kevin Spear

Book Designers
Scott Cook and Amy Adams of DesignLab

Indexer
Lisa Wilson

Layout/Proofreading
Terri Edwards
Liz Johnston
Donna Martin
Jeannette McKay

Contents at a Glance

Contents

Foreword

The Bible is arguably the most mysterious book ever written. Nearly every page bristles with enigma. Its stories refer to unknown people and places. Its numerous authors are largely anonymous. Even the process by which the Bible came to be in book form remains largely unknown. To be sure, scholars are much better off today than they were even 50 years ago, thanks to a wealth of archaeological data and changes in the way we approach the text. Despite centuries of study, though, many of its secrets continue to evade them.

Where exactly is Noah's Ark? Or the Ark of the Covenant? When and how did the Exodus take place? Did the events depicted in the Bible ever really happen? Are Abraham, Moses, and Jesus historical figures? Who wrote the Dead Sea Scrolls? These are just a few of the questions that millions have pondered while exploring the richness of the Biblical texts.

In the last century, such questions have become the focus of heightened interest and often have led to fanciful claims of discovery. One of the most fascinating, from a psychological and sociological point of view, has been the unsubstantiated assertion that the Bible contains hidden numerical codes—secrets about the assassination of Abraham Lincoln, the first lunar landing, and more recent events. But there have been many unique claims. In the last 20 years alone, the Bible has been seen as a series of algorithms, as a testament to the Big Bang Theory and as proof of the existence of extraterrestrial life. Such competing claims often tell us more about a person's desire to harmonize the Biblical world with their own than they do about the Bible.

Recently, full-scale archaeological expeditions have been launched in search of a colossal boat made of gopher wood and a griffin-gilded box containing two clay tablets. The discovery of a copper "treasure map" among the Dead Sea Scrolls has fueled a similar fervor among writers and gold diggers. Television specials and Web sites continue to teem with sensationalist archaeological and interpretive discoveries. Yet, once examined closely, such discoveries often remain elusive. Perhaps the biggest Biblical mystery of all is why the Bible continues to evoke so many differing interpretations.

In this book, *The Complete Idiot's Guide to Biblical Mysteries,* Donald Ryan, scholar and professional archaeologist, takes us on an exploration of the Bible's many mysteries. With knowledge of the ancient world and a healthy sense of humor, Ryan excavates the many layers of history that cover the Bible's mysteries, continually brushing away fiction from fact. In brief and judicious paragraphs, Ryan moves from mystery to mystery, describing each of their origins, the various attempts to solve them, and the current view of scholarship on the subject. This book is as much fun to read as it is interesting. Just as an archaeologist often discovers new mysteries while solving older puzzles, this book reveals that while Biblical scholarship has solved many long-standing enigmas, many new and more fascinating mysteries remain.

Scott B. Noegel, Ph.D.

Dr. Scott B. Noegel is Assistant Professor of Ancient Near Eastern Languages and Civilizations at the University of Washington–Seattle, where he teaches Biblical Hebrew, hieroglyphic Egyptian, Akkadian, Ugaritic, and Aramaic. He received his Ph.D. in Near Eastern Languages and Literatures from Cornell University in 1995. Dr. Noegel is the author of more than 30 articles on diverse topics concerning ancient Near Eastern languages and literature, three dozen book reviews, and a monograph on wordplay in ancient Near Eastern texts. He is the recent editor of *Puns and Pundits: Wordplay in the Hebrew Bible and Ancient Near Eastern Literature* (CDL Press, 2000). Dr. Noegel has consulted for the History Channel, for the Discovery Channel's *Nile: Passage to Egypt* CD-ROM, and for a number of books and films. His Web site, "The Okeanos," is a premiere resource for browsers interested in the ancient world. Visit at faculty.washington.edu/snoegel/okeanos.html.

Introduction

Welcome to the fascinating and mysterious world of the Bible. While there are lots of books providing commentary on each individual character and story in the Book, we're going to concentrate on some of the more unusual, controversial topics, many of which are outright perplexing. We'll start out by looking at what the Bible is, who wrote it, and how it came to be what it is today. This involves the world of scholars such as archaeologists and theologians, and we'll learn a little about how they do their detective work.

God is, of course, the main character of the Bible, so it's important for us to attempt to figure out the Supreme Being before considering such controversial subjects as the Creation. Among God's creations are the often mischievous humans God deals with and gives rules to, punishes, and protects. In the midst of all this are miracles and extraordinary events aplenty.

We'll take a look at such great stories as Noah's Ark, the Exodus, and the events occurring in the Promised Land. And as archaeologists, we'll explore what artifacts or other evidence might remain. For Christians, the New Testament is a precious collection of writings that describe and comment on the life and teachings of Jesus of Nazareth. A part of this book is devoted to this extraordinary individual and his followers.

The Bible is, at its most basic, a book written on paper. We're going to look at some of the more extraordinary discoveries of ancient manuscripts and also some of the questionable documents that weren't included in the final version of the book. And to round things off, we'll take a look at mysterious Bible codes and numerology, angels and devils, the unusual and the odd, and the provocative Book of Revelation, which some say describes the end of time.

Obviously, with a book of this size it's only possible to skim the surface of these weighty issues, which have occupied the minds of scholars and ordinary individuals for thousands of years. Writing a book of this sort is not necessarily easy. There are numerous interpretations and spins on interpretations for nearly every topic. A single Bible verse or piece of related evidence can often be construed in many, sometimes contradictory, ways.

Religion and the Bible can be sensitive issues, dear to the hearts of many people. As such, I ask the reader to approach this book with an open mind. Ideas might be presented with which you disagree or which you might even find shocking, but there is no requirement for you to accept or believe one thing or another. The people who object most strongly to anything, I have found, are those who believe that there is only one way of thinking, and that way is their own. I hope you'll enjoy this volume as it's meant to be taken—as an exploration of some of the many wonders and mysteries of a fascinating and influential book, the Bible.

By the Way ...

Throughout the book you'll find little boxes, or sidebars. These contain explanations, elaborations, or additional facts or quotes.

Logos

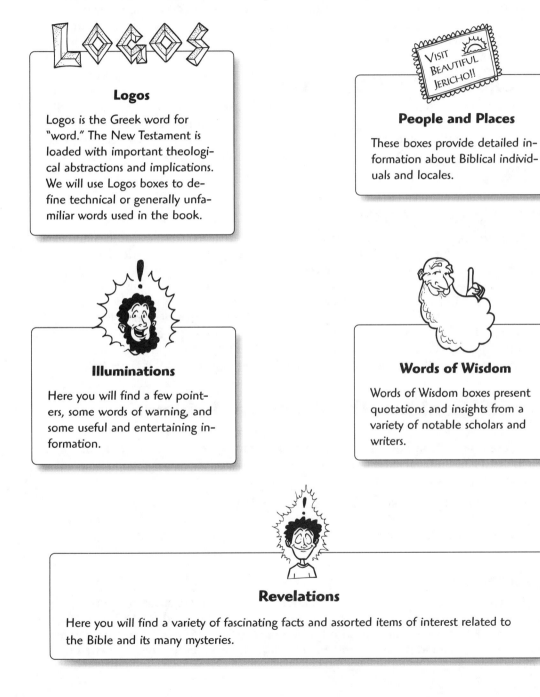

Logos is the Greek word for "word." The New Testament is loaded with important theological abstractions and implications. We will use Logos boxes to define technical or generally unfamiliar words used in the book.

People and Places

These boxes provide detailed information about Biblical individuals and locales.

Illuminations

Here you will find a few pointers, some words of warning, and some useful and entertaining information.

Words of Wisdom

Words of Wisdom boxes present quotations and insights from a variety of notable scholars and writers.

Revelations

Here you will find a variety of fascinating facts and assorted items of interest related to the Bible and its many mysteries.

Some Bible Notes

The Bible has been translated into English many different times. New discoveries and varying interpretations have produced a number of different ways of presenting the same text. In this book, the translation known as the Revised Standard Version (RSV) will be used unless otherwise noted. On occasion, you might find a quote from the classic King James Version (KJV) or the New International Version (NIV).

A Wonderful Biblical Artist

Throughout the book, you'll find some lovely illustrations by an individual named Gustave Doré. Doré was a popular French artist who lived between 1832 and 1883. Although he illustrated many fine books during his lifetime, his drawings of Biblical scenes are among his best-known works, and continue to be cherished by many to this day.

Acknowledgments

Many thanks are extended to Sherry Ryan and my little assistant, Samuel; Mary Russell, John Jones, Gary Krebs, Amy Zavatto, Christy Wagner, and the other fine Alpha Books people involved in the production and editing of this book; Mr. and Mrs. M. D. Schwartz; my various scholarly cohorts, including Brian Holmes, Mark Papworth, Thor and Jacqueline Heyerdahl, and Barbara Mertz; my many excellent colleagues in the Humanities Division at Pacific Lutheran University; John Petersen, Josh Miller, Chris Tyler, and Barrie Schwortz; my loyal supporters, including Mr. Jeffrey Belvill, Johnny Rockne, Patricia Armstrong, and Jane Ho; and special thanks to two wonderful Biblical associates: Rabbi Mark Glickman and Rev. Hugh Crowder.

Special Thanks to the Technical Reviewer

The Complete Idiot's Guide to Biblical Mysteries was reviewed by an expert who double-checked the accuracy of what you'll learn here, to help us ensure that this book gives you everything you need to know about the Bible and its many mysteries. Special thanks are extended to John Jones.

Jones holds a Ph.D. in Religious Studies from Yale University, and has edited several *Complete Idiot's Guides*. He was also the technical reviewer for Jay Stevenson's *The Complete Idiot's Guide to Angels*.

Part 1

Laying the Foundations

Before launching into a consideration of the many mysteries of the Bible, it's a good idea to know a little about the Book itself. What's in it? Who wrote it? How did it come to be? Are its claims true? And finally, how do you go about examining its contents?

In this section we'll look briefly at these questions, and you'll see that the mysteries of the Bible start fairly early on. Next, we'll take a look at the most profound topic of all: the Bible's main character, God. Who or what is God? Does God really exist? It's a subject that tends to drive one to contemplation!

Chapter 1

Introducing the Book of Mysteries

In This Chapter

- What's so special and mysterious about the Bible?
- What is the Bible and what's in it?
- How did we get today's text?
- Who wrote the Bible?
- Some useful terms and information

Many call it "the Good Book," but just how good is it? More than a billion copies of the Bible have been printed in thousands of languages—more than any other book ever published. Most homes in the Western world have at least one copy (whether they read it or not), and its words are constantly quoted. Its laws and values make up the Judeo-Christian ethic that forms the foundation of Western Civilization, and its stories have been retold for numerous generations.

What Is the Bible?

Despite its popularity, the Bible is one of the most mysterious books in existence. We're not sure who wrote it, and there is no universal agreement about what it means or to what degree it is an accurate reflection of reality.

Illuminations

Apart from the hundreds of millions of Bibles printed in such major languages as English, Spanish, and French, the Book has been translated into such obscure languages as Mta Manobo in the Philippines, the Peruvian Amuesha language, and the Hanga language of Ghana, Africa.

Words of Wisdom

"What a book! Great and wide as the world, rooted in the abysmal depths of creation and rising aloft into the blue mysteries of heaven ... Sunrise and sunset, promise and fulfillment, birth and death, the whole human drama, everything is in this book ... It is the book of books."

—Heinrich Heine, *Ludwig Boerne* (1840)

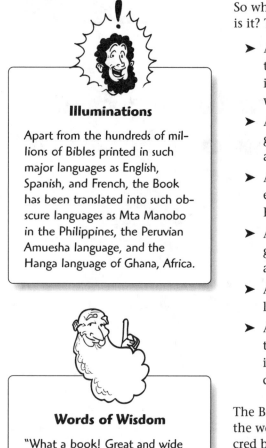

So what's special about this book? What kind of book is it? The Bible is ...

- A book of origins that explains, in its own way, the beginnings of our planet and everything on it, and offers insights into why things are the way they are.
- A book of laws, morals, and values that provides guidelines for individual behavior and private and public justice.
- A history book that tells the story of some of the events that took place in Palestine and the Near East until about 2,000 years ago.
- An inspirational book that has provided hope, guidance, and motivation for human goodness, and occasionally for human evil.
- A book of fine literature that ranges from thrilling sagas to beautiful poetry.
- A book of wonders. Miracles and divine interventions abound in the Bible, supporting the faith of its believers and bolstering the incredulity of its detractors.

The Bible is held in high regard by a large portion of the world's population. The Hebrew Bible is held sacred by 15 million Jews as well as over a billion Christians, who have added additional Scriptures to the volume. Although one billion Muslims view their special book, the Koran (Qur'an), as the ultimate word of God, they revere the Bible as a source of earlier divine revelations.

Apart from being the most printed book in the world, the Bible is also the most studied. For centuries, theologians and other scholars, and the average humanoid, have continually studied the Bible in order to ferret out its mysteries and meanings. Every word has been examined over and over again, and there are probably more books written about the Bible than any other subject. As a matter of introduction, let's take a quick look at this fascinating book.

A Whole Library

To begin, we need to sort out what we mean by "the Bible." It's really not one book, but a library of books. The early compilation of books is often simply called the Hebrew Bible, since it was written predominantly in Hebrew. This is often referred to by Christians as the Old Testament, as opposed to the New Testament, which contains other books describing the life and teachings of Jesus of Nazareth and some of his early followers. The New Testament was composed primarily in Greek.

Some people don't like the term "Old Testament," because it implies that the text is old and has been superseded. To Jewish people, who don't accept the New Testament as scripture, it is the *only* Bible, "the Hebrew Bible." Some have suggested using the expressions First and Second Testament, or Hebrew Scriptures and Christian Scriptures. The term Old Testament has been in use for such a long time, however, that its use as the name for the Hebrew Bible is commonly accepted.

Let's take a brief look at what is to be found within the Old and New Testaments.

Logos

The word **Bible** is derived from the Greek word *biblos,* which means "book." The word has its origins in the Phoenician port of Byblos, which was known for its papyrus in ancient times.

The Old Testament, or Hebrew Bible

The Old Testament, or Hebrew Bible, is sometimes divided into three sections: the Torah (law), the Prophets, and the Writings. The Torah consists of the first five books and is considered the fundamental source of law for the Jewish people.

Its first book, Genesis, tells the story of God's creation of the earth and all living things, especially people, who often disappoint their Creator. At one point in Genesis, God destroys most life on the planet in a great flood and starts over.

Eventually, God chooses a mortal, Abraham, with whom an agreement, or *covenant,* is struck. In exchange for exclusive worship and obedience to the One God, God in turn will bless Abraham and his descendants, who will become known as the Hebrews, the Israelites, or the Jews.

Logos

Tanach is the Hebrew term for the Hebrew Bible, or Old Testament. **Torah** refers to the first five books of the Hebrew Bible. It is also known by its Greek name, the **Penteteuch.**

In the next book of the Torah, Exodus, the Hebrews are delivered from slavery in Egypt. God then presents a series of commandments and laws for living and worship. The Torah lays the foundation for the rest of the Old Testament, and the spiritual development of the descendants of Abraham.

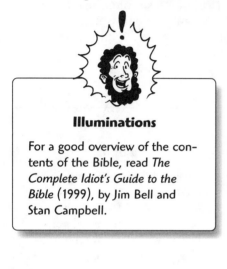

Illuminations

For a good overview of the contents of the Bible, read *The Complete Idiot's Guide to the Bible* (1999), by Jim Bell and Stan Campbell.

The succeeding books of the Old Testament contain historical and prophetic stories that describe the successes and foibles of God's people, and God's reactions to them. Both marvelous blessings and tragic setbacks occur, and in the midst of the history are prophets who foretell the future and provide warnings about what will happen if God's laws are not obeyed. Other books contain wise adages, poetry, and praises to God.

Throughout the Old Testament, the power of God is demonstrated through miracles and divine interventions, while humans struggle to behave properly and deal with the notion of one Supreme Being. We'll be dealing with many of these mysteries in the pages ahead. The religion that developed within the context of the Old Testament is Judaism, and the Jewish people continue to thrive in a modern world radically different from their origins during Biblical times.

The New Testament

The New Testament contains the story of the life of Jesus of Nazareth and some of his followers, who believed that Jesus was the Son of God sent to earth as prophesied in the Old Testament. The first four books are referred to as the Gospels; they tell of great miracles performed by Jesus and record his teachings. They conclude with the execution of Jesus, followed by his marvelous resurrection from the dead.

After the Gospels comes the Book of Acts, which tells the story of the followers of Jesus in the immediate aftermath of his death and resurrection. Jesus ascends to Heaven with a promise to return, and the miracles continue as his followers begin to spread the Word.

Much of the rest of the New Testament consists of letters, most of which are said to be written by a believer and missionary named Paul—they elaborate upon the teachings of Jesus. The final book, Revelation, is a highly symbolic work which is often used to predict dire times preceding the return of Jesus, also known as the Second Coming.

Revelations

Followers of Jesus are referred to as Christians, and among Christians, there are several different sects with varying beliefs. Protestants are Christian groups that broke away from the Roman Catholic Church or the Church of England due to political and doctrinal differences. Orthodox Christian churches are those that developed east of Rome, such as those found in Greece, Armenia, Egypt, and Russia.

Not All Bibles Are the Same

All Christian Bibles contain both the Old and New Testaments. And although they include all the books of the Hebrew Bible, different versions arrange the books in a different order. Additionally, Catholic Bibles contain several books, known as the Apocrypha, that aren't included in modern Hebrew and Protestant Bibles because non-Catholics don't regard them as having high spiritual value or a credible origin.

In the Beginning

Like many things in it, the Bible's origins are a subject of controversy. The earliest material, containing the Creation story and stories of the first people, along with genealogies, was probably passed down by oral tradition for many generations. Writing is only about 5,000 years old, which is much too late even for those who believe that the earth is only about 6,000 years young.

It's not known when the texts of the Bible were first actually written down, although one tradition states that it was the scribe Ezra who gathered many of the Old Testament books into their standardized form around the fifth century B.C. They were probably written on papyrus. Later, vellum or animal hides became the preferred writing surface.

Illuminations

The works of the *Apocrypha,* which literally means "hidden things," are additional books found in some Bibles but not universally accepted. Although they appear in Roman Catholic Bibles, they are not found in Hebrew Bibles or most Protestant Bibles.

Logos

A **scroll** is a rolled-up manuscript which is unrolled for reading. A **codex** consists of a group of flat pages typically bound in book form.

The earlier texts were rolled into *scrolls,* although eventually the *codex,* or flat page form, became quite common. We don't have the original manuscript of any of the books of the Bible, but instead have copies that might date from a couple of hundred to a few thousand years after the events that are described in them. We'll be talking more about some of the earliest Bible manuscripts later in this book.

A rabbi scrutinizes a portion of the text of the Torah hand-written on a scroll.

(Photo by Joshua Miller)

Logos

Canonization is the process by which potential parts of a book, or a group of books, are accepted or rejected on the basis of their appropriate merits.

Sorting It Out

The Hebrew Bible, a.k.a. the Old Testament, was written primarily in Hebrew and also in Aramaic. Around 250 B.C. it was translated into Greek by a group of 72 scholars assembled in Alexandria, Egypt, to do the work. The result was called the Septuagint, which presents a surviving rendition of the Old Testament of that time.

Although the Septuagint contained the books of the Apocrypha, those books were later eliminated from the official collection of the Hebrew Bible. This process of accepting or rejecting candidates for inclusion in the Holy Book is known as *canonization,* and was completed by A.D. 70 for the Hebrew Bible.

The Leningrad Codex

The authoritative, complete text of the Old Testament today, in Hebrew, is based on a manuscript known as the Leningrad Codex, now housed in St. Petersburg, Russia. The Codex was compiled and edited by a group of Jewish scholars known as the Masoretes, who not only carefully copied the text of the old books, but made numerous insightful scholarly notations in the margins. They also added vowels to the Hebrew letters, Hebrew being a script that doesn't necessarily require vowels to be written.

The fact that this, the earliest complete Hebrew Bible, dates to only as recently as A.D. 1010 has fueled controversy about how different our current Bible might be from the very earliest. The discovery of the Dead Sea Scrolls has gone some way towards addressing that issue (see Chapter 16, "Scrolls in the Desert").

Books of the Bible

Hebrew Bible/Old Testament

Genesis
Exodus
Leviticus
Numbers
Deuteronomy
Joshua
Judges
Ruth
1 Samuel
2 Samuel
1 Kings
2 Kings
1 Chronicles
2 Chronicles
Ezra
Nehemiah
Esther
Job
Psalms
Proverbs
Ecclesiastes
Song of Solomon
Isaiah
Jeremiah
Lamentations
Ezekiel
Daniel
Hoseah
Joel
Amos
Obediah
Jonah
Micah
Nahum
Habakkuk
Zephaniah
Haggai
Zecharia
Malachi

New Testament

Matthew
Mark
Luke
John
Acts
Romans
1 Corinthians
2 Corinthians
Galatians
Ephesians
Philippians
Colossians
1 Thessalonians
2 Thessalonians
1 Timothy
2 Timothy
Titus
Philemon
Hebrews
James
1 Peter
2 Peter
1 John
2 John
3 John
Jude
Revelation

Picking the Good Ones

As with the Old Testament, there were serious debates about what should be included in the New Testament, and what should not. There are a good number of "gospels," Christian letters, and other writings that simply didn't make the cut (see Chapter 17, "Alternative Scriptures and Fabulous Fakes"). The books composing the New Testament were canonized by the mid-fourth century A.D., and both the Old and New Testament were translated into Latin by a Christian scholar named Jerome by the year A.D. 405.

Visit
Beautiful
Jericho!!

People and Places

Jerome, also known as Eusebius Hieronymus Sophronius (ca. A.D. 240–420), was commissioned by Pope Damasus I to make a Latin translation of the Bible. Jerome was an expert in reading both Greek and Hebrew, and his Latin translation, called the Vulgate, was a standard for centuries.

Divine Penmanship

Until the invention of the printing press, all Bibles were copied by hand. In Jewish tradition, there are very strict rules regarding the copying of religious texts to insure accuracy. Even today, handwritten Torah scrolls are used in synagogues. Christian monks labored for years to produce copies of the books, and it must have been a relief to everyone when the movable-type printing press was invented by Johann Gutenberg in 1456. The first book printed on that press was the Bible, in Latin.

Visit
Beautiful
Jericho!!

People and Places

John Wycliffe (d. 1384), who translated the Bible into English in the fourteenth century, was put on trial by church authorities 40 years after his death. He was proclaimed a heretic and his body was dug up, burned, and thrown into a river.

A Dangerous Book

In Christian Europe, the fact that the Bible was printed in Latin gave a certain power to the relatively few who were literate and could read it. Keeping the Bible out of the hands of the masses was one way of controlling the interpretation of the Great Book.

Eventually, copies of the Bible were translated into such languages as English and German, though initially against the wishes of the authorities. William Tyndale (1494–1536), who translated, printed, and distributed copies of the New Testament in English, was pronounced a heretic by English church officials and burned at the stake.

German theologian and reformer Martin Luther (1483–1546) not only translated the Bible into German, but insisted that it be written in the kind of language that the average individual could understand and appreciate. Eventually, the powers that be would come to accept that the Bible could indeed be a book for all people. From then on, the mysteries of the Bible would be made public for all to examine and contemplate.

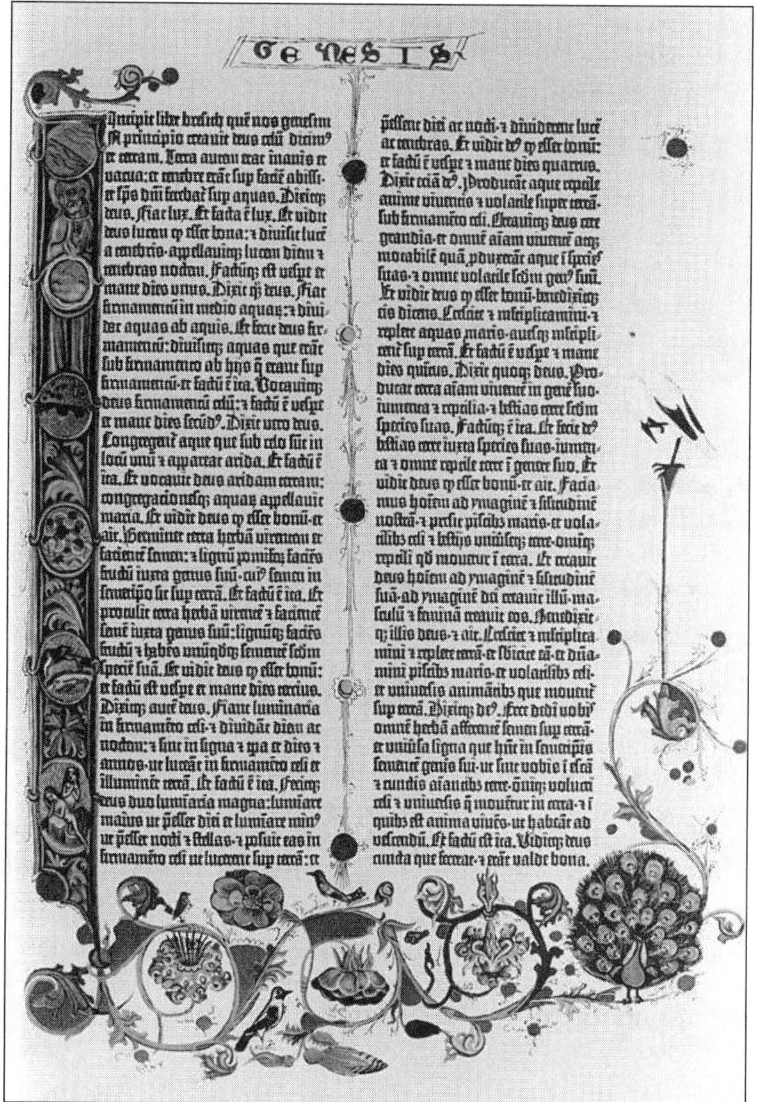

A page from the Gutenberg Bible.

(Photo by Joshua Miller)

King James Starts a Trend

A great milestone was achieved when an official English language translation of the Bible, commissioned by the English monarch King James, was published in 1611. The King James Version became a standard that's still in use today. There are many who claim that this translation was inspired by God and is the authoritative version of the Bible.

Another important translation, the Revised Standard Version, appeared in English in 1952 after years of work by scholars. Others followed, and a recent visit to the local religious bookstore revealed an amazing variety of translations. Here's just a sample: *The New International Version,* the *Jerusalem Bible,* the *New Living Translation,* the *New American Standard Bible,* and the *New King James Version.*

Revelations

There are many specialty editions of the Bible addressed to specific audiences. They include the *Life Recovery Bible,* the *Daily Walk Living Bible,* and the *New Adventure Bible* for young people. The text of the Bible can be found on audio cassettes read by the likes of Charlton Heston, and it's also available on CD-ROM for computer study.

Who Wrote the Book of Many Mysteries?

Having seen how popular and influential the Bible is, one might expect an easy answer to one of the most important questions: Who wrote it? Well, like much of what you'll find in the Bible, it's not that simple. Some of the books have their authors identified by name; the book of Isaiah, for example, is presumed to have been written by Isaiah, the book of Luke by Luke, and so forth.

Others have a traditional author; for example, Moses is traditionally thought to be the writer of the Torah. For several books, the authors are decidedly unknown. But as you'll see below, there are always more questions. First, let's look at some general issues regarding the author or authors of the Bible. There are a number of possibilities across a broad spectrum, including the following:

- The Bible was written by God and dictated to the likes of Moses, who recorded it verbatim.
- The Bible is the inspired Word of God transmitted through human scribes who, being human, aren't necessarily infallible and are capable of creating and perpetuating errors.
- The Bible was written by wise and pious people as a profound expression of their understanding of their origins and God's will.
- The Bible was written by humans but nonetheless contains timeless wisdom and items of historical and literary interest.
- The Bible was written by humans belonging to particular cultures at a particular time and is not necessarily a universally relevant document.

The first couple examples perceive the Bible as infallible, or nearly so. Proponents of this view believe that the Word of God is accurate as written, and this being the case, there's little to argue about with critics regarding its authority. At the other end of the spectrum, someone who holds the last viewpoint might regard the Bible as an interesting collection of antique Near Eastern myths, legends, and superstitions.

Words of Wisdom

"Holy Scripture is so exalted that there is no one in the world ... wise enough to understand it so fully that his intellect is not overcome by it. Nevertheless, man can stammer something about it."

—Blessed Angela of Foligno (1248–1309), *Book of Vision and Instructions*

Under the Microscope

Of all the books of the Bible, the first few of both the Old and New Testaments have received the most scrutiny. The Torah, made up of the first five books of the Old Testament, is often referred to as the Five Books of Moses, yet many scholars question whether only one individual was involved in the writing. After studying the text in depth, they have suggested that there might be four or more different authors, whose texts were combined by yet another individual.

Different writing styles can be detected, including preferences in the use of the name of God, and one of the writers has a detailed knowledge of priestly practices. A separate author for the last book of the Torah, Deuteronomy, has also been suggested. Can it be proved? No, but it can be argued. Does this detract from the possibility that it might be God's Word? Not necessarily.

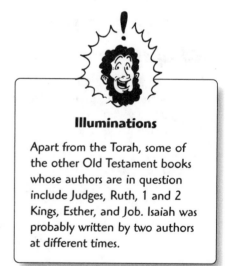

Illuminations

Apart from the Torah, some of the other Old Testament books whose authors are in question include Judges, Ruth, 1 and 2 Kings, Esther, and Job. Isaiah was probably written by two authors at different times.

The Mysterious "Q"

A similar situation exists with the first four books of the New Testament, known as the Gospels. Three of the books, Matthew, Mark, and Luke, are amazingly similar in places—so similar, in fact, that some scholars believe that Matthew and Luke are mostly copies of portions of Mark and another document, referred to by scholars as "Q." There is no known copy of "Q," but the internal evidence in the texts makes a strong case for its existence.

Finding Your Way Around

As you can see, the very nature of the Bible is a fascinating and controversial topic, and this is just Chapter 1! From the Bible's earliest days, believers and detractors have been arguing and speculating about, refining, rejecting, and accepting every word and detail found within the Book.

As we discuss various marvels and incidents to be found in the Bible in the chapters ahead, there are a couple of things to get used to, in case you aren't already in the know: how to find things in the Bible, and a little dating vocabulary.

Revelations

The question has often been asked: How could Moses be the author of the Torah when one of the books describes his own death? Some have explained this problem by suggesting that such parts were added later by his successors. Some who believe that the Bible is absolutely without error have claimed that Moses was aware of the circumstances of his own death as foretold by God.

Chapter and Verse

The Bible is composed of many books, each with a given name. These books have been further divided into numbered chapters and verses that enable us to precisely locate a given word, phrase, or story of interest. For example, John 3:16 refers to the sixteenth verse of the third chapter of the Book of John.

Name Your Source!

Keep in mind, though, that there are lots and lots of different translations of the Bible from which to choose, so when quoting a Bible verse, it's a good idea to let people know which version you're using. Here are some abbreviations you might find, all used in this book, which will tell you the source of a quotation:

- **KJV.** The King James Version
- **RSV.** The Revised Standard Version
- **NIV.** The New International Version

It's About Time

As we are dealing with a lot of events that take place in time, we need to review just a few dating terms in order to place things in their historical context. The calendar in common use today was created by Christians and begins its numbering system with the birth of Jesus. This requires the use of some special terms to help keep things in order:

- B.C. "Before Christ." Refers to the number of years before the birth of Jesus.
- A.D. *Anno Domini.* Refers to the number of years after the birth of Jesus.

Many people think that because B.C. means "Before Christ," then A.D. must mean "After Death." Not so. First of all, if that were the case, you'd have to add about 33 years to your actual date to account for the tenure of Jesus' life on earth and then come up with a special term for dealing with those years. And, from a theological point of view, Jesus was only dead for a couple of days before being resurrected anyway.

Fortunately, we don't have to worry about all that: A.D. is actually an abbreviation for two Latin words, *Anno Domini,* which mean "Year of Our Lord." From the perspective of a Christian calendar-constructor, every year since the birth of Jesus would be a Year of Our Lord.

Now some folks out there don't care for the theological bias of these terms. Perhaps they don't share Christian beliefs or simply feel that religion should not be imposed on such a universal apparatus as a calendar. To address those concerns, there is an alternative pair of terms that essentially mean the same thing. The terms recognize that our current Christian calendar is entrenched and in common use and is not going away, but the theological implications are neutralized:

- B.C.E. "Before the Common Era." Means the same as B.C.
- C.E. "Common Era." The equivalent of A.D.

The term "Common" refers to the calendar dates that we all use in common, regardless of their origin and irrespective of our personal beliefs. The B.C./B.C.E. and A.D./C.E. distinction is mostly known in academic circles, where it is unevenly applied. It's often a matter of personal choice and occasionally it is an editorial policy, but B.C.E. and C.E. are being used more frequently, so it's best to recognize and understand them for what they are.

Illuminations

When our present calendar was created, a mistake was made that miscalculated the date of the birth of Jesus by a few years. Although this doesn't much affect our ability to organize and discuss time, it has some interesting implications regarding the celebration of the new millennium and predictions for the end of the world. (See Chapter 22, "Revelation: The End?" for more details.)

The important thing is to have a system that everyone can understand. In this book, we will use the traditional B.C./A.D. terms, which are familiar to more people.

Words of Wisdom

"You can learn more about human nature by reading the Bible than by living in New York."

—William Lyon Phelps, in a 1933 radio speech

Counting Backward

Another occasionally useful way of noting a point in time is with a B.P., or "Before Present," date. Essentially, B.P. means "years ago." So if this is the year A.D. 2000, and I'm talking about 10 years B.P., I'm referring to the calendar year A.D. 1990. Or, to make matters slightly more complicated, if this is the year A.D. 2000, and I'm talking about 2500 B.P., I'm referring to the year 500 B.C.

Why would anyone want to do this? As you'll see when we discuss dating techniques in the next chapter, some methods, like radiocarbon dating, assess the age of an object from the time of the laboratory procedure. A date produced in the laboratory 10 years from now would be different (by 10 years) from a date provided today.

Round About Then

One last term of time is *circa,* usually abbreviated with a simple "ca." Circa means "about that time." It is useful for rounding off dates for a general discussion or for referring to dates we can't pin down exactly.

The Least You Need to Know

- The Bible is the most published book on Earth and has been translated into thousands of different languages.
- The Bible is composed of two "libraries" of books: the Hebrew Bible, or Old Testament, valued as Scripture by both Christians and Jews, and the Christian books of the New Testament.
- The Bible contains a variety of different kinds of literature emphasizing people's relationships with God and their attempts or failures to follow God's laws and plans. The Bible also includes lots of purported history.
- The Bible was assembled over a long period of time, and the Bible we can read today is the result of a lengthy process of writing, canonization, copying, printing, and translation.
- Despite its popularity, the Bible remains one of the most mysterious books known. Even its authorship has been questioned, and its spiritual authority is subject to wide interpretation.

Chapter 2

The Bible Detectives

In This Chapter

- Scrutinizing the text of the Bible
- Making sense of ancient languages
- Biblical archaeologists dig for insights
- The debate about Biblical archaeology

The Bible is not the easiest book to understand. It was written over a period of hundreds of years by many authors in times and cultures far removed from our own. So how do we make sense of these profound and provocative texts?

This challenge has been addressed continuously over the centuries by theologians and other scholars, as well as the average reader. There are a number of ways of trying to grasp the truth, and in this chapter, we're going to see how some students of the Bible carry out their search for meaning and understanding.

Studying the Texts

Despite centuries of study and hundreds of thousands of books and articles on the subject, there is little consensus about what the Bible or any of its numerous books might really mean. Two scholars analyzing the same Bible verse might come to completely opposite conclusions, while others will say that the message can't be studied directly anyway, and you need to read between the lines.

At the very root of any study, of course, are the words themselves. As I mentioned in the last chapter, the Bible as we know it was written primarily in Hebrew and Greek. If you want to be a real Bible scholar, you'll have to be able to read and comprehend those languages if you hope to evaluate the source material on your own. Otherwise you'll have to rely upon a translation, as most people do.

Revelations

Hebrew and Greek belong to two very different language families. Hebrew is a Semitic language that is related to languages such as Arabic, Aramaic, Akkadian, and Phoenician. Greek is an Indo-European language with relatives that include Latin, German, and English. There are, in fact, many words in the English language with Greek roots.

Excuse Me, Do You Speak Akkadian?

There are also some Old Testament texts written in Aramaic, a language related to Hebrew, and some early Christian writings can be found in languages other than Greek, such as Syriac and Coptic. If you have a broad interest in the ancient world of the Bible, other languages of the old Near East might also be of interest, including Akkadian (the language of the Babylonians and Assyrians) and Egyptian.

Illuminations

In a lot of old Greek texts, there is no separation between words, so the letters just run together. It takes a real expert to sort out where one word ends and another begins!

It may seem strange that some scripts, such as Hebrew, Arabic, and ancient Egyptian, routinely don't write their vowels. For example, CN Y RD THS SNTNC? If you know the language, however, patterns in the words or the context of a sentence usually make it clear which vowel is appropriate. Just to make things more difficult, unlike European languages, these languages are typically written from right to left.

As you can see, if you want to study the old texts, a background in ancient languages is very helpful. And being able to read these languages is just the beginning. To make sense of them, you need to understand what the words mean not just now, but when they were written. Words can change meaning through time, and their use in other cultures can be very different.

Even the English language has changed substantially since the classic King James Version of the Bible, still in wide use today, was written. There are many words in that classic translation of 1611 that are no longer used today or now have different meanings. Few people today go around addressing each other in terms of "thee" and "thou," for instance, and when was the last time you "spoketh unto" anyone?

ΕΥΑΓΓΕΛΙΟΝ

ΚΑΤΑ ΙΩΑΝΝΗΝ.

Ἐν ἀρχῇ ἦν ὁ λόγος, καὶ ὁ λόγος ἦν πρὸς τὸν θεόν, καὶ θεὸς ἦν ὁ λόγος. Οὗτος ἦν ἐν ἀρχῇ πρὸς τὸν θεόν. Πάντα δι' αὐτοῦ ἐγένετο, καὶ χωρὶς αὐτοῦ ἐγένετο οὐδὲ ἕν, ὃ γέγονεν. Ἐν αὐτῷ ζωὴ ἦν, καὶ ἡ ζωὴ ἦν τὸ φῶς τῶν ἀνθρώπων· Καὶ τὸ φῶς ἐν τῇ σκοτίᾳ φαίνει, καὶ ἡ σκοτία αὐτὸ οὐ κατέλαβεν. Ἐγένετο ἄνθρωπος ἀπεσταλμένος παρὰ θεοῦ, ὄνομα αὐτῷ Ἰωάννης· Οὗτος ἦλθεν εἰς μαρτυρίαν, ἵνα μαρτυρήσῃ περὶ τοῦ φωτός, ἵνα πάντες πιστεύσωσι δι' αὐτοῦ. Οὐκ ἦν ἐκεῖνος τὸ φῶς, ἀλλ' ἵνα μαρτυρήσῃ περὶ τοῦ φωτός. Ἦν τὸ φῶς τὸ ἀληθινόν, ὃ φωτίζει πάντα ἄνθρωπον, ἐρχόμενον εἰς τὸν κόσμον. Ἐν τῷ κόσμῳ ἦν, καὶ ὁ κόσμος δι' αὐτοῦ ἐγένετο, καὶ ὁ κόσμος αὐτὸν οὐκ ἔγνω. Εἰς τὰ ἴδια ἦλθε, καὶ οἱ ἴδιοι αὐτὸν οὐ παρέλαβον. Ὅσοι δὲ ἔλαβον αὐτόν, ἔδωκεν αὐτοῖς ἐξουσίαν τέκνα θεοῦ γενέσθαι, τοῖς πιστεύουσιν εἰς τὸ ὄνομα αὐτοῦ, Οἳ οὐκ ἐξ αἱμάτων οὐδὲ ἐκ θελήματος σαρκὸς οὐδὲ ἐκ θελήματος ἀνδρός, ἀλλ' ἐκ θεοῦ ἐγεννήθησαν. Καὶ ὁ λόγος σὰρξ ἐγένετο καὶ ἐσκήνωσεν ἐν ἡμῖν, καὶ ἐθεασάμεθα τὴν δόξαν αὐτοῦ, δόξαν ὡς μονογενοῦς

The opening lines of the Gospel of John in Greek.

What Does It All Mean?

With Biblical texts, there are a variety of things to sort out, especially with the older documents. Who wrote them, and when, and where? Some surviving ancient manuscripts are fragmentary or otherwise damaged and difficult to read. But apart from these sorts of questions and problems, the ultimate goal is to determine what it all means. What are the words trying to tell us? This process of analyzing the text of the Bible is called *exegesis*.

Logos

The King James Bible uses the word **corn** to describe what Americans know as wheat. The word is still in common use today in Britain to describe wheat, while **maize** is the word used there for the New World plant. This has caused some confusion and has led at least a few Americans to think that the Bible people were making popcorn and tortillas!

Competent members of the clergy will study a text in great detail before developing an interpretation and sharing their views with their congregations, eager for enlightenment. Such studies include a word-by-word and grammatical analysis, hopefully in the original language, along with a consideration of the historical, cultural, and even geographical context of the verses. What comes before and after the verses is important, as is the location of related material elsewhere in the Bible.

Fortunately, there are many good reference works that make this seemingly intimidating effort less difficult. The huge range of interpretations possible, however, clearly demonstrates that exegesis is not an exact science, but a scholarly process.

Make No Apology

This might be an appropriate time to bring up a special term that is useful in describing the debate about the various mysteries of the Bible. The word is *apologetics,* and those who engage in apologetics are called *apologists.*

Logos

Exegesis is the process of analyzing the text of the Bible. **Apologetics** is the defense of one's beliefs. **Apologists** are the practitioners of apologetics.

Now in modern English, that word "apology" means that one is sorry for something or remorseful. Not so when it comes to Bible study. The earlier meaning of the word has to do with defense, and Biblical apologists are those who ardently defend the integrity of the Book, ideas found therein, or their personal faith.

Are they sorry? No way! They'll gladly serve up some answers to your most challenging questions, and then it's up to you what to make of it. Some of the masters of apologetics are outstanding debaters, so if you want to pick a fight, you had better be prepared with some intellectual and spiritual ammo! And you'd better know your Bible!

Outside Sources

Apart from the Bible itself, there are other written sources that can shed some interesting light on the Bible and its people and times. There are inscriptions and documents from places such as Mesopotamia, for example, that occasionally help explain, if not actually confirm, certain things in the Bible.

Apocryphal and other books not in the Biblical canon can also sometimes prove useful, as can local traditions which survive today in some of the Bible lands. Ancient historians occasionally provide additional commentary, as do collections of Jewish religious commentary and tradition, as well as the Koran.

Putting It in Context

Cultural anthropology, which is the study of human cultures, also has much of interest to say to those examining the Bible. Anthropologists observe and attempt to explain culture, typically in an objective, nonjudgmental way. Such scholars might ask what roles religion and history serve in a culture, or what social, intellectual, and psychological needs they meet.

In addition, to understand a figure such as Jesus, for example, and what he was saying and doing, you really need to understand the historical and cultural context of the times. Knowing what it means that Jesus was a Jew living in Palestine under Roman occupation adds a wealth of detail to your understanding of his story.

Words of Wisdom

"It is one of the glories of the Bible that it can enshrine many meanings in a single passage .... Each man marvels to find in the divine Scriptures truths which he has himself thought out."

—St. Thomas Aquinas, *De Potentia* (1263)

Biblical Archaeology: Digging Up the Mysteries

The field of archaeology has contributed mightily to the study of the Bible. Archaeology is the study of the remains of the human past, and the examination of such leftovers as ancient artifacts, bones, and texts can provide some real insights.

Given the controversial nature of the Bible, it's not surprising that attempts to apply archaeology to "test its truth" have led to great arguments. Ask two archaeologists working on the subject, and you'll probably get three opinions!

Words of Wisdom

"We ought to listen to the Scriptures with the greatest caution, for as far as understanding of them goes we are as but little children."

—St. Augustine, Tractate 18 in Joann, P.L. 35 (ca. 416)

Define Your Territory

At face value, the notion of "Biblical archaeology" doesn't appear to be a difficult one. Biblical archaeologists are interested in what archaeology can tell us about the Bible. But there are others who prefer other terms. Since the majority of the story involves the life and history of the Jewish people in the area of modern-day Israel, there are some who prefer to call it the archaeology of the land of Israel.

Others find that term politically charged, and these people might prefer the term Syro-Palestinian archaeology, or *Palestinian* archaeology. Still others see that term as too restrictive, given that the Bible includes tales of Egypt, Mesopotamia, and other places in the region, and refer to themselves as archaeologists of the lands of the Bible or the Near East.

Modern-day Israel is virtually one big archaeological site. Interest in archaeology is a matter of national pride, and numerous excavations take place there every year. Biblical archaeology is popular in much of the rest of the world as well. Several glossy magazines cater to a public thirst for more information, and many scholarly journals address the subject, under its various names. To keep things simple, let's just use the term *Biblical archaeology* to refer to any archaeology that relates to the Bible and its peoples in both the Old and New Testaments.

The Land of the Bible

The term *Palestine* refers to a geographical region which more or less incorporates the area of the modern state of Israel and the territory east to the Jordan River. The word has its roots in the word *Philistine,* which was the name for a group of people who lived along the coast. The name was in general use to describe the region until the modern state of Israel was formed in 1948.

Palestine, where much of the Biblical story takes place, is located at a wonderful crossroads between Egypt and a large number of ancient civilizations to the north and east, including the Phoenicians and the Mesopotamians. Located on the Mediterranean, Palestine was accessible by sea and was also readily traversed by land. These qualities made it a valuable territory, and it was often overrun by other powers within the region.

VISIT
BEAUTIFUL
JERICHO!!

People and Places

Although many of the Arabs of the region of modern Israel refer to themselves today as Palestinians, the geographical term itself is politically neutral. The area was, in fact, known by that name until the state of Israel was declared in 1948.

Rock of Ages

Now that we've sorted out the geography of Biblical archaeology, let's take a look at a different way of organizing information—chronologically. The archaeological history of the Palestine region is organized into the following groupings, which are based on time and technology.

- **Paleolithic** (ca. prior to 8000 B.C.). A time period when humans were primarily hunters and gathers making use of stone tools.
- **Neolithic** (ca. 8000–4000 B.C.). The time period when humans began to develop agriculture and settle in permanent villages.
- **Chalcolithic** (ca. 4000–3150 B.C.). The Neolithic period with the addition of the use of the metal copper.
- **Bronze Age** (ca. 3150–1200 B.C.). The time period in which bronze metal technology was available. It tends to appear with the building of cities.

- **Iron Age** (ca. 1200–332 B.C.). The time period in which iron technology becomes available; iron is a metal superior in some ways to bronze.
- Time periods can also be identified by referring to the dominant power in the region at the time: for example, the Persian Period, the Hellenistic Period, and the Roman Period.

The basic time classification scheme was developed in Europe in the early nineteenth century and then applied to various places as archaeology developed. In Biblical archaeology, many of these "ages" are further subdivided into specific time periods. For example, Late Bronze Age IIb refers to the years 1750 to 1550 B.C., and Iron Age I is 1200 to 1000 B.C., although the dating is occasionally subject to dispute.

Digging Deep

People have been living in the area of Palestine for tens of thousands of years, and Neanderthal remains have been found in Israel. Perhaps it was a route for early humans such as *Homo erectus* as they spread from Africa into Europe and Asia. Many of the archaeological remains in Palestine survive in the form of big mounds, or *tells,* which are the accumulated debris of human occupation over the millennia.

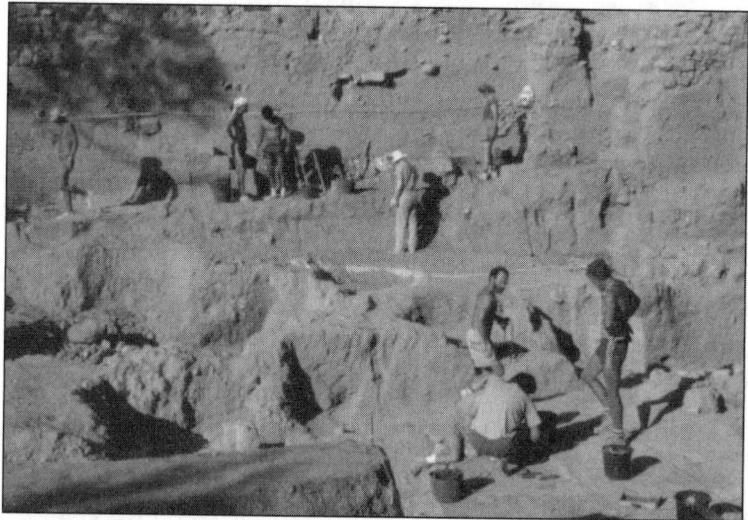

Archaeologists at work excavating a big tell in Israel.

(Photo by author)

Just as in Mesopotamia, and here and there in Egypt, the mounds tend to look like big hills, and the archaeologist who dares to excavate these places will probably find an amazingly complex series of layers, features, artifacts, and structures. Trying to relate one part of a site to another can be complicated, and digging a tell can be like sorting out a massive three-dimensional puzzle.

Early Days

Some of the earliest attempts to explore the ancient world were inspired by the Bible. Nineteenth-century excavations in places such as Palestine and Mesopotamia were often inspired by the desire to demonstrate the accuracy of the Bible and learn more about the people described therein. Many of these early excavations were crude by modern standards and were mostly dirt-removal exercises in search of interesting objects.

Logos

A **tell** (also spelled **tel**) is a mound made up of the accumulated debris of human occupation. Tells are commonly found all over the Near East.

A lot has changed since, and archaeology has evolved into a sophisticated science. Great care is used today in an effort to extract as much information from the remains of the past as possible. Specialists abound, and some are experts in such subjects as dating pottery, reading inscriptions, and studying bones, soil, and plant remains.

The Archaeological Record

Illuminations

For an easy introduction to the subject of archaeology, buy a copy of the author's *The Complete Idiot's Guide to Lost Civilizations* (1999). Thank you very much.

It's certainly not the purpose of this book to describe the how's and why's of the many facets of archaeology. Such details can be readily found elsewhere. But a couple of things will be important in understanding some of the issues in the chapters ahead. One is a basic understanding of what we call the *archaeological record*. The other is a general knowledge of how archaeologists tell how old things are.

First of all, what archaeologists are really digging up are some of the material remains of the human past. Note that I used the word "some." It's very important to understand that not everything that people do leaves a mark or record we can find later. A lofty conversation, for example, leaves no trace in the ground.

Furthermore, many things don't survive very well through time. Depending upon environmental conditions, all, some, or none of what has resulted from human behavior might survive the ages. It can take a good bit of detective work for the archaeologist to make sense of what does survive.

How Old Is It?

Determining the age of an artifact or other item of archaeological interest is a crucial element in archaeology, and there are a number of ways to go about it. We'll take a quick look at three of the most important dating techniques that are used in Biblical archaeology. They are …

- Stratigraphy.
- Stylistic analysis.
- Laboratory analysis.

The first, *stratigraphy,* involves analyzing layers, or strata, in an archaeological site. By looking at how layers of dirt and debris are positioned in relation to one another, one can usually tell which layer is older: The older ones tend to be below the younger ones.

Of course, it's not always that easy. Things can get mixed up through a variety of processes, from people reusing building materials to a dog burying a bone. Even worms can confuse the issue by churning up the layers and even moving small objects around! But in general, stratigraphy is a good way to determine the relative age of the layers and artifacts in a site.

In Style

Another important way to date old objects is by their *style.* You can tell that a Model T automobile is older than a Camaro by the way it looks. So, too, with many other kinds of objects, since styles have always tended to change through time.

This concept allows an expert to pick up a piece of pottery and tell whether it is a tenth-century Philistine pot or a much later Roman amphorae. With old texts, the writing style and the choice of words can often identify when a document was written.

Logos

Stragigraphy is the analysis of layers, or **strata,** in an archaeological site to see how they are related to each other. Older layers are usually, but not always, below younger ones. **Style** refers to the special characteristics of an object or piece of writing that help identify its origins.

Famous and Radioactive

Stratigraphy and style both tell us how old one object is in relation to another, but they don't necessarily give us its actual age. For that, we need to turn to laboratory analysis. One of the best-known methods is radiocarbon dating, or carbon-14 dating. Without going into a lot of detail, this dating method is based on the notion that all living creatures absorb a kind of radiation from the atmosphere. When they die, this radioactive material begins to decay at a known rate. The amount of radioactive material remaining in a sample can be measured to determine how many years it has been since the sample was alive.

Although this technique works very well, it is not perfect. It's only accurate on uncontaminated organic materials, and the older the sample, the wider the spread of possible dates. The technique is good only for objects that are between about 400 and 50,000 years old—luckily, this isn't much of a problem for items of Biblical interest.

The most important thing to understand about radiocarbon dating is that the dates are meaningful only to the extent that the sample is meaningful. For example, if I am trying to date an old building with a wooden beam, I had better take into account the possibility that the wooden beam could be an old piece of wood reused from an earlier structure. If that is the case, the radiocarbon date would tell me how old the beam itself is, but not necessarily the age of the building in which it was found.

Is Biblical Archaeology a Good Idea?

Is it appropriate to use archaeology to attempt to prove the accuracy of a book such as the Bible? That's a very good question. It really comes down to a matter of individual faith and expectation. In essence, archaeology is merely a tool that can shed light on the past. It can't on its own impart spirituality or prove the nature of miracles or the nature of God.

Illuminations

The Bible contains many stories of God's direct intervention in human affairs that we call miracles. Miracles, however, are very difficult to prove in the archaeological record. We can't see the handprints of God on the walls of Jericho, for example, but what does that prove? Mostly that if you're looking to dig up miracles, you're probably wasting your time.

Taking It to the Max

Among those who study archaeology and the Bible, there are two widely different views on the appropriateness of Biblical archaeology, and lots of other folks in the middle who believe something in between. The Biblical *maximalists* believe that the Bible is an accurate account of history and that archaeology can, does, and will confirm this truth. Many of these scholars, but not all, subscribe to the fundamentalist belief that the Bible is the inspired word of God and that every word should be taken literally.

Keep It to a Minimum

On the opposite extreme are the Biblical *minimalists,* who see the Old Testament in particular as historically unreliable, and as such, believe that much of it is best viewed as cultural mythology, fable, and literature.

Minimalists argue that there is little archaeological evidence for much of what is said in the Bible. Where are the ruined cities of Joshua's conquest, they'll argue, and where is the evidence for the likes of King David, not to speak of hundreds of other Biblical characters? Deluxe skeptics they are, with a "show me the archaeological evidence" approach. They certainly seem to enjoy a vigorous debate.

As you can see, the study of the Bible is a vibrant process with a variety of disciplines contributing to the search for understanding. The more we learn about the dynamics of the past, the more insights we might gain from the texts—yet another good reason for studying archaeology and history, no matter what your spiritual viewpoint.

Logos

Biblical **maximalists** believe in the general historical accuracy of the Bible, while skeptical **minimalists** argue that there is little compelling evidence to show that many of the events described in the Bible actually happened.

The Least You Need to Know

- Scholars use various methods to explore the Bible, including analyzing texts and studying the history and culture of its times.
- The Bible wasn't originally written in English, so scholars who analyze its text need a good knowledge of languages such as Greek and Hebrew.
- Archaeologists have been excavating in the lands of the Bible for many decades now and have added much to our knowledge of the human past.
- Archaeology can assist in the understanding of Biblical times and places, but can't be expected to prove miracles or their divine origins.
- You can expect lots of interesting discoveries and insights from the dynamic field of Biblical archaeology.

Chapter 3

God: The Biggest Mystery of Them All

In This Chapter

- Who or what is God?
- What does God do?
- What does God want?
- Is there actually a God?

The biggest mystery in the Bible is also its principal subject: God. What or who is God? What does God do and what does God want? Outside of the Bible, does this God actually exist? These provocative questions continue to stimulate debate, especially in our modern world, where the freedom to discuss such topics is generally (but not entirely) widespread.

The One and Only

In any discussion of God, it is important to realize that the Bible is based on a radical idea for its time: The God of the Bible considers himself to be the one and only. Although other supernatural beings are mentioned in the Book, including angels, demons, and such, God is regarded as the only and true deity, despite the fact that most peoples worshiped dozens of gods during Biblical times.

This one God is the same one worshipped by Jews, Christians, and Muslims, although each have some different ideas about the details. The basic and all-important concept, though, is called *monotheism:* the belief in one God. This is opposed to *polytheism,* which is the belief in many gods. The basic statement of monotheism is found in Deuteronomy 6:4:

> Hear, O Israel: the Lord is our God, the Lord is one.

Logos

Monotheism is the belief in one God. **Polytheism** is the belief in many gods.

1 + 1 + 1 = 1?

Christians tend to believe that God is composed of three entities: God the Father, God the Son, and God the Holy Spirit. God the Father is the Great Creator and the God of the Old Testament. Christians believe that God sent His son, Jesus, to Earth for various theological reasons, and that Jesus was one and the same as God the Father.

The Holy Spirit is seen as yet another manifestation of God that can work through humans in special ways. This idea of God as three entities in one is known as the *Trinity,* and it is a difficult concept to grasp.

Meet Me in Nicaea

When the early Christian church was developing, there were great debates regarding who Jesus was and what his relationship might be to God. Some thought that Jesus was just a special man sent by God, while others saw him as literally the son, or offspring, of God. A special meeting was held in A.D. 325 at Nicaea in what is now Turkey. There the official, basic beliefs of Christianity were laid down and the Trinity concept was officially endorsed.

Revelations

Both Jews and Muslims have a difficult time with the Trinity. Judaism and Islam are strictly monotheistic, and they see this concept of God being three as sufficiently confusing to be suggestive of polytheism.

Old Man with a Beard?

So what is the nature of God, and what does God look like? In art, God has often been depicted as a wise old man. This, of course, is based primarily on the Biblical creation story that reports that humans were made in the image of God: therefore, God must have human features.

This picture of God also includes the notion of age and wisdom, and if God was the Creator, then he's certainly older than the rest of us. He's also occasionally addressed as "our Father," and the masculine pronouns used in the Bible add to the picture.

A few people in the Bible are said to have seen God. Moses saw his back, and Jacob might have wrestled with him. And if Jesus is God, then a lot of people have seen him.

Looking After the Flock

God as described in the Bible looks after those who follow him, and is powerful, just, merciful, eternal, loving, all-knowing, and all-present. But don't make him mad! There's a lot of mayhem in the Old Testament caused by God when he's angry! And even in the New Testament, Jesus vividly describes the punishment awaiting those who reject God.

Jews and Christians, however, believe that although humans will always be sinful and break his laws, God is also forgiving. Why? We'll talk about that concept on the Christian side when we get to Jesus (see Chapter 13, "A Miraculous Life").

One of the most popular and poetic descriptions of God is given in Psalms 23, in which people are likened to sheep tended by God, a dutiful divine shepherd:

> The Lord is my shepherd; I shall not want. He maketh me to lie down in green pastures; he leadeth me beside the still waters. He restoreth my soul; He leadeth me in the paths of righteousness for His name's sake. Yea, though I walk through the valley of the shadow of death, I will fear no evil; for thou [God] art with me; thy rod and thy staff [protective tools of the shepherd] they comfort me. (23:1–4, KJV)

Illuminations

There are two books in the Bible that do not mention God: Esther and the Song of Solomon. He's mentioned in Ruth but doesn't appear as a character.

Yes Sir, God

If God is considered by many to be the supreme Creator and ruler of the Universe, then it's no surprise that he is regularly treated with the utmost respect. You may have already noticed that the word "God" in this book is given a little extra special treatment. For example, the first letter is capitalized, as opposed to the lowercase "g" typically used when describing a run-of-the-mill god or gods.

Another tradition is the use of the male pronoun "he" (also often capitalized) to refer to God. In the Hebrew text of the Bible, God is referred to in such a way, so it is in keeping with the translation. There are some people, however, who strongly object to God being referred to as a male. Terms like that, they claim, serve to neglect or oppress women and to limit God in unreasonable ways.

Logos

Some of those who have rejected the use of male terminology for God in the Bible have produced their own Bible translations which use "gender-inclusive" terminology. Some refer to God as "our Father and Mother in heaven" and to Jesus as "Child of God," rather than "Son of God."

On the other hand, one might argue that if God is all-powerful and all-knowing, then he could have chosen a different people than the Hebrews, with their patriarchal social system, through whom to share the Bible with all people for all time. Then again, there are those who believe that the Bible is flexible enough to adapt to changing times. Overall, though, God seems to transcend gender, and for many people is most comfortably perceived as a great spirit with both masculine and feminine characteristics.

The Sacred Name

There are many names for God in the Bible. The most important, though, is YHVH, a word that is probably related to the Hebrew verb "to be." So what's with the four letters? These four letters, as found in Hebrew, represent the personal name of God. It is sometimes referred to as the *Tetragrammaton,* and is written with vowels as "Yahweh" or "Yahveh."

This name, though, is considered very sacred, and in Jewish tradition it is never pronounced nor spelled out with vowels, so that this special name won't be abused. When the name is encountered while reading the Bible out loud, the word "Adonai," which means "the Lord," is substituted in its place. We will respect this tradition in this book from here on.

Logos

The four Hebrew letters YHVH represent the personal name of God. They are called the **Tetragrammaton.** They are also the source for the popular but mistranslated name of God used in the King James Bible: Jehovah.

YHVH: the personal name of God. Treat it with respect.

The name YHVH is also the source for the translated name of God found in the King James Bible: *Jehovah*. As well known as this name is, and as beloved as the King James Bible is, this important word is actually a bit of a mistranslation.

The Hebrew scribes wrote the vowels for the word Adonai under the letters of the Tetragrammaton to remind readers that that's how the name should be read. The King James scholars translated the name with the incorrect vowels.

Among the many names for God found in the Bible, YHVH is combined with other words that provide us with descriptive insights. Here are just a few:

- **YHVH-Yireh.** "The Lord will provide."
- **YHVH-Rophe.** "The Lord who heals."
- **YHVH-Shalom.** "The Lord of peace."
- **YHVH-Tsidekenu.** "The Lord of our righteousness."

Other names for God include:

- **El.**
- **Elohim.**
- **El-Elyon.** "God most high"
- **El-Shadai.** "God judges"
- **Kadosh.** "Holy one"
- **Melekh.** "King"

All of these names are interesting because they describe some of the traits of God. They show us the mighty role of God as the all-powerful and divine ruler, judge, and parent.

Illuminations

One traditional Jewish way of referring to the sacred name of God is by using the word HaShem, which literally means "the Name."

What Does God Want?

Yet another age-old question is, what does God want? The Bible spells out a number of things:

> ... What doth the Lord thy God require of thee, but to fear the Lord thy God, to walk in all His ways, and to love Him, and to serve the Lord thy God with all thy heart and with all thy soul, to keep the commandments of the Lord, and his statutes, which I [God] command thee. (Deuteronomy 10:12–13, KJV)

In the book of Micah (6:8), we also learn that God requires one to "do justly, and to love mercy, and to walk humbly with thy God ...." (KJV) The commandments and statutes we'll deal with in Chapter 8, "Laying Down the Law."

Interestingly, unlike the gods of many polytheistic religions, the Biblical God can communicate his wishes to individual human beings without the intervention of special priests, oracles, or omens. There are many people who believe that God has a special purpose for their lives, whatever it might be. Some think they've found it, others are still looking.

Revelations

In the Bible, God seems to work in mysterious ways, often seemingly beyond the understanding of mere mortals. Take the story of Job, for example. Job was an extremely good man who steadfastly worshiped God and obeyed the rules. The story tells how God allowed Satan to attempt to break Job's loyalty to God by imposing on him nearly every imaginable hardship and tragedy. Yet Job remained loyal and continued to worship God, although he couldn't ascertain God's purpose in all of this. The story does have a happy ending, however, and many good things come Job's way.

Does God Exist?

Now here's a huge question that has been on the minds of scholars and ordinary human beings alike for thousands of years: Does God exist, and if so, how can you prove it? There have been many attempts to answer this question. Following are just a handful.

I Am Therefore I Am

At one point in the Bible, God refers to himself as "I am," a mind-boggling two-word concept that gives rise to this idea: God exists because the very concept of God exists. Or, as a variation, God exists at least in name and as a concept, whether or not he exists in reality. This notion is not particularly satisfying to those who want to demonstrate absolutely the existence of a mighty force called God.

Words of Wisdom

"Without the slightest doubt there is something through which material and spiritual energy hold together and are complementary. In last analysis, somehow or other, there must be a single energy operating in the world."

—Pierre Teilhard de Chardin, *The Phenomenon of Man* (1955)

Getting the Ball Moving

Then there's the "in the beginning" theory. If a ball rolls, it does so due to some outside force. If a fish swims, it does so because various processes are in motion that work together to allow its scaly body to move effortlessly through the water. When the universe came into existence, there must have been some sort of force that started it all, and this force, some will say, was God, whatever the exact nature of God might be.

The Great Architect

Perhaps the most widely accepted argument for the existence of God is what is often called "the argument from design." Take a walk in the forest, look at a flower, or observe a sunset at the beach. Glance at a millipede with its dozens of coordinated legs or marvel at the amazing creature known as a human baby, which began nine months earlier as a couple of cells.

The complexity of the world is staggering, and it's hard to imagine that there was not some sort of intentional design somewhere, at some time, that ensured that all of the parts would work together so well.

The marvelous beauty found in nature or the amazing complexity of the universe can inspire a belief in a Supreme Being.

(Photo by Joshua Miller)

Doing the Right Thing

Another argument for the existence of God arises from this question: Are humans in the absence of God's divine rules capable of behaving in a moral fashion? Some say that the answer is no, and that left to our own devices, the world would be chaos. Instead, humans are often capable of dramatic acts of self-sacrifice and kindness. A belief in a moral and wise God with supreme authority, therefore, is a necessity.

Critics might claim that humans are more than capable of establishing moral laws if for no other reason than group survival. There are hundreds of human societies that have managed to get along with each other without knowledge of the God of the Bible. Their rules might be a bit different, but many demonstrate fairness and kindness. And aren't any rules which command us not to lie, steal, and murder good rules for living?

Words of Wisdom

The brilliant and influential scientist Albert Einstein (1879–1955) has this to say on the subject of God:

> "A conviction, akin to religious feeling, of the rationality or intelligibility of the world lies behind all scientific work of a higher order. This firm belief, a belief bound up with deep feeling, in a superior mind that reveals itself in the world of experience, represents my conception of God."
>
> —In *The American Weekly* (1948)

The Bible Is a Masterpiece

Here's an argument for the existence of God based on the Book itself. Some people are so impressed by the Bible and its contents that they believe that humans are incapable of producing such a wealth of wisdom, beauty, theological abstraction, and historical truth. Some say that there are even secret codes embedded in the text that prove this book cannot be merely a human product (see Chapter 18, "Reading Between the Lines"). Others are not so confident. The Bible has its critics, who claim that it is full of errors and human brutality.

Hedging Your Bets

Blaise Pascal (1623–1662) came up with a different reason for believing in God. Pascal argued that the benefits of believing in God, which include a good afterlife, outweigh any disadvantages this belief might involve. He arrived at his theology as the best option given what he saw as all the possible scenarios:

- God doesn't exist and you don't believe in him, and it's all over when you die.
- God doesn't really exist, but your belief in him causes you to lead a decent life anyway.
- God does exist and you believe in him, and are rewarded for your belief.
- God does exist, and if you guess wrong and don't believe in him, you could burn in hell.

The gambler in Pascal chose to believe in God, because the price of believing was low, but the price of not believing was high.

There are problems with Pascal's system. For one, it's pretty darn insincere. Choosing to believe in God because it might possibly have the better payoff in the long run makes one question if such a gambler is actually capable of a real belief in anything.

Secondly, Mr. Pascal seems to think he knows what the outcome of each option will be. But if God is all knowing and all powerful, perhaps he will choose to punish Pascal for being a cynic and instead reward the well-behaved and sincere nonbeliever.

Individual Experiences of God

Many people believe in God without benefit of outside theories. Their belief has its origins in personal experiences that have left a lasting impact on them. Perhaps they believe their lives or their loved ones have been miraculously spared or healed, for example.

Some have been led to a belief in God for no other reason than having experienced the improbable or the unexplainable. Some scientists who were formerly atheists have come to acknowledge the possibility of the existence of God after witnessing events that even their scientifically trained minds couldn't match up with the known laws of the universe.

Words of Wisdom

"One must be convinced of God's existence, but one need not prove it."

—Immanuel Kant, *The Only Possible Ground of Proof for a Demonstration of the Existence of God* (1763)

Faith

Many people believe in God through sheer faith. They put their trust in the Bible and feel satisfied with their personal relationship with God. It's hard to argue about this with such individuals; it's their special choice.

Why Not Believe in God?

In a free society, where people have a choice as to what to believe or not to believe, the option of not believing in God is always present. There are several reasons people might choose not to believe in God. Here are a few:

- They feel that a supernatural being such as God is unnecessary to explain the existence and workings of the universe.
- They don't believe that the Bible is a credible document.
- They can't believe that a loving God would allow so much pain in the world.
- They rebel against the various atrocities carried out through history by humans in the name of God.
- They rebel against the religion of their parents, or object to the perceived excesses of organized religion or such entities as televangelists.

Logos

Atheists are individuals who don't believe in God. **Agnostics** are those who acknowledge the possibility that God might exist, and **deists** believe in the general concept of the existence of God.

According to German philosopher Friedrich Nietzsche (1844–1900), God is dead. According to social philosopher Karl Marx (1818–1883), whose writings inspired various Communist regimes, God never existed, and religion is merely an "opiate of the masses" that has no permanent place in a progressive society.

These basic *atheistic* propositions are by no means uncommon today. Still others claim to be *agnostics*, or *deists*. The former acknowledge the possibility that there is a God, but aren't sure, while the latter believe in God, but aren't sure what God is.

How's God Doing?

So what role might God play in the world today? At least a few billion people believe in God in one way or another. But is God actively involved in the world today, or is he taking a break? Does God answer prayers and intervene on request, and if so, under what circumstances? Many people claim that God plays an active role in their daily personal lives. Who am I to dispute that?

Words of Wisdom

"God is dead." (Nietzsche)

"Nietzsche is dead." (God)

—Bathroom graffiti

The purported word of God as expressed in the Bible has had a tremendous impact on world history and upon individuals, and that alone makes the subject interesting and worthy of consideration. The big questions have not been solved to everybody's satisfaction. Not everybody believes in the existence of God, and not all who do claim to understand the full meaning of God's will in the world today. God is indeed mysterious!

The Least You Need to Know

- God as described in the Bible is the one and only God, a concept known as monotheism.
- God goes by many names, and is characterized as, among other things, just, wise, and all-powerful.
- According to the Bible, God wants his followers to acknowledge his supremacy and obey the rules. Many of the other details are elusive.
- The existence of God is a major philosophical question. Some choose to believe and some don't, for a variety of reasons.

Part 2

In the Beginning

The very first book of the Bible, Genesis, contains some of the most important, interesting, and profound storiesw in the entire collection. Therein we find tales that explain our origins and give insights into why we are the way we are. And even in our so-called sophisticated times, the Bible story of creation continues to thrive, often in conflict with modern science.

Apart from creation, Genesis talks about some of the amazing adventures and antics of early generations. Human nature is frequently stripped bare, and God is regularly disappointed with the result. Consequently, we find a little mayhem here and there. In the most dramatic example, God destroys the earth in a giant flood, sparing just enough life to carry on in its aftermath. The reality of some of these stories continues to be debated, while archaeologists and adventurers search the deserts and mountains for physical evidence.

Chapter 4

The Creation Controversy

In This Chapter

- God creates the earth
- Scientists present other options
- A big debate
- A little advice

Some of the most enduring questions that humans pose about themselves involve origins. Where do we come from? Where did the world come from? How did things come to be the way they are? These kinds of questions are what keep biologists, geologists, archaeologists, historians, and parents busy for years.

The Bible has its own answers for these questions, but, as with much else in the Bible, there is great disagreement about what those answers mean. And when it comes to the question of the ultimate origins of the universe and life on earth, the fur can really fly!

In the Beginning

The opening lines of Genesis, the first book of the Bible, contain some of the most provocative words ever written:

> In the beginning, God created the heavens and the earth .... (NIV)

It sounds simple enough, right? Except that ...

- ➤ It assigns the origins of the universe to a supernatural being.
- ➤ It raises this question: If the Universe was indeed created by a Creator, then who, if anyone, created the Creator?
- ➤ The details, such as issues of method and timing, seem to fly in the face of many accepted scientific findings about how the universe might have been created.

Three Profound Words

Words of Wisdom

"In the beginning, God created the heavens and the earth. The earth was without form and void, and darkness was upon the face of the deep; and the Spirit of God was moving over the face of the waters."

—Genesis 1:1–2

If the whole notion of Creation by God is controversial, it is so to its very core. Just in the first three Hebrew words of Genesis, *b'reshit barah Elohim,* we find profound theological implications. Here is a sample:

B'reshit is often translated as "in the beginning." This seems to suggest the beginning of time or existence. But another way to translate these first three words is, "When God began to create," which can suggest that God had been around for a long time before deciding to create the universe or this particular universe.

Barah is a form of the Hebrew verb "to create." It is, however, in the verb form that indicates a single male, yet it is matched up with a name for God that has a plural ending, "Elohim." And through much of the creation story God refers to himself in the plural, for example "Let us make man in our own image." Is this just the way of speaking reserved for royalty, a "majestic plural"? Or is God addressing heavenly beings such as angels and so forth? Is this plural name a reflection of the Christian trinity?

Let There Be Light

The story continues with a sequence of six acts of creation over a period of six days: light, elements of the universe, the earth, plants, animals, and a final crowning achievement on the last day, humans. Then God took a break. The story is quite amazing. Unlike many Near Eastern creation stories which typically involve gods who mate and create other gods, the God in Genesis speaks the universe into creation:

> And God said, Let there be light! And there was light! God saw that the light was good. (1:3–4, NIV)

בְּרֵאשִׁית בָּרָא אֱלֹהִים אֵת הַשָּׁמַיִם וְאֵת הָאָרֶץ׃ וְהָאָרֶץ
הָיְתָה תֹהוּ וָבֹהוּ וְחֹשֶׁךְ עַל־פְּנֵי תְהוֹם וְרוּחַ אֱלֹהִים מְרַחֶפֶת
עַל־פְּנֵי הַמָּיִם׃ וַיֹּאמֶר אֱלֹהִים יְהִי אוֹר וַיְהִי־אוֹר׃ וַיַּרְא
אֱלֹהִים אֶת־הָאוֹר כִּי־טוֹב וַיַּבְדֵּל אֱלֹהִים בֵּין הָאוֹר וּבֵין
הַחֹשֶׁךְ׃ וַיִּקְרָא אֱלֹהִים לָאוֹר יוֹם וְלַחֹשֶׁךְ קָרָא לָיְלָה וַיְהִי־
עֶרֶב וַיְהִי־בֹקֶר יוֹם אֶחָד׃

The opening verses of the Book of Genesis in the Hebrew Bible.

One Big Bang!

Many scientists find it difficult to incorporate such a metaphysical concept as God into their theories about the origins of life and the universe. One widely accepted scientific theory says that it all began with an immense explosion, which is popularly known as the Big Bang.

According to this theory, at one time, perhaps 15 billion years ago, a ball of matter and energy exploded, giving birth to an expanding universe. Various chemical elements and material structures were formed as a result, including stars and the other features of the cosmos.

In the right physical conditions, such as those found on earth, the chemical elements needed to create the simplest of life-forms came together to ultimately develop through biological evolution into the living world we experience today.

This theory, which in detail is quite complex, has undergone various modifications over the years, as do many scientific theories. Always lurking in the background, however, is this question: From where did the original matter originate, and what, or perhaps who, set the Big Bang into motion?

The Bible Tells Me So

Up until about 150 years ago or so, many people in Western countries (Europe and North America) weren't particularly interested in deep discussions about Big Bangs or human origins, as these sorts of matters were adequately covered in the Bible. God created heaven and earth, and that was explanation enough.

Other issues, such as the age of the earth, for example, or any other such question you might wish to answer, could be figured out by using information available in the Bible. Those who today believe in the literal truth of the Biblical creation story are called *creationists*.

Logos

Creationists are those who believe that God created the earth as described in the Book of Genesis.

Archbishop Ussher Dates the Earth

Using Biblical information such as genealogies and theological ideas about time, Irish archbishop James Ussher (1581–1656) in 1654 calculated the date of the creation of the Earth to the year 4004 B.C. This was for a long time the accepted date from which to calculate the age of our planet. Although scientists today might add a few billion years to that figure, we should be careful not to scoff at the archbishop, who arrived at a reasonable conclusion given the beliefs and tools of his time: the Bible and a trust in its literal truth.

Revelations

Archbishop Ussher's date of 4004 B.C. for the Creation was later elaborated with the exact day: October 23. That was the date on which the Jewish New Year, or Yom Kippur, occurred during that year.

Mammoth Crossing

The occasional discovery of fossils or the petrified bones of unknown creatures deep in the ground proved no obstacle to a Biblical interpretation. The story of Noah and the Great Deluge could explain how the creatures became interred in sediments during a global flood (see Chapter 6, "Nautical Noah and the Ark").

Illuminations

In traditional Jewish calendars, the number of years are counted from the date of Creation, which was estimated at 3761 B.C.

As for the remains of huge, unknown animals, some believed that living representatives of the giants' bones could be found in places as yet unexplored by Europeans, such as the African interior or the New World. American President Thomas Jefferson, who collected fossils, asked the explorers Lewis and Clark to keep their eyes open for animals such as mastodons and giant ground sloths on their expedition across the North American continent.

"And God said: Let there be light!"

(Illustration by Gustave Doré)

What Mr. Darwin Says

The comfortable Biblical explanation for the creation of life received an earth-shattering challenge with the publication of Charles Darwin's *Origin of Species* (1858). The book provided an alternate theory to explain how various and diverse life forms, including humans, came into being, all without requiring the direct involvement of God.

The subject of human origins was particularly provocative because the theory suggested that humans were distantly related to apes and other primates, and had, in fact, evolved from ape-like ancestors.

This idea seemed to discount the Biblical creation story and was seen as an insult to God, in whose image the Bible said humans were created. Besides, many people were revolted at the thought of being somehow related to hairy, gregarious, and arguably homely monkeys and apes.

In summary, Darwin's theory states that the various species of animals we see today, including humans, evolved over time through a process known as natural selection. Natural selection works because there is a certain amount of variation found within any species: Some individuals are taller, some have black fur and some have brown fur, and so on. In certain conditions, some of these variations will be advantageous and persist, while others will die out.

Visit
Beautiful
Jericho!!

People and Places

Charles Darwin (1809–1882) is considered to be the founder of modern evolutionary theory. His book, *Origin of Species* (1858), had a profound effect on science and religion.

Take for example a group of giraffes, some taller, some shorter. Let's say a drought occurs that kills the lower leaves on the giraffes' favorite trees. The long-necked giraffes will probably survive, because they will be able to reach enough food to avoid starvation. The short-necked giraffes probably won't survive, leaving the long-necked giraffes to make more baby long-necks, while the short-necked genes will likely die out. Survival of the fittest, as they say.

Revelations

Biologists have classified humans, along with all other forms of life. Here is where you stand: You're an animal as opposed to a plant. You're a vertebrate because you have a backbone, and you're a hairy, warm-blooded, milk-drinking mammal. You fit in well with monkeys and apes in the Primate order. Your genus is *Homo* and your species is *sapiens*.

The BIG Fight!

So what's the big deal? Well, aside from that thing about being related to apes, Darwinian evolutionary theory doesn't require God to be directly involved in the act of creation. The most adamant of creationists argue that the Bible is the infallible word of God, and what it says in there is what happened—period. Scientists, they claim, perpetuate a lie, and their propaganda must be countered.

The usual approach is to attack the weaknesses of evolutionary science, and this they do at times with great vigor! There are creationist institutes that make it their business to discover how the findings of scientists conform to the Biblical notion of creation, and to refute the data that doesn't.

This has its helpful side. Pointing out weaknesses in science can lead to their correction, no matter whether the results are favorable to creationist viewpoints or not. And scientists certainly have made some mistakes in their time. Let me say that the Creation vs. Evolution literature is vast, and you're only going to get a small sample of the contents here.

A favorite tactic of creationists is to point out some of the serious goofs made by evolutionists over the years, particularly when it comes to misidentified fossils. Here are just a few:

- **Nebraska Man.** In 1922, the fossilized tooth of an extinct peccary formed the basis for the reconstruction of a kind of prehistoric man. In this embarrassing incident, an artist even went so far as to reconstruct this husky, hairy fellow, much to the chagrin of evolutionists, who are repeatedly reminded of this gaff.
- **Piltdown Man.** Between 1912 and 1915, a fragment of a fossilized human skull was found in a gravel quarry in England along with what appeared to be a matching ape-like jaw bone. Some scientists believed that they had found the missing evolutionary link between apes and humans. Piltdown Man was a regular feature in textbooks until the whole thing was found to be a hoax in 1953. Someone—and there are several prominent suspects—planted the human skull fragments with the jaw of an orangutan. Ouch!
- In the early 1980s a skull fragment of a young donkey was initially identified as a very ancient European and in 1983, a purported human fossil collar bone was exposed as a dolphin rib.

Visit
Beautiful
Jericho!!

People and Places

Richard Dawkins (b. 1941) is one of the most eloquent spokesmen for scientific evolutionary theory. One of his most famous books, *The Blind Watchmaker* (1986), argues that a supernatural force is not necessary to account for the intricacies of nature. The process of evolution, he says, is perfectly capable of producing the diversity and complexity of all life on the planet.

Words of Wisdom

"In my most extreme fluctuations I have never been an atheist in the sense of denying the existence of God."

—Charles Darwin, *Life and Letters,* Volume 1 (1887)

As ridiculous as all of these incidents are, we need to give the scientists a little credit. In most cases, they are quick to acknowledge their mistakes and move on. After all, they, like the rest of us, are fallible, and science is by definition an ever-evolving process of discovery and modification.

The Age of the Earth

In addition to the human/ape question, there are a number of specific issues that really irk the creationists. The age of the earth is a major one. Creationists might argue that the earth is only about 6,000 years old, or maybe even older, but certainly not the four billion or so years that geologists have claimed. Geological and other scientific methods for dating the earth and the human past are radically flawed, they claim, and produce inconsistent results.

From a scientific perspective, yes, results are occasionally inconsistent. But this doesn't mean the whole system is flawed. Techniques such as radiocarbon dating can sometimes be cross-checked with other methods such as tree-ring dating, which produces an accurate calendar date.

Creationists also disparage the scientific assumption known as Uniformitarianism, a theory that says that the processes seen at work today are similar to those that were at work in the past. For example, if a deep river valley is now eroding at an average of an inch a year, it can be assumed that it was also eroding at about the same rate in the past. This means that a very long time indeed would have been required to produce the modern deep valley.

To explain these apparent long-term geological processes, creationists will often propose great earth upheavals or catastrophes, such as the global flood described in Genesis. Or they might suggest that many of the dramatic landforms we see today were manufactured at the time of creation. There are a number of creationists highly trained in science who in fact attempt to use science to make their point. These folks are sometimes referred to as *scientific creationists.*

Logos

Scientific creationists are believers in God who look at the findings of science to demonstrate and confirm their belief in Biblical creation.

The Fossil Record

One big thing that many creationists focus on is fossils. If evolution were true, then you might expect to find evidence of smooth transitions from one type of creature to another, but that's not usually the case. Where is such evidence?

Furthermore, creationists take great delight in pointing out the differences between textbooks of the past and those of the present, which show a marked difference in the proposed sequence of human evolution from ape-like creatures to modern man. Most scientists, however, readily admit that ideas have changed.

To really look at this issue, we need to know something about how things become fossils. Of the untold billions of creatures that ever inhabited the earth, only the remains of a tiny fraction have managed to survive as fossils. And of those, only a minute fraction have been discovered by scientists.

So with that being the case, it is not surprising that even if fossil evidence for transitional species exists, it isn't readily found in abundance. It also explains why the ideas about evolutionary sequences are always changing with the chance discovery of fossils here and there.

Revelations

Although Charles Darwin is best known as the founder of evolutionary theory, another man, Alfred Russel Wallace (1823–1913), had on his own and at about the same time arrived at the same conclusions. Darwin's promptness in getting his theory out resulted in his enduring fame today, while Wallace's contribution is not very well known.

Dinosaurs in the Neighborhood

Another thing often claimed by creationists, along with a young earth, is the coexistence of humans with extinct creatures such as the dinosaurs. If evolution is a sham, and all of the animals were created together, followed by humans, then it follows that they all lived together. There are a few strange "artifacts" that have been used to support this argument.

Near Glen Rose, Texas, for example, there are allegedly fossilized human tracks found next to those of dinosaurs. Scientists counter this claim by arguing that these are not human tracks at all, but the muddy fossilized prints of a smaller dinosaur. (Some modern entrepreneurs selling carvings of human footprints at the site didn't help matters.)

And then there is the question of where the dinosaurs are now. If God created these creatures, why would he cause them to go extinct? Some have argued that the earth was destroyed twice and the dinosaurs were taken out in the first instance.

Some Middle Ground?

There are many profoundly religious people who with a clear conscience can accept both the existence of God and the approaches of science. There are many ways of looking at the Bible and stories such as the ones in Genesis. Rather than a literal six days of creation, could the story not be more abstract than that? Could not the process of evolution be God's tool for populating the planet with a diversity of life over a long period of time?

While there are those who insist that everything was created in six 24-hour days, others point to a poetic description of God's view of time found in Psalms 90:4:

> For a thousand years in thy sight are but as yesterday when it is past, or as a watch in the night.

Words of Wisdom

"Instead of lessening the dignity of man's origin, evolution actually exalts it, by placing it far above the moistened dust or mud of the earth to living creatures endowed by God with sentiency and a form of intelligence."

—John A. O'Brien, *The Origin of Man* (1947)

In 1996, Pope John Paul II surprised many with his comments that "new knowledge has led to the recognition of the theory of evolution as more than a hypothesis." While such a statement seems to endorse scientific claims, the Pope emphasized that evolution does not explain the spiritual nature of humans, nor did he discount a role in the process for the Creator.

Another approach is to look at science and the Bible as apples and oranges. Science cannot tell you what your purpose on earth is, other than mating and perpetuating your genetic material. The Bible, however, can suggest a higher purpose for your existence and the ultimate source for all things. Science can attempt to describe how and when it might have happened; religion can provide the why.

Illuminations

The Scopes trial was the subject of a highly praised theatrical stage production written by Jerome Lawrence and Robert E. Lee entitled *Inherit the Wind,* which was also made into a major motion picture in 1960.

Monkeys on Trial

Occasionally, the debate between science and creationists leaves the church halls and printed page to become a serious legal matter. What should children be taught in schools? In America, where the separation of church and state is considered a basic principle, the role of the Bible in public government-funded schools is a hot topic. In a couple of classic cases, the Bible and evolution have had their day in court.

In 1925, the state of Tennessee passed a law banning the teaching of evolution in the classroom. In an effort to challenge this law, a public school science teacher, John Scopes, volunteered to be put on trial. The famous Scopes Monkey Trial took place in that same year and became a great public spectacle as religious fundamentalist prosecutor and former presidential candidate William Jennings Bryan faced the defendant's lawyer Clarence Darrow in a theatrical courtroom battle. Each side dramatically presented their case for and against evolution and in the end, Scopes was convicted and fined $100. The case was later overturned on a technicality.

Can't We All Just Get Along?

The controversy certainly didn't end with the Scopes trial! In August 1999, the Kansas Board of Education ruled to give evolution a back seat in their public school curricula. Although it can be mentioned in the classroom, it won't be discussed in depth as the primary biological theory that explains the diversity of life. Other bits of this new ruling also give a boost to creationist notions.

As you can see, the Creation/Evolution debate can be nasty. Here are a few tips that I would like to offer on this discussion.

VISIT
BEAUTIFUL
JERICHO!!

People and Places

Dr. Duane Gish is one of the most outspoken of the scientific creationists. He has written numerous articles discounting evolutionary theory and is very skillful in debating scientists. He is the director of an organization called the Institute for Creation Research, which is dedicated to supporting Biblical notions of creation.

Hey Evolutionists!

Give those Creation people some slack! Much of their argument is from faith, which isn't very debatable. Furthermore, they're dealing with certain concepts, like God, that aren't readily measurable in a laboratory. They're also defending their deeply held beliefs, which they fear might be suppressed by scoffing skeptical secularists. You can also accept the fact that a lot of creationist folks are just as smart as you are, but maintain a different belief system.

Words of Wisdom

"When a certain shameless fellow mockingly asked a pious old man what God had done before the creation of the world, the latter aptly countered that he had been building hell for the curious."

—John Calvin, *Institutes,* I (1536)

Hey Creationists!

These scientists aren't all religion-hating atheists. Many believe in God, but maybe not exactly the same way you do. Also, learn a little more about the scientific process, which is subject to change as discoveries are made. A clear idea of the details of dating methods and of evolutionary theory would help a lot.

And quit bringing up all of the old dirty laundry like Nebraska Man that has long been acknowledged as an embarrassing mistake. Come up with some new stuff once in a while, and quit quoting from out-of-date science textbooks. Planting doubts in people's heads might be good for your cause, but ultimately, faith in a good and just God is more important than nitpicking the scientists.

Hey Both of You!

Stop the ridicule and hostility. It doesn't help your case in the eyes of thoughtful people, and it doesn't contribute to a credible debate.

Teaching Tolerance

When I teach courses in archaeology or anthropology, I am very aware that there is a mix of all viewpoints in my classroom. I'll often begin by reading a bit of Genesis, in Hebrew, and explaining to the students that no matter what they personally believe, the stories in Genesis have been an important part of explaining the past for many centuries. Genesis is thereby acknowledged. No matter what you might personally believe about God, the Biblical creation story was and is very influential.

When I go on to explain evolutionary theory, I make it clear that no matter what you believe, a well-educated individual should be aware of the contending theories regarding the origins of the earth and its creatures. In short, I don't care what individuals personally believe, but an awareness of other's ideas is always worthwhile. Consider the arguments and make up your own mind!

The Least You Need to Know

- The question of Creation is an incredibly controversial and complex subject.
- Creationists believe that God created the earth exactly as described in the first chapter of Genesis.
- Some creationists believe that the earth is only about 6,000 years old, while most scientists contend that it's in the billions.
- Scientists often explain the origin of the earth in terms of an original cosmic explosion, and the variety of life in terms of evolutionary processes.
- Although scientists and creationists often disagree, it's also possible to see religion and science as providing their own answers to different kinds of questions.

Chapter 5

The Wonders of Genesis

In This Chapter

- God creates humans, who disappoint him
- Adam and Eve get kicked out of Paradise
- The tongue-twisting Tower of Babel
- Abraham strikes a deal
- Sodom and Gomorrah

Of all of the books in the Bible, one could easily argue that Genesis is the most diverse and amazing. The story of Creation, of course, is utterly remarkable. But it doesn't end there. Genesis goes on to explain in its own way a lot of other things that are both mysterious and enlightening. A talking snake leads to pain and suffering; humans try to build a skyscraper to heaven and end up utterly confused; God totally wipes out a city full of wicked people; and a whole lot more. Let's take a look at a few of these wonderful events.

In God's Image

At the end of the Creation story in Genesis, God creates a couple of humans, one male and one female. The first man is created from dust, and God breathes life into him. The man is given the name Adam, which is related to the Hebrew word "earth," because he was taken out of the earth. He is then put under divine anesthesia, and a female companion is created from him out of one of his ribs!

It's quite clear that Adam and Eve are created separately from the rest of the earth's creatures, and God puts them in charge of the planet. Now this is an interesting thing, and you can look at it at least two ways. If all of this great stuff on earth is yours as a gift from God, then it's okay to suck up all the fish into drift nets, dig strip mines wherever it's convenient, and chop down trees whenever it seems useful. On the other hand, you can argue that to be given jurisdiction over the earth is an awesome responsibility that requires care, skill, and good judgment.

Revelations

Kids love this old riddle: An archaeologist finds an intact, ancient tomb. Inside there are no artifacts and no inscriptions—only two perfectly preserved naked human bodies laid out on stone slabs, one male and one female. The archaeologist immediately declares that this is the tomb of Adam and Eve! Why? Since Adam and Eve were not born but were created by God, they have no bellybuttons!

Illuminations

I've heard a couple of people tell me that men have one fewer rib in their skeleton than women. They get this idea, of course, from the story in Genesis. Not so! Both men and women have the same number of bones in their body: 206 in the adult skeleton.

No Place Like Home

Genesis tells us that Adam and Eve lived in a wonderful garden where they could frolic naked in a safe and worry-free environment. So where was this Garden? The Bible actually gives some geographical clues in Genesis 2:10:

> A river flowed out of Eden to water the garden, and there it divided and became four rivers.

- **The Pishon**, which flows around the land of Havilah, where, according to the Bible, gold and other precious materials can be found.
- **The Gihon**, which flows around Cush.
- **The Tigris**, in Mesopotamia.
- **The Euphrates**, also in Mesopotamia.

This places the Garden somewhere in a fairly large area in the Middle East—some say right in the vicinity of modern-day Iraq! And what's left of this place today, you ask? Most likely nothing to speak of! The whole region is generally hot, dry, and occasionally troublesome. Run around naked there today and you'll either get the worst sunburn of your life or be thrown in jail for public indecency!

Adam's First Wife?

Some old Hebrew stories that aren't in the Bible describe a wife for Adam before Eve. This woman, named Lilith, refused to be dominated by or even equal to Adam and left him to become a bit of a demoness with the power to torment newborn babies. Eve was then created as a suitable replacement.

Eve Meets Science

It would be fair to say that most scientists don't take the story of Adam and Eve literally. Some believe, however, that there could be a common female ancestor for all *Homo sapiens*. A recent study examined the mutations found in a type of DNA (the genetic code found in all human cells) transferred from mother to child, called Mitochondrial DNA, and announced that such a common ancestor existed in Africa around 200,000 years ago.

Not surprisingly, this controversial idea has its critics, some of whom claim that it's difficult to gauge how much time has passed using genetic mutations. Despite the theory's flaws, however, most evolutionary scientists agree that all humans had their origins in Africa.

VISIT
BEAUTIFUL
JERICHO!!

People and Places

The character of Lilith has become something of a symbol in some parts of the feminist movement, representing strength without dependence upon men.

Revelations

Mitochondrial DNA, or mtDNA, is a type of DNA found outside a cell's nucleus. This sort of DNA is thought to be inherited unmixed from one's maternal line and has given scientists hope of tracking ancient relationships and migrations of people.

Illuminations

What were the first words spoken between humans in the Garden of Eden? One amusing suggestion is that the first man introduced himself to his new partner using a palindrome: "Madam, I'm Adam." (A palindrome is a phrase that is spelled the same frontward or backward.)

Logos

Original sin is the concept that humans have inherited the sinful nature of Adam and Eve.

Forbidden Fruit

Wherever the Garden of Eden was, life there was pretty good. God gave Adam and Eve only one rule: Don't eat the fruit from a particular tree. This was the Tree of Knowledge of Good and Evil. But Eve passed by the tree one day and a mysterious talking snake convinced her to have a sample. She did so, and offered a bite to Adam, and the first known sins were committed. The fruit had its effect and their carefree days were over. They realized they were naked and ran for the fig leaves.

This story is loaded with controversy. Was Eve, and metaphorically all women, a gullible temptress who lured Adam into doing a bad thing? On the other hand, Adam had a choice, and that might be what this story is really about: free will. Given the options of good and not good, humans have a choice.

Now this gets into some heavy philosophical and even biological territory. Do we really have free will, or are some of our choices determined by our environment, upbringing, or even our genetic code? The story is also loaded with implications about the nature of sin—in this case, disobeying God's rules—and also about the human capacity for temptation.

By the way, the fruit of the Tree of Knowledge is often popularly depicted as an apple. The Bible doesn't specify exactly what kind of fruit it is, but apples are suitably attractive if you happen to be drawing a picture.

Bad Snake!

Adam and Eve made their mistake and were apparently aware of it, because they hid from God when He came to visit. Adam blames the woman, of course, and Eve blames the snake, and God punishes all three. Snakes are cursed and condemned to crawl along the ground. Childbirth will be unpleasant for Eve. Adam's life on the gravy-train is over. From now on, he's going to have to work hard for a living! And they're kicked out of the Garden. And just in case they try to sneak back in, an angel with a flaming sword is placed at the entrance.

Adam and Eve get kicked out of the Garden of Eden for bad behavior.

(Engraving by Gustave Doré)

Some theologians will say that this story of Adam and Eve wonderfully illustrates human nature. For those seeking to understand why humans are the way they are, and why most of our lives aren't a free ride, the story has some interesting insights.

In Roman Catholic doctrine, all humans have inherited the guilt of their oldest ancestors, Adam and Eve: a concept known as *original sin*. Instead of believing that all humans when born are a blank slate with the capacity to do good or evil, the notion of original sin says that you're bad when you're born, so you need a forgiving God, and Jesus in particular, to overcome your sinful nature.

Illuminations

In Genesis (1:28), God commands Adam and Eve to "be fruitful and multiply." This is considered the first of the 613 commandments traditionally recognized by Jews in the Torah.

Words of Wisdom

"God delights in our temptations, and yet hates them; He delights in them when they drive us to prayer; He hates them when they drive us to despair."
—Martin Luther, *Table Talk*

Paradise Lost

So Adam and Eve had to work for a living, but soon they gained some helpers when they had a couple of kids. Cain, their firstborn, became a farmer. His brother was named Abel and raised sheep. Both made offerings to God. An argument arose between the two brothers and Cain killed Abel: the first murder, of untold millions to follow. God punished Cain and exiled him to a miserable life.

God also places a mysterious mark on Cain lest someone find him and decide to murder him as well. In doing this, God might be showing a kind of mercy. What is this mark? No one knows for sure, but the story has more than once been twisted around by racists to justify abusive behavior. (For example, the "mark of Cain" might be dark skin, so dark-skinned people are the cursed descendants of Cain.)

Cain's New Career

Here's another big mystery: In Genesis 4:17, Cain's wife is mentioned. Where did she come from if Adam and Eve had only sons? This question is usually answered by saying that Adam and Eve must have had other kids and Cain married one of his sisters. Anyway, Cain is said to have gone out and built a city, which he named Enoch after his son.

The stories of Genesis from the Garden of Eden through Cain's building of a city are interesting from an anthropological point of view. In studying early civilizations, anthropologists have noted that the first humans were hunters and gatherers who lived off the land and in harmony with nature. Similar societies today are generally egalitarian, share their resources, and have a lot more leisure time than you might expect.

Out of some of the early hunting and gathering groups, about 10,000 years ago, the first villages arose, and these were supported by agriculture and domesticated animals. Some argue that this change in lifestyle, although it had some benefits, encouraged some of the worst of human behavior, including theft and envy of personal property, along with power inequities brought about by the uneven distribution of wealth.

From some of these early agricultural societies would arise the first cities and civilizations. In a sense, the Genesis story follows a similar developmental sequence: Adam and Eve begin in harmony with nature in the Garden. They're kicked out and begin a much harder life, and bad things such as the murder of Abel occur. Cain builds the first city.

Illuminations

After Cain murdered Abel, God asked Cain where his brother might be, and Cain answered, "Am I my brother's keeper?" (Genesis 4:9) This question, referring to one's responsibility to other humans, is a question that continues to be asked and discussed to this day.

The Tower of Babel

We're going to skip a couple of wonderfully puzzling Genesis stories, and get back to them later (the famous story of Noah's Ark is featured in the next chapter, and we'll also take a look at some great genealogies featuring some very old people). For now, let's look at a truly strange construction project.

By the time we get to Genesis 11:1–9, there are a whole bunch of people around, and they're acting a bit arrogant. So arrogant, in fact, that they attempted to build a brick skyscraper tall enough to reach heaven! This is a preposterous thing to do, but it doesn't stop them from trying.

God doesn't approve of this sort of behavior, so he messes up their building project in a very clever way. Instead of wrecking the place, he causes the workers to speak mutually unintelligible languages and scatters them over the face of the earth.

What Did You Say?

This story serves as an explanation for the multitude of languages found on the earth today. Many linguists see the real story as being a little more complicated than that, but perhaps at one time there was a single human language that originally diverged when groups became separated and their languages evolved independently.

Revelations

The number of the world's languages today is estimated to be around four to five thousand. Many of the smaller languages are dying out, while English-speakers grow in number. One of the rarest languages is a Biblical one, Aramaic, which is today spoken in only two villages in Syria.

Ancient Skyscrapers

The story of the Tower of Babel is thought to have taken place in Babylon, a region and city in Mesopotamia, in the vicinity of modern-day Iraq. The ancient people of Mesopotamia were known to build tall temple platforms known as *ziggurats,* and the ruins of a number of these impressive structures survive. Nineteenth-century travelers through the region saw some of these remains and went so far as to identify at least one as the famous Tower.

Although a few ziggurats are tall, there are none to be found of sufficient size and height to identify with the story. And even if there were, we still couldn't be sure it was the original Tower. But it is certainly possible that the ziggurats, or something like them, were the inspiration for an interesting lesson, whether or not a literal Tower of Babel was ever attempted.

The Tower of Babel.

(Engraving by Gustave Doré)

A Divine Covenant

One of the most important characters in Genesis, and certainly in the Jewish religion, is Abraham, a nomad from Ur in Mesopotamia with whom God struck a deal. In return for Abraham's obedience and exclusive worship of the one true God, God would look after Abraham and his descendants.

Of course there was a little more to it than that. In fact, there were two parts to the deal, or covenant. Part one was the spiritual contract between God and Abraham. Part two was a physical contract: Abraham and his male descendants were required to be circumcised. This would be a mark that would distinguish their people from others.

Why Not a Tattoo?

Circumcision is an interesting idea, when you think about it. Why not a tattoo, a funny hat, or some other distinguishing mark or attribute? And God asked that the operation be performed on the eighth day after the birth of a baby boy. Abraham didn't have that option, so he did it to himself with a flint knife when he was 90 years old!

The practice of circumcision still goes on today in the Jewish community, and on the eighth day if at all possible. In fact, the event is often celebrated with a ceremony called a Berit Milah, or *bris,* which includes family, friends, and a nice buffet. Interestingly, some medical studies have claimed that the eighth day is indeed optimal for the procedure.

Logos

A **bris** is the Jewish circumcision ceremony. It is performed by a person specially trained to perform a circumcision, called a *mohel.* While there are plenty of good mohel jokes to be found in Jewish humor, the bris is a profoundly meaningful ceremony for Jewish families, and has been for many centuries.

A Promise Fulfilled

In many areas of North America, circumcision is routinely performed on infant boys, regardless of religion. Although it has been practiced for thousands of years, circumcision has recently become controversial. While some claim that it has worthwhile health and hygiene benefits, others claim that it is a form of unnecessary mutilation inflicted on infants. For Jewish people, however, it is a link through time back to Abraham and the original covenant, and the fulfillment of a divine commandment.

Abraham and Isaac

Abraham became a father and the ancestor of a great nation, but it took a miracle to do it. God told Abraham and his wife Sarah that they were going to have a son. (Genesis 18) Sarah laughed, because Abraham was 100 years old and she was 90.

But, according to the story, a son did come, and they named him Isaac. Abraham had already had a son by one of his maidservants, Hagar. That child was named Ishmael, and is traditionally considered the ancestor of the Arabs, while Isaac is the ancestor of the Jews.

Speaking of Isaac, he is featured in one of the most disturbing stories found in the Bible. As a test of Abraham's willingness to obey God, God orders him to take his beloved son up to a mountain, build an altar, and sacrifice the boy. (Genesis 22) Abraham is just about to do the deed when he's told to stop, and a ram is found nearby to be sacrificed instead. This troubling story has engaged theologians for decades.

Illuminations

Muslims believe that it was Ishmael who was the favored son of Abraham and that he was the son who was bound on the altar in God's test.

Words of Wisdom

"No virtue is ever so strong that it is beyond temptation."

—Immanuel Kant, *Lecture at Konigsberg* (1775)

Sodom and Gomorrah

Genesis features another well-known story about how God dealt with evil people. There were two cities with horrible reputations: Sodom and Gomorrah. The people were apparently engaging in all manner of depravity, and God had had enough and told Abraham so. Abraham was a bit concerned about God's plan to destroy the cities, because his nephew Lot, a decent fellow, and his family were living in Sodom.

A couple of angels were sent to have a talk with Lot, and a riot nearly broke out when the local men wanted to have a little fun with the divine visitors. Lot would have nothing of the sort. He even offered his two virgin daughters to the lustful mob, but they insisted that he hand over the angels. The angels blinded some of these rioters as they attempted to beat the door down.

The Pillar of Salt

The angels warned Lot to remove his family from the city, and the next day they escaped. Sodom, along with Gomorrah, was destroyed in a "hail of fire and brimstone." Lot's family had been told to leave the city and not look back, but Lot's wife apparently couldn't resist taking a look at the city under destruction. The Bible says that she was transformed into a pillar of salt.

The sites traditionally identified with Sodom and Gomorrah are found at the southern end of the Dead Sea near the Israeli-Jordanian border. The area is interesting geologically, with very high concentrations of salts and other chemicals. There is even a rock formation that has been given the name "Lot's wife."

God Is in the Details

Recently, a couple of geologists speculated that an earthquake may have swallowed up the cities as the shaking land liquefied. Others have suggested that volcanic or geothermal activity contributed to the hail of fire and brimstone said to have demolished the cities.

Although it can't be positively determined that any ancient remains there are indeed the actual cities, the nature of the area certainly inspires thoughts of fire, brimstone, and salt! Like so much else in the Bible, there are intriguing suggestions, but it can be pretty hard to pin down the details.

The Least You Need to Know

- The book of Genesis is full of stories that illuminate the human condition.
- The story of Adam and Eve illustrates that given free will, humans have the capacity for both good and evil.
- The story of the Tower of Babel shows the dangers of arrogance and explains the diversity of languages in the world.
- A covenant struck between Abraham and God formed the foundation for the monotheistic beliefs shared by Jews, Christians, and Muslims to this day.
- In the Old Testament, when God gets tired of human excesses, watch out. Sodom and Gomorrah are a prime example.

Chapter 6

Nautical Noah and the Ark

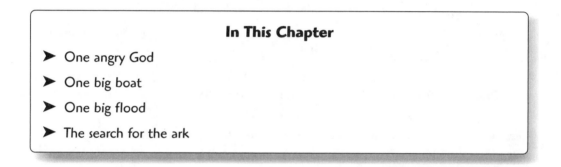

In This Chapter

- One angry God
- One big boat
- One big flood
- The search for the ark

Yet another of the marvelous and sometimes baffling stories of Genesis is that of Noah's Ark. (Genesis 6–8) In the clash between scientists and those who believe in a very literal interpretation of the Bible, this story is nearly as volatile as that of Creation.

In the last chapter, I wrote a little about how God became seriously angry with a group of misbehaving humans, the citizens of Sodom and Gomorrah, and leveled the place. The story of Noah and the Flood actually takes place well before Abraham, Lot, and company, but because it is such a special story, it deserves its own chapter.

God Has Had Enough

Here's the story. In Genesis 6:5–6, it is written:

> The Lord saw that the wickedness of man was great in the earth, and that every imagination of the thoughts of his heart was only evil continually. And the Lord was sorry that he had made man on the earth, and it grieved him in his heart. So the Lord said, "I will blot out man whom I have created from the face of the ground, man and beast and creeping things and birds of the air, for I am sorry that I have made them."

Verse 11 goes on to say that "the earth was corrupt in God's sight, and the earth was filled with violence." Look what Adam and Eve started! Given free will and a little temptation, the habit of bad behavior has been carried on in following generations. God decides it's time to start over.

> I have determined to make an end of all flesh; for the earth is filled with violence through them; behold, I will destroy them with the earth … I will bring a flood of waters upon the earth, to destroy all flesh which is the breath of life from under heaven; everything that is on the earth shall die.

Noah, however, was righteous and "walked with God," so he is chosen for a special job. He is instructed to build a boat which will save him and his wife, along with their three sons and their wives, from the impending deluge.

First Build a Boat

God gave Noah specific instructions for building the boat:

- It should be built of gopher wood.
- It should be 300 cubits long, 50 cubits wide, and 30 cubits high.
- It should have three decks.
- It should have rooms.
- It should be covered with pitch inside and out.
- It should have a roof.
- There should be a door on one side.

First of all, let's look at the building material. We really don't know what "gopher wood" is. It certainly has nothing to do with the modern rodent we call the gopher. The wood gets its name from the literal pronunciation of the Hebrew word as it appears in the Bible, and the word appears only in this story.

It's possible that this wood is cypress. It's also possible that "gopher wood" might be sturdy bundles of reeds, whose natural buoyancy would be further preserved with a coating of pitch. Boats of papyrus and reeds were known to have been used in Biblical lands.

Visit
Beautiful
Jericho!!

People and Places

Noah is listed in the New Testament book of Hebrews as one of the giants of faith for taking God at His word and building the ark.

Illuminations

Given the wicked nature of the people of his day, Noah and his family must have been the butt of intense scoffing and ridicule for their mammoth, and probably high and dry, building project. Noah, though, would have the last laugh.

A Really Big Boat

To figure out the size of the boat, we need to know how big a "cubit" is. Traditionally, it was a distance from the elbow to the end of the fingers and was probably about 17½ to 20 inches. If we take 18 inches for a rough estimate, then Noah's boat would be 450 feet long, 75 feet wide, and 45 feet high! That's a big boat.

There have been many attempts to reconstruct the ark based on the scant information provided in Genesis. It is often depicted as rectangular because of the dimensions given in the Bible, but it's possible that it could have been wider in the middle, like many wooden boats.

Illuminations

Boats of reeds are mentioned in Isaiah 18:1–2. In the late 1960s and 1970s, Norwegian explorer and scholar Thor Heyerdahl tested the seaworthiness of ancient boats by crossing the Atlantic in a boat of papyrus reeds and later traveling about the Persian Gulf and beyond on another reed ship. Most of his attempts were successful: They really do float!

Room for All

It's a roomy boat because not only will Noah's family be aboard, but male and female pairs of all the animals, as well, to repopulate the earth after life is destroyed. In Chapter 6, God commands Noah:

> And of every living thing of all flesh, you shall bring two of every sort into the ark, to keep them alive with you; they shall be male and female … two of every sort shall come in to you, to keep them alive. Also take with you every sort of food that is eaten, and store it up; and it shall serve as food for you and them.

This explains the need for all of those rooms—to keep the various beasts separated, not to mention providing storage space for their food!

All Aboard!

So the world is going to be destroyed, and a pair of each animal is needed to get things going again later. That's a heck of a lot of animals, even for a massive ship like Noah's! Furthermore, there's another description in the story that states that God wanted even more animals:

> Seven pairs of all clean animals … and a pair of the animals that are not clean … and seven pairs of the birds of the air also.

This is a whole bunch of animals, given the thousands of species that abound today. And what happened to the idea of just two pairs, anyway? Things are getting complicated.

Revelations

Noah's boat is traditionally called an ark, but this word can be confusing. It's an English translation of the Hebrew word *tevah,* which is also the word used for the floating, tar-sealed basket in the story of Moses. The word "ark" is also applied to another famous Biblical artifact: the Ark of the Covenant, a special box likewise created with specific instructions from God (see Chapter 11, "The Ark of the Covenant"). The Hebrew word for this object, though, is *aron*. Today, the word "ark" is also used for the alcove in a synagogue that holds the Torah scrolls.

How Many Beasts?

Defenders of the literal truth of the story sometimes argue that representative varieties of the different animals were placed aboard the boat, rather than a pair of each species. This idea, however, would require some sort of evolutionary repopulation mechanism, or a flood that wasn't world-wide.

And what about the seven pairs? Some speculate that the seven pairs of clean animals might refer specifically to those species that were used in sacrifices. If you didn't have some extras around, after all, you'd lose a whole species just by being pious.

Illuminations

There was no need for big aquariums on the ark. Apparently fish weren't affected by the Flood.

Who Rooms with Rex?

For those who subscribe to the young earth theory and believe that dinosaurs and humans co-existed, there seems to be a real space problem when it comes to huge beasts such as the mighty Brontosaurus or the fierce, carnivorous *Tyrannosaurus rex.* One fellow explained to me that yes, the dinosaurs were also aboard the ark, but they took baby ones to save on space.

The Big Flood

In any case, Noah, who was 600 years old at the time of the flood, proceeded to load up the ark, and the flood began. According to Genesis 7:

> All of the fountains of the great deep burst forth, and the windows of the heavens were opened. And it rained forty days and forty nights .... The waters increased and prevailed and increased greatly upon the earth; and the ark

> floated on the face of the waters. And the waters prevailed so mightily upon the earth that all the high mountains under the whole heaven were covered; the waters prevailed above the mountains, covering them fifteen cubits deep.

The flooding continued for 150 days, and the ark came to rest on a mountain. Noah sent out a raven and then a dove to search for land. Finally, after almost a year, Noah and company left the ark when things were sufficiently dry. He then built an altar and made a sacrifice to God.

Fountains of the Deep

Now building a big boat is one thing, and Noah's age might raise a few scientific eyebrows, but a world-wide flood that destroyed everything on the earth except the passengers of the ark is a leading bone of contention between religious fundamentalists and many scientists. How could the entire earth be covered with water? Mount Everest is 29,028 feet tall! And where did all the water come from—and where did it go afterward?

Let's look at some of the explanations people have suggested over the years:

- One theory is that the phrase "fountains of the great deep" refers to water trapped under pressure beneath the earth in the *antediluvian,* or pre-flood, environment, which may have been quite different from the world in the aftermath of the great Deluge.
- Another idea is that in Noah's day, the atmosphere was quite different from what it is now, and featured a "water vapor canopy" encircling the earth that provided a second source for the huge amounts of water necessary to flood the entire surface of the planet to a great depth.
- Others believe that a comet hit the earth, causing huge catastrophic effects including changes in the weather, radical alteration of the earth's surface, and massive flooding. Subscribers to the young earth theory would have this happening about 5,000 years ago.

VISIT
BEAUTIFUL
JERICHO!!

People and Places

The wettest spot on the face of the earth is Mount Waialeale on Kauai in the Hawaiian Islands. It rains there most of the time. And people in Seattle can certainly relate to what 40 days and 40 nights of rain is all about!

LOGOS

Logos

The **Deluge** refers to the great flood recorded in the book of Genesis. **Antediluvian** refers to the world before the Deluge.

Pulling the Plug

And where did the water go afterward? It now makes up the oceans, goes one theory, because along with the flood came a major reshaping of the earth's surface: Mountain ranges rose, big valleys and canyons were scoured out, and deep basins opened for the oceans. Huge mountains like Everest were lifted up, and the flood waters drained to the deep areas below.

As we saw with the Creation story, the Bible has long been used to explain various episodes of the distant past. The Great Flood is a particular favorite, providing the explanation for the various human and animal fossils buried in the ground, including the curious phenomenon of fossil sea shells found in geological strata high up in the mountains.

Modern geology, however, tells quite a different story, seeing the planet's present state as the result of various processes taking place over hundreds of millions, if not billions, of years.

Visit
Beautiful
Jericho!!

People and Places

It was left for Noah's family to repopulate the earth. Noah's eldest son, Shem, is considered the ancestor of the Hebrew people. His name is the source of the word "Semitic," which has been applied to the language family which includes Hebrew, and to speakers thereof.

Floods of Epic Proportions

Although geologists will dispute that there ever was a world-wide flood, legends about big floods are common in many cultures around the world, including others in the Middle East. There, in 1872, a dramatic discovery was made of an ancient text that contains a story very much like the one in Genesis.

The text was found on a clay tablet excavated from the site of Kuyunjik in Mesopotamia and is part of a popular saga known as the *Epic of Gilgamesh.* In this story an immortal man named Utnapishtim tells Gilgamesh a story that is dramatically similar to Noah's.

Long ago, the story goes, the gods were displeased with humans, so they decided to destroy all living things on the earth. But one god gave his friend Utnapishtim advance warning so he could build a boat big enough for his family, belongings, and a selection of living creatures. A storm raged for seven days, bringing massive flooding.

The boat came to rest on a mountain, and three birds were released to check for dry land. When it was safe to leave the boat, Utnapishtim built an altar and made a sacrifice to the gods. Is this independent confirmation of the Biblical story, in a slightly distorted version? Did the author of Genesis borrow from Gilgamesh? Or was the flood story part of a wider regional myth, legend, or historical memory?

Digging for Sediments

In the 1920s, while excavating at the site of Ur in Mesopotamia, British archaeologist Leonard Woolley found a very thick deposit of flood debris which generated much excitement. Could this be archaeological evidence of the Biblical Deluge?

Revelations

The *Epic of Gilgamesh* survives in several copies written on clay tablets in the Sumerian and Akkadian languages of Mesopotamia. The epic describes the adventures of a part-man/part-god hero named Gilgamesh. At one point, Gilgamesh seeks the survivor of the great flood, Utnapishtim, to try to find the secret of his immortality. Gilgamesh was unsuccessful in achieving a similar status.

A big flood certainly had taken place at one time at Ur, but a check of other sites in the region didn't turn up the same evidence. Besides, the deposits found at Ur were much too late to have been related to the Great Flood. This flood had been more or less local, and in Mesopotamia, a flood plain in the midst of two rivers, the occurrence of a flood is not that surprising.

A More Limited Viewpoint

It is also possible that the flood that the Bible describes was not world-wide, after all. The Hebrew word used in the Bible for the flooded area is *eretz*, which can mean not only "the earth," but also "the land." This being so, perhaps the story was actually describing a more local event.

If the flood was immense and regional, then it might indeed appear to Noah that all of his world was inundated. Some Biblical literalists heartily reject this more explainable situation, however, in favor of a global catastrophe.

More Science

Is there any other evidence for large-scale flooding that might support the Genesis story? Well, relatively recently, in geological terms, the Ice Age had a profound effect upon the shaping of the earth. After the last period of glaciation, melting ice contributed to a global sea-level rise of about 300 feet! Large sections of land that were once exposed became submerged as a result. Could the story of Noah be an ancient memory related to these earth phenomena?

Whether the details of the account of Noah and the flood are literal or a great tale that illustrates God's judgment and redemption, it is, nonetheless, a fascinating story that will continue to inspire Bible readers and ark-hunters. The end of the narrative is especially touching. God promises Noah that he will never again destroy the earth with a flood. As a reminder of His promise, God placed a bow in the sky as a sign—the rainbow that is seen in the sky when sun and mist come together.

Noah's Ark grounded on Mt. Ararat.

(Engraving by Gustave Doré)

Illuminations

Most people probably don't give much thought to the shape of the rainbow, but its curved arch is in the shape of the weapon known as a bow, as in bow and arrows. It is this sort of bow that God refers to in the story of Noah.

The Search for the Ark

The Bible says that the ark came to rest on the mountains of Ararat, so if we can identify this place, might we not be able to find the remains of the ark itself? Finding Noah's Ark could be the most important and amazing archaeological discovery of all time! But there are a couple of things to consider first:

- We must assume that what the Bible says in the story of Noah is literally true, and not a metaphor or some other literary device.

- We would have to assume that the ark was deposited in an environment conducive to its long-term survival. This is by no means guaranteed, especially if it was built of perishable materials.

With these assumptions met, we might confidently go out looking for the big boat.

Revelations

Some recent research has produced convincing geological evidence for a massive flood in the area of the Black Sea around 5600 B.C. Perhaps as a result of rising sea levels following the Ice Age, the waters of the Mediterranean Sea poured forcefully into the Black Sea, which at the time was a fresh-water lake surrounded by farmland. Could such a dramatic phenomenon inspire tales of a great flood?

Which Mountain?

The Bible says the ark ended up in the mountains (plural) of Ararat, and the most likely region is that known as Urartu in ancient times, an area north of Mesopotamia. There one might expect to find the ark firmly lodged on a tall mountain, and the all-time favorite candidate is a mountain in eastern Turkey called Agri Dagh, or Ararat.

The Koran, the holy book of Islam, gives a different location for the ark: "Mount Judi," which is usually identified with a mountain called Cudi Dagh in southern Turkey. Although not nearly as high as Agri Dagh, this mountain appears to have a much older tradition as the site of the ark's resting place.

VISIT
BEAUTIFUL
JERICHO!!

People and Places

The mountain in Turkey traditionally identified as Mount Ararat is a volcano and stands 16,940 feet tall. Its Turkish name, Agri Dagh, means "Mountain of Pain."

Ancient Reports

Ark hunters are encouraged by mentions of the boat's survival dating back a couple of thousand years. A Chaldean priest named Berossus wrote in the third century B.C. that pieces of the ark still survived and people could scrape pitch off of them for use on amulets.

The first-century Jewish historian Josephus mentions reports that the remains of the ark were still in existence. Subsequent reports by Christian and Muslim writers continued to mention that ark remains could be found on mountains that are named as, or fit the description of, Ararat, or alternatively Judi.

Recent Sightings

Several twentieth-century eyewitnesses claim to have actually seen the ark on Mount Ararat. A Turk named George Hagopian said that around the year 1905, when he was a young boy, he was taken by his uncle to the site of the ark. It was located on a ledge at the edge of a cliff, and was made of some rock-hard material.

Logos

Arkologist is a term used for those who are interested in locating the remains of Noah's ark.

The boy thought the structure was stone until he was told otherwise by his uncle. The skeptic in me might suggest that this was indeed some sort of stone structure of undetermined origin, which was believed by locals to be part of the ark.

Another fascinating report was made by a Russian pilot named Roskovitsky, who allegedly flew his plane near Ararat in 1916 and spotted a boat at the edge of a frozen lake. The story goes on to say that a subsequent Russian expedition to investigate this report found the ark and explored its interior, which contained hundreds of rooms of different sizes. A detailed description of the ark is said to have been written, and photographs taken, but alas, all was lost in the Russian revolution in the following year.

Several decades later, an American serviceman, Ed Davis, reported being taken by locals high up on Ararat to see a large fragment of the ark. No pictures were taken. In the 1950s and 1960s a Frenchman, Fernand Navarra, visited Ararat several times and returned with some interesting samples of wood which he claimed were taken from a structure embedded in ice high up on the mountain. When the wood was radiocarbon dated, however, it dated mainly to around A.D. 600 to 800.

The ark has on other occasions been "spotted" from the air, but searches on the ground have yet to reveal anything substantial. A few years ago, a startling claim was made that the ark had indeed been discovered, but again documentation was lacking. The camera with the photographic proof fell down the side of the mountain. In time, this story proved to be a complete hoax.

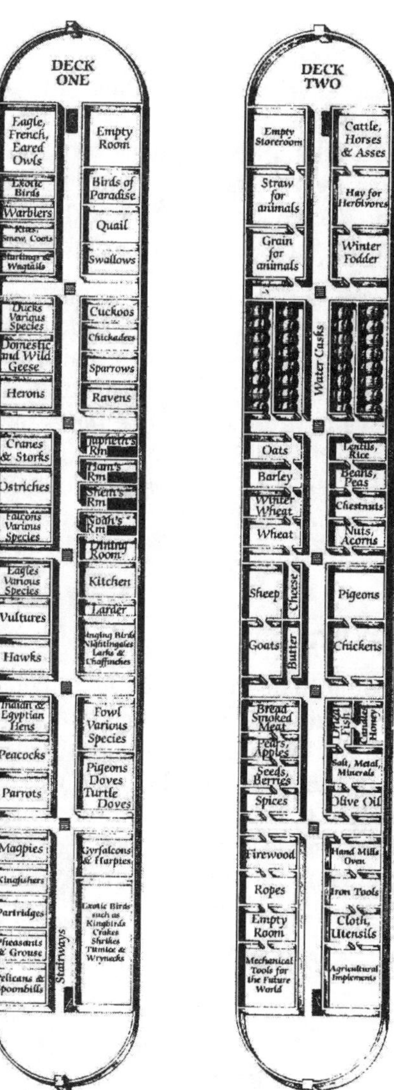

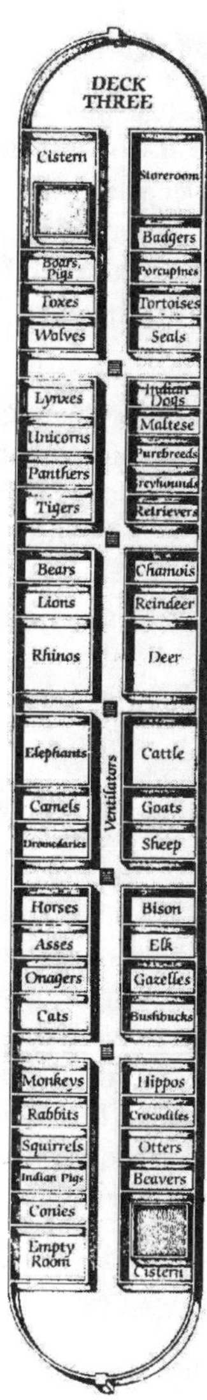

A speculative floor plan of the three levels of Noah's Ark as imagined by Athanasius Kircher in 1675.

A Ghost Ship?

Sometimes photographs aren't the best evidence. In the late 1950s, aerial photographs revealed an amazing site about 15 miles from the base of Mount Ararat. A huge boat-shaped outline could be readily observed at a place known as Durpinar. Could this be the remains of the ark, carried by the forces of nature to the foot of the mountain?

Despite the claims of a few arkologists that they can detect the remains of boat ribs and metal fittings, geologic studies of the Durpinar "ark" have indicated that it is merely a geological feature. It's also too big to fit the Biblical description, unless you subscribe to the possibility of some sort of extra-large "divine cubit."

Modern Expeditions

The search for Noah's Ark continues, and sophisticated scientific equipment has been enlisted, including high-resolution infrared aerial photography, ice coring, and ground-penetrating radar. Occasionally, yet another ark hunter will make a big announcement, followed by a groan of disappointment when the weak or nonexistent evidence is presented. Perhaps the search is in vain. In any event, many of the eyewitness reports are the result of hearsay or the misinterpretation of natural features, along with a few hoaxes.

Visit
Beautiful
Jericho!!

People and Places

American astronaut Colonel James B. Irwin (1930–1991) is perhaps the most famous of the arkologists. After a career which included a visit to the moon in *Apollo 15*, Irwin participated in five expeditions searching for the ark.

The search is complicated by the fact that the region of Mount Ararat is at present a somewhat dangerous place. Kurdish nationalists in the vicinity aren't always pleased to have visitors, and kidnappings of arkologists have taken place. Some visitors to the mountain have been given military escorts, but only after a special permit from the Turkish government has been obtained.

Watch Your Step

As both an archaeologist and a mountain climber, I have a little advice to give any would-be arkologists out there. First of all, a lot of expeditions are well-intentioned and Biblically inspired, but very weak on mountaineering skills. The glacial terrain can be hazardous, and searching some of the more dangerous places requires specialized skills. Injuries are not uncommon. Exploring this terrain requires the involvement of good climbers. If need be, the Bible guys can direct the climbing experts from a safe location.

Show Me Some Coprolites

Second, even if a big wooden structure is found on a mountain such as Ararat, a careful scientist cannot automatically conclude that Noah's Ark has been found. The find would have to be thoroughly examined and subjected to tests, and a proper argument developed.

It is always possible that it could be some other kind of structure, after all; a holy mountain might easily have had shrines built on its slopes over the years. On the other hand, the case for an ark is enhanced if the newly discovered structure is found to contain 10 tons of elephant dung.

And finally, if you do find Noah's Ark, take some pictures, note the location as precisely as possible, and then hang on to your camera and don't lose the map! I'll be happy to look at your evidence—when you can show me the boat.

The Least You Need to Know

- According to the Bible, a disappointed God destroyed most of life on earth with a big flood.
- Noah and his family, along with representatives of the different animal species, survived the Flood in a huge ark and then repopulated the earth.
- Many scientists and Biblical literalists are at odds over the truth of the story of Noah's Ark and the fact of a world-wide flood.
- Despite numerous attempts to locate the ark, there is no credible evidence that it has yet been found or even survives.

Part 3

Seeking the Promised Land

The story of the Exodus is one of the most dramatic and vital stories found in the Bible, and it has implications that affect us to this day. God's people are enslaved and then delivered to a Promised Land. And on the way, they receive a set of laws that continue to shape our modern society. It is a story of miracles and the promise of God fulfilled.

The compelling narrative in the Bible tells a heroic story, but what really happened, and who was involved? What about all of the miracles? What kind of physical evidence remains for archaeologists and other scientists to examine? The complexity of these issues might surprise you, and the details rarely fail to prove intriguing.

Chapter 7

Let My People Go!

In This Chapter

- The descendants of Abraham are enslaved
- Moses becomes a reluctant leader
- Horrible plagues and magnificent miracles unfold
- Searching for clues to the Exodus in history and nature

In the last couple of chapters, we looked at some of the wonderful stories found in Genesis. The book that follows it is called Exodus, and it contains another of the world's great stories, full of miracles and wondrous occurrences.

The story of the Exodus is a tale of primary importance for the Jewish people and others who follow the God of Abraham, because it shows God making good on the promise he made to look after his people.

A Struggling Family

In order to set the stage for Exodus, we still have a little unfinished business to deal with in Genesis. As you may recall, Abraham had a son named Isaac by his wife Sarah. Isaac grew up and had twin boys, Jacob and Esau, by his wife Rebekkah.

Without going into details, the two brothers were extremely competitive, and Jacob ended up cheating his brother out of his inheritance, thereby becoming the family patriarch. You can read the sordid details about Jacob and his hairy brother Esau in Genesis, especially chapters 25 to 27.

Jacob's life story is quite amazing. At one point, he actually wrestled with God, or possibly an angel, all night long. This was an exhausting experience, and just to make sure Jacob knew who won, he received a gratuitous hip displacement before it was all over. Afterward, he was given another name, *Israel,* meaning "struggles with God."

Logos

The term **Hebrew** refers to the descendants of Jacob's 12 sons, each of whom became the patriarch of his own tribe, known as the 12 tribes of Israel, or Israelites. **Israel** is another name for Jacob, and means "struggles with God." Today these people are called **Jews,** after the tribe of Judah. The name of the modern country of Israel is a reflection of its ancient heritage.

Joseph Moves to Egypt

Jacob had a number of sons, 12 to be exact, and he favored one in particular, whose name was Joseph. This, of course, stirred up all kinds of sibling rivalry, and one fine day Joseph's brothers threw him into a well and told their aging father that animals had eaten him. They actually sold him as a slave, and Joseph ended up in Egypt.

Joseph's wisdom and dashing good looks got him a nice job, but when he turned down the naughty advances of his employer's scheming wife, he ended up in jail. There, he came to the attention of Pharaoh, the ruler of Egypt, because of his ability to interpret dreams and predict the future. Joseph was rewarded with a job as one of the highest officials in Egypt. (Genesis 41)

Illuminations

The ruler of Egypt is often referred to as Pharaoh, which literally means "Great House," a reference similar to our modern use of "the White House" or "10 Downing Street" to refer to the administration of the U.S. President or the Prime Minister of Great Britain.

Family Reunion

Meanwhile, there was a dry spell in Palestine, and Joseph's brothers traveled to Egypt to stock up on food. After a few dramatic encounters with his clueless brothers, where Joseph hid his true identity, he revealed himself to them, and it was happy reunion time. The whole family, which included Jacob and numerous descendants, immigrated to Egypt.

The Exodus Begins

Genesis ends on a cheery note, as the thriving Joseph blesses his brothers shortly before his death. The tone shifts quickly, however. The book of Exodus, the second book of the Bible, begins in Egypt some 400 years later. The situation is not so hot for the numerous descendants of Jacob and his 12 sons, now known as the

12 Hebrew tribes, or the Israelites. They have been enslaved by the Egyptians, and there are so many of them that the Egyptians fear a slave revolt.

An order is given to exterminate all newborn Hebrew boys, to try to keep things under control. One mother saved her son by putting him in a waterproof basket and floating him down the Nile, where he is discovered by a bathing princess. The boy is given the name Moses and raised in the royal household.

Go Down Moses

Moses grew up and eventually killed a brutal foreman over some slave abuse and went into exile. Eventually, when Moses was 80 years old, God contacted him through an amazing talking burning bush. God ordered the fugitive to go back to Egypt to save his people, who were still enslaved.

Moses was understandably reluctant, but with assurances that God would help him, he set out and confronted Pharaoh. A new pharaoh had come to power since he left, but the memory of Moses was still alive in Egypt. Pharaoh scoffed at Moses' demand to free the Hebrew slaves, and then the miracles began.

Logos

The name **Moses** is not an uncommon one in Egypt. Several kings had the name Rameses or Thutmoses, the "moses" or "meses" part meaning "born of"—in these cases, the Egyptian gods Ra and Thoth.

What Is a Miracle?

The Bible is full of wonders and miracles, and the book of Exodus contains one after the other. But what is a miracle? Perhaps we can define it as an event that occurs outside the realm of the known laws of the physical universe.

This nice definition, however, is not necessarily adequate, because not all of the amazing occurrences fall outside the realm of nature. In fact, especially in Exodus, there are a number of things, such as plagues of locusts and flies, that can and certainly do occur in nature.

Illuminations

Contrary to popular belief, the pyramids of Egypt were not built by Hebrew slaves. The Great Pyramid at Giza was already 1,000 years old at the time of Moses.

The difference, though, is that the events are attributed to God. To believers, God is using the forces of nature to carry out a miracle. One thing to consider when evaluating natural miracles is whether their appearance, timing, or intensity is unnatural or unexpected.

What might a nonbeliever say about these miracles? Perhaps the miracles as reported in the Bible are the observations or embellishments of startled and superstitious people. A well-timed earthquake might seem divine, as might a rash of annoying insects appearing at an opportune, or inopportune, moment. And what about miracles that defy the known laws of the universe? Some say that perhaps the "miraculous" events are completely natural, but we simply don't know all the natural laws.

Revelations

In Mesopotamia, a legend tells the story of the warlord Sargon of Akkad, who, like Moses, was put in a waterproof basket in a river for later discovery. Unlike Moses, who was raised in the royal household, Sargon was found by Akki the drawer of water and later became Akki's gardener. Despite such inauspicious beginnings, Sargon became king, with the help of his girlfriend, the goddess Ishtar. The Sargon known from history (ruled ca. 2334–2279 B.C.) conquered the sophisticated Sumerians, and he and his successors ruled Mesopotamia for about 150 years.

Plagues and Miracles

Whether you believe miracles are divine intervention or lucky coincidence, they certainly caused a lot of trouble for the Egyptians. Moses and his brother Aaron confronted the pharaoh with their outrageous demands to free the Hebrew slaves, and were, understandably, turned down. So Moses, occasionally with the help of Aaron, attempted to bend the will of the king by demonstrating the might of his God with a series of 10 miserable plagues (beginning in Exodus 7:14).

- **Blood!** First, the water of the Nile River was turned to blood, making the water undrinkable and killing all the fish. The royal magicians were able to duplicate this effect, so Pharaoh remained unimpressed.
- **Frogs!** The second plague involved frogs. Frogs everywhere—even in the Pharaoh's own bed and in the bread ovens. Interestingly, the king's own magicians were likewise able to convince some frogs to come out of the water. Pharaoh promised to release the Hebrews if Moses could get God to destroy the frogs at a given hour. He did, and masses of frogs died the next day and were piled into stinking heaps. But Pharaoh reneged, and God inflicted another plague …

- **Gnats!** This must have been incredibly unpleasant! The king's magicians were unable to duplicate this feat, but Pharaoh was still unconvinced, so another plague occurred.
- **Flies!** Swarms of flies descended upon all of the houses of the Egyptians, again including the royal household, but not those of the Hebrews. Again ineffectual. Next!
- **Affliction!** An affliction killed the Egyptian's livestock, but not that of the Hebrews. Pharaoh remains unmoved.
- **Boils!** The next plague, boils on Egyptian man and beast, required Moses to throw a handful of kiln ashes into the air. Pharaoh remained stubborn, so Moses tried ...
- **Hail!** Moses warned Pharaoh about this one, and those who heeded the warning took shelter. Those who didn't were destroyed in a fearsome display of hail, thunder, and lightning, although the weather remained fine where the slaves lived.
- **Locusts!** Not impressed? Then how about some locusts? Locusts so thick that they darkened the surface of the land, eating anything edible that might have survived the hailstorm. Still not enough to persuade Pharaoh.
- **Darkness!** Would three days of darkness do the job, then? Nope!

Illuminations

During their first confrontation with the pharaoh, Moses' brother Aaron tried to dazzle the king by throwing down his walking stick, which then turned into a snake. The unimpressed pharaoh had his magicians perform a similar stunt. Aaron's feat, though, proved to be a real miracle when his snake gobbled up all of the others! Read about it in Exodus 7:8–12.

The book of Exodus makes it clear that God was offering an awesome demonstration of his power over the multitude of Egyptian gods, to the point of ridicule. This must have been terrifying to the Egyptians. Nevertheless, Pharaoh refused to free the Israelites.

Pass over This House

In the face of Pharaoh's stubbornness despite nine utterly nasty plagues, one final, awful plague was threatened—the first-born sons of all the Egyptians would die. (Exodus 11–12)

The Hebrews were instructed to kill a lamb and smear its blood on the doorposts and lintels of their homes. This would serve as a sign to pass over the homes of the Hebrews when God was dealing out death to the Egyptians.

This final horrible plague had the proper effect. The Hebrews quickly packed up and left, with Pharaoh's permission. The Israelites were miraculously guided in their journey by a cloud during the day and by a pillar of fire at night. All was going well until Pharaoh decided to give chase just as the Hebrews approached a body of water known as the Sea of Reeds.

Parting the Waters

Here, one of the most magnificent miracles of Exodus occurs. The Hebrews are trapped between the water and the marauding Egyptian army. God causes the waters to part, allowing the Hebrews to cross safely, before the waters came crashing down again and drown the Egyptians. (Exodus 14)

From there, the Hebrews would wander for 40 years before engaging in a campaign of conquest to settle themselves in the promised land of Canaan in the region of Palestine.

Illuminations

The Bible says 600,000 men, plus women and children, were released from slavery in Egypt. That would probably make for well over a million people!

Natural Explanations

There has been lots of speculation about the many incredible events in the Exodus story, particularly because most of them seem to be the kinds of things that can occur on their own in nature.

Some have suggested that the Nile turning to "blood" and becoming undrinkable could be a result of an algae infestation or reddish mud or silt flowing from a southern source downstream. The magicians of Pharaoh were able to create a similar effect, perhaps with a common magic trick that is still performed today (with a chemical catalyst).

VISIT
BEAUTIFUL
JERICHO!!

People and Places

A few speculators have tried to equate Moses with the curious Pharaoh Akhenaten (reigned 1353–1335 B.C.). Akhenaten upset the religious establishment by advocating the worship of a supreme god in the form of the sun disk. This, however, was not the same as Hebrew monotheism. Akhenaten himself was worshipped as a living god among a host of other lesser gods.

It's even been suggested that many of the subsequent plagues might be a reaction to a temporarily polluted Nile. Frogs get out and die, flies abound, and animals and humans get sick. As far as atmospheric phenomena are concerned, hail is known to be very damaging to crops. In Egypt every year there is the khamseen season, a time when sandstorms are prevalent. Some of these storms can radically affect visibility and perhaps explain the darkness.

Defenders of the Bible, of course, will claim that the timing and the intensity of these events is a demonstration of God's power. They support their views with the fact that the Hebrew slaves were spared all of these things. And the last plague, they say, the death of the first-born Egyptians, does not follow any known natural phenomena.

Illuminations

In the New Testament, Jesus turns water red, but in that case, it's very drinkable—it's wine!

The Pillar of Fire

There have been attempts in recent years to explain the guiding cloud, the pillar of fire, and the parting of the waters as effects of the eruption of a Mediterranean volcano. This volcano, named Thera, exploded violently and had a severe, although not clearly defined, impact on some of the cultures of the region.

VISIT
BEAUTIFUL
JERICHO!!

People and Places

There's not much left of Thera. The remaining rim of its blown-out crater forms the present island of Santorini, where archaeologists have discovered incredibly well-preserved ancient remains under a blanket of old volcanic ash.

The theory is that the escaping Hebrews saw the massive volcanic plume of the erupting volcano and could likewise see its fireworks by night. The parting of the sea might be a result of a huge tidal wave or tsunami that would cause the water to withdraw before closing. Then again, these just might be miracles!

The Sea of Reeds

Although the body of water the Hebrews crossed has often been called the Red Sea, the words in the Hebrew Bible are actually *yam suf,* or Sea of Reeds. This suggests a marshy area such as those found in the northeastern delta region of Egypt. It would be a lot shallower and perhaps shorter than the Red Sea route, depending upon where the crossing took place.

Illuminations

When the Hebrews exited Egypt, they also took with them a mummy—that of their founding ancestor, Joseph, who would be buried in the Promised Land (see Joshua 24:32).

On the other hand, there are those who insist that the yam suf is indeed the great body of water known as the Red Sea, and the Hebrews might have crossed in the narrows of its westernmost arm before entering the Sinai Peninsula.

Who's That Pharaoh?

So who was the pharaoh who was responsible for all this? The Bible talks about two pharaohs:

- The Pharaoh of the Oppression
- The Pharaoh of the Exodus

The former is the fellow in charge when the book of Exodus begins; the latter is the one who dealt with Moses and the plagues. A tremendous amount of discussion has been aimed at trying to figure out who these pharaohs might be, and thus tie the Exodus firmly into a historical chronology.

Ramses the Great

After years and years of discussion, there is still no consensus about who the Biblical pharaohs were, but there are a few clues. The Bible mentions that the Hebrew slaves were working on the twin store-cities of Pithom and Pi-Ramses, both of which have been located in the Nile Delta where the Hebrews were likely settled.

The name "Pi-Ramses" is the big tip-off, as there were several kings named Ramses during the Egyptian 19th and 20th Dynasties (ca. 1307–1070 B.C.). One king in particular, Ramses II, was a great builder and a formidable military leader, and is a favorite candidate for the Pharaoh of the Exodus.

VISIT
BEAUTIFUL
JERICHO!!

People and Places

Ramses II (reigned 1279–1213 B.C.) was rather fond of building impressive monuments to himself, the remains of which can be found all over Egypt today.

The Woman Pharaoh

Other guesses include the famous Pharaoh Hatshepsut. Hatshepsut (reigned ca. 1473–1458 B.C.) was actually a woman, the wife of Pharaoh Tuthmosis II. When her husband died, she became ruler of Egypt, having apparently usurped the throne from her very young stepson, who was the rightful heir. Hatshepsut ruled Egypt for about 20 years, and her time in power was characterized by magnificent building projects and expeditions of exploration.

In a very elaborate theory, eminent Egyptologist Hans Goedicke proposed a scenario that would put all of the pieces together. A prime piece of evidence is an Egyptian text of Hatshepsut that might covertly mention the drowning of the soldiers in the Red Sea, for which Goedicke blames Thera and a destructive tidal wave.

When it was first announced, this fascinating theory received a good bit of public and scholarly attention, but it has been widely dismissed. Although there are several elements of great value in the good professor's idea, the very fact that it is so complex has made it a field day for the nitpickers.

Examining the Evidence

There is but one mention of the Israelite people in Egyptian texts. It is found on a large inscribed stone table, or stele, dating to the reign of Merneptah, the successor of Ramses II. Merneptah's stele gives a list of names of cities conquered by the Egyptians in Palestine. Along with these cities is the name Israel, and it is written differently than the other names.

Rather than using the special hieroglyph at the end of the word which would indicate that it is the name of a city, the word "Israel" uses the heiroglyphs that indicate a people. This is fascinating. It indicates that the Hebrews were already established by that time in the region of Palestine, and for some, this causes some serious timing problems.

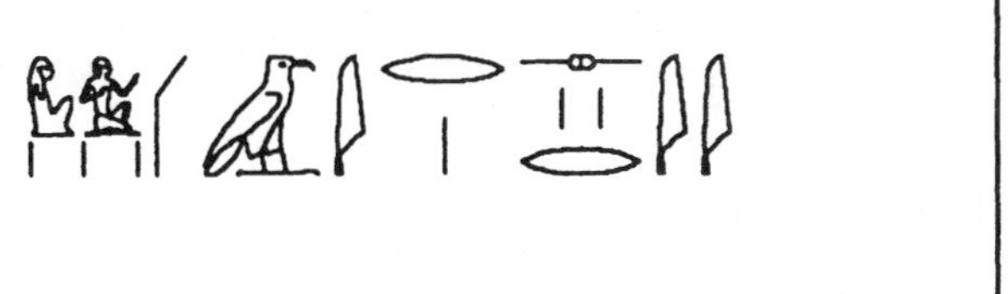

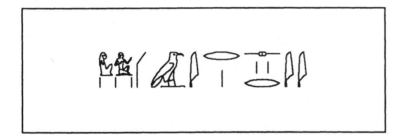

The name of Israel as it appears in Egyptian hieroglyphs on Merneptah's stele.

In the last few years, it has been noted that there might also be a picture of the Israelites on an Egyptian temple! The picture is part of a damaged inscription of Merneptah that seems to repeat the victories recorded on his stele, with the addition of illustrations of the vanquished people.

There's a good argument for this being the case, but it's hard to prove because in this example, the name Israel is not specifically mentioned. Even so, it's the closest thing to a picture of the ancient Hebrews that we might have.

Revelations

Moses and his people were so happy to have miraculously crossed the Sea of Reeds that they sang a song of praise to God, which can be found in Exodus 15:1–21. Here is just a sample:

> I will sing to the Lord, for He has triumphed gloriously; the horse and his rider He has thrown into the sea. The Lord is my strength and my song, and He has become my salvation; this is my God, and I will praise Him, my father's God, and I will exalt Him.

Getting a Date

Some scholars have tried to date the Exodus by dating the eruption of the volcano Thera. If Thera really was the source of the cloud, the pillar of fire, and the Red Sea parting, then it should be a simple matter to match the date of the eruption to the relevant pharaoh.

Unfortunately, dating the eruption has been neither easy nor conclusive. The generally accepted date of around 1600 B.C. is pretty early for some of the details in the Exodus story, such as the building of the stores cities of Pi-Ramses and Pithom. And this assumes, of course, that the volcano was actually involved in the story!

A portrait of Ramses II by Winifred Brunton. Could this be the Pharaoh of the Exodus?

(From W. Brunton, Kings and Queens of Ancient Egypt, *1926)*

Negative Evidence

There is no lack of Exodus theories, but all of them are difficult to prove. To those of faith, however, no proof is required. I should also mention that there are those who say that the Exodus never happened, none of it, and it was all made up many years later. I'll talk a little about that in the next chapter.

Critics might point to a lack of Egyptian evidence for the details of the Exodus, but then again, the Egyptians were not known for admitting their mistakes. Would a grandiose pharaoh such as Ramses II brag that his army was defeated by a ragged group of slaves? Hardly. When the Egyptians won a battle they tended to boastfully exaggerate their success, while their failures were rarely, if ever, mentioned.

A few expeditions have sought to prove the accuracy of the Biblical Exodus story by searching for the remains of the drowned Egyptians and their chariots in the Red Sea. I have seen pictures of what are supposed to be coral-encrusted chariot wheels, and I'm not impressed. The location of the Red Sea crossing is a big question to begin with, and how well any artifacts would survive from the event is also questionable.

Revelations

The miraculous and wonderful story of the Exodus is precious in Judaism. It tells how God kept his promise to look after his people, and delivered them from slavery. The story is commemorated every spring in the Jewish observance of *Pesach,* or *Passover,* one of the most important of the Jewish festivals.

Passover actually takes place over the space of a week. The most notable event is a dinner, called a seder, which occurs on the first night. During the seder, the Exodus story is retold and relived, and symbolic food is consumed. This annual dinner, shared by family and friends, assures that this story will not be forgotten.

Art Imitates Life Imitates Art

There have been several films produced about the Exodus, the three most famous being the two versions of *The Ten Commandments* produced by Cecil B. DeMille and the recent animated tale *Prince of Egypt.* DeMille had a penchant for doing things in a big way, even in his first *Ten Commandments,* which was a black-and-white silent film released in 1929.

Illuminations

The story of the Exodus as retold during the Passover dinner does not even mention Moses. The glory and credit is given to God alone, lest people exaggerate the status of Moses and come to see him as a god.

A lot of effort was put into building huge sets that would indicate the might and power of the Egyptian pharaoh, including palace facades and an avenue of sphinxes. The 1959 color version, starring Charleton Heston and Yul Brynner, was even more spectacular and involved the fabled "cast of thousands."

In an odd twist of archaeology meeting fantasy meeting modern times, a group of archaeologists set out to locate the remains of the old 1929 movie set, which had been buried in sand at Guadalupe Dunes in California.

Using sophisticated equipment that can help locate underground structures, they have found major pieces of the set and are beginning to excavate them as valuable relics of early film-making. Some might think this is truly bizarre—an "archaeological" expedition to uncover the film set that replicates a real civilization—but it sounds like a lot of fun to me!

The Least You Need to Know

- The book of Exodus tells the story of how the Hebrews were enslaved in Egypt and were freed with the help of a remarkable man named Moses.
- It took a series of nasty plagues to convince the Egyptian ruler to release the Hebrew slaves.
- The plagues have been explained in various ways. Some see them as acts of nature, others as God working through nature.
- It is not known for sure who the Pharaoh of the Exodus story is, but Ramses II has long been a strong candidate.
- The wondrous tale of God's deliverance of his people is retold annually in the Jewish holiday of Pesach, or Passover.

Chapter 8

Laying Down the Law

In This Chapter

- The Israelites wander in the desert and Moses receives the law
- The Ten Commandments and other rules
- Let's talk kosher
- The search for Mount Sinai

As incredible as the stories in Exodus are, with their miracles and plagues, the departure of the Israelites from Egypt was really just setting the stage for much more to come. Deliverance from the Egyptians was a demonstration of God's concern for his people. Now that they were free, it was time to give them a little structure. In this chapter, we'll resume where we left off, and take a look at some of the rules that God handed down to Moses to distribute; rules that have been passed down through the ages to our present day.

Travels with Moses

In our last chapter, we saw how the Bible describes the Hebrew tribes' release from slavery in Egypt. After crossing the Sea of Reeds, the Israelites found themselves wandering in a stark desert wasteland, and many began to complain. Wasn't the food and drink a heck of a lot better back in Egypt?

After all, there's not much to eat and drink in the desert for a huge number of people. Fortunately, miracles continued to be plentiful. For one thing, Moses occasionally struck a rock with his staff and out gushed water—a handy thing to have in the desert.

Manna from Heaven

As for food, sufficient numbers of quail became available in the evening to feed everyone, and a mysterious substance called *manna* appeared on the ground in the morning. In Exodus 16:14, manna is described as "a fine, flake-like thing, fine as hoar-frost on the ground" in the aftermath of morning dew.

What exactly manna might be is unknown, although some suggest it might be some sort of tree or shrub resin. One idea is that manna is a sweet sap that oozes from tamarisk trees when their bark is penetrated by beetles.

Logos

Manna is a kind of food that miraculously appears on the desert ground in the morning to feed the wandering Hebrew people. The Hebrew word has sometimes been translated to mean "what is it?"

Illuminations

Moses had the golden calf ground into dust and mixed with water. He then ordered the Israelites to drink it.

The Sacred Calf

The Hebrew tribes under the leadership of Moses wandered for years in the wilderness—40, the Bible says—but the highlight of the experience occurred at a place called Mount Sinai. Here at this high desert mountain, God called Moses to receive the laws that would govern the behavior of his people.

Moses climbed the mountain and returned with a pair of stone tablets on which the laws were written. Meanwhile, in his absence, the Israelites became discouraged and restless and resorted to idolatry. They gathered some gold together, make a golden calf, and proceeded to worship it.

Even Aaron, the brother of Moses, was in on it! When Moses descended and saw the fiesta going on below, he smashed the tablets, and then had to climb up again to receive a second set. The laws are known as the Ten Commandments, and they are some of the most influential words ever written.

The Big Ten

Even though the Ten Commandments were received by Moses over 3,000 years ago, their impact has had tremendous longevity. These basic rules were inherited by the followers of Jesus, and when Christianity came to dominate Europe and Western civilization, the Ten Commandments traveled with it.

They have had a tremendous impact on the way many societies are structured, and they continue to play an important role today. Let's take a brief look at each of these commandments. (Exodus 20, KJV)

Moses descends Mount Sinai with the Ten Commandments.

(Illustration by Gustave Doré)

Rule Number One

> I am the Lord thy God, which have brought thee out of the land of Egypt, out of the house of bondage. Thou shalt have no other gods before me.

There is no doubt who's speaking here. It's YHVH, the God of Abraham, letting everyone know who's the boss, and including a not-so-subtle reminder of who got the Israelites out of slavery in the first place.

This commandment recognizes that at that time people were worshiping all manner of different gods, and makes it clear that this is unacceptable to the one true God. By extension, some modern theologians believe that this commandment can be violated by obsession with things—cars, drugs, whatever—that in essence serve as substitute gods.

Words of Wisdom

"Oh senseless man, who cannot possibly make a worm, and yet will make gods by the dozen."

—Michael de Montaigne, *Essays*, Book 2, Chapter 12 (1580)

Off Your Knees

> Thou shalt not make unto thee any graven image, or any likeness of any thing that is in heaven above, or that is in the earth beneath, or that is in the water under the earth. Thou shalt not bow down thyself to them, nor serve them.

This commandment is pretty clear: Don't worship any statues, and don't make any statues that might be worshiped. The bits about heaven, earth, and water refer to ancient beliefs about the nature of the cosmos, which is the dwelling place of gods, angels, demons, and other supernatural beings.

Jews and Moslems take this commandment very seriously. You will not find a painting or statue of God in a synagogue or mosque. Instead, the awesome power of God is often expressed through architecture or even calligraphy.

If you have ever been in a Roman Catholic or Eastern Orthodox church, however, you will typically find loads of statues and paintings depicting Jesus on the cross, his mother Mary, and various saints. This sometimes rubs Protestant Christians the wrong way. Catholics make it clear, however, that they are not worshiping these statues, but rather venerating them or using them as a focus for prayer.

Here Comes the Bar of Soap!

> Thou shalt not take the name of the Lord thy God in vain.

Remember when your mother would give you all kinds of trouble for saying things like "God d**n it"? These days, arguably, this commandment is the least observed. Now you can hear all kinds of cursing and swearing on television and the radio, when just decades ago this stuff was taboo in a big way.

Even words such as "damn" or its derivatives, such as "dang," could invite a hearty rebuke. After all, the literal meaning behind "damn" is that you wish to sentence someone to hell. But who are you to order God to do anything? It is out of respect for this commandment, and out of respect for God, that Jews traditionally avoid saying God's name, instead substituting words such as *Adonai* and *HaShem*.

Take a Break!

> Remember the sabbath day, to keep it holy. But the seventh day is the sabbath of the Lord thy God: In it thou shalt not do any work …. For in six days the Lord made heaven and earth, the sea, and all that in them is, and rested the seventh day: wherefore the Lord blessed the sabbath day, and hallowed it.

Illuminations

Misspelling the name of God is definitely undesirable. Sometimes the word God is found printed as G-d in some Orthodox Jewish writings and newspapers, which also makes it hard to pronounce.

God gives everyone a day off! In the Western world, we are pretty spoiled by having a two-day weekend (and some want three!), but I assure you this isn't the case in much of the world. Squeaking out a poor living can be a seven-day-a-week job. One day off is good.

The traditional Jewish Sabbath begins at sundown on Friday and lasts until sundown on Saturday. Later tradition has developed many specific rules about what is and isn't permissible to do on the Sabbath. Driving, using money, turning on electricity, and cooking are among the things not permitted in Orthodox households.

It's not a big problem, though, and most Jewish families who observe the Sabbath look forward to it as a glorious time for family, rest, and an opportunity to worship God. In other words, it's an opportunity to spend some time devoted not to making a living but to doing some living in very meaningful ways.

For Christians, Sunday has become the day they regard as the Sabbath, as one way of emphasizing the importance of their belief in the resurrection of Jesus, which is thought to have occurred on a Sunday. For Muslims, Friday is the big day.

You're Grounded, Mister!

> Honor thy father and thy mother.

Listen to your ma and pa! This is the commandment that many teens have a rough time with—and maybe it was written with them especially in mind. It recognizes respect for one's elders and encourages family harmony.

VISIT
BEAUTIFUL
JERICHO!!

People and Places

In modern Israel, it helps to know who is who because on Friday, the Muslim shops are closed, on Saturday, the Jewish shops are closed, and on Sunday, the Christian shops are closed.

Put Down the Gun

> Thou shalt not kill.

This important commandment has been mistranslated in the King James Bible, which has led to some confusion. The Hebrew word here translated as "kill" really means "murder." You should not murder. The Bible is full of killing, both of people and of animals. There are wars in which God helped out and instances in which God himself killed a lot of people. A murder, however, is an illegal killing.

Hands Off

> Thou shalt not commit adultery.

This is pretty self-explanatory. In America, though, you might never know this was one of the famous Ten Commandments, because adultery seems to be the favorite theme of the entertainment industry.

Leave My Stuff Alone!

> Thou shalt not steal.

We all know what this means, but a lot of people do it anyway.

Do You Swear to Tell the Truth?

> Thou shalt not bear false witness against thy neighbour.

This law is oh so important. Telling untrue stories about other people can cause a lot of mayhem, whether it be idle gossip or false testimony in a court of law. In many ancient societies, making false accusations had severe consequences. It was generally up to the accuser to prove the point.

I Want It, I Want It, I Want It!

> Thou shalt not covet thy neighbour's house; thou shalt not covet thy neighbour's wife, nor his manservant, nor his maidservant, nor his ox, nor his ass [donkey], nor any thing that is thy neighbour's.

Being envious or desirous of things that aren't yours or that you can't have can lead to great disappointment, or maybe even cause you to break one of the previous commandments.

The commandments can be looked at as falling into two groups: those which govern the relationship between humans and God, and those which govern the relationships among humans. The latter ones, especially, make a lot of sense even to nonbelievers, and I think that most people would agree that murder, stealing, and adultery do not contribute to a healthy, peaceful society.

Revelations

The Ten Commandments have been arranged differently over the years. Various groups have divided or combined the first commandments, dealing with monotheism, or the last commandments, dealing with coveting. Either way, they add up to 10!

603 More to Go!

Whereas most people have heard of the Ten Commandments, you might not be aware that Jewish tradition counts a total of 613 commandments, all found in the first five books of the Bible, a.k.a. the Torah. Three hundred and sixty-five are considered negative commandments—"Don't do this"—while the rest are positive.

Many of these laws have shaped the attitudes prevalent in Western civilization, and some have formed the basis of legal statutes. Here are just a few of the more obscure rules found in the book of Deuteronomy:

- "Cross-dressing" is considered bad form in much of Western society. Here's a verse that might have influenced this attitude: "A woman shall not wear anything that pertains to a man, nor shall a man put on a woman's garment; for whoever does these things is an abomination to the Lord your God." (22:5)
- "You shall not wear a mingled stuff, wool and linen together." (22:11) So much for polyester, spandex, and other mingled modern "miracle fabrics"!

Illuminations

Jewish people believe that along with the laws found in the Bible, Moses also received an "oral Torah" that contains more rules, some that offer specific instruction as to how to properly pray, observe the Sabbath, and so on.

- "There shall not be found among you any one who burns his son or his daughter as an offering, any one who practices divination, a soothsayer, or an augur, or a sorcerer, or a charmer, or a medium, or a wizard, or a necromancer." (18:10–11) So stay way from that Ouija board, and quit calling the psychic hotline!
- "Cursed be he who misleads a blind man on the road." (27:18) This goes to show that mean-spirited people have been around for thousands of years!

And while you're at it, don't sleep with your stepmother, stepsiblings, parents-in-law, or beasts.

A Different Legal Standard

In many instances, the Torah stands out as clearly different from other law codes known from the ancient Near East. In Babylonia, for example, there was a law that stated that if you accidentally killed someone else's son, your own son would be put to death.

In Deuteronomy 24:16, we find that "The fathers shall not be put to death for the children, nor shall the children be put to death for the fathers; every man shall be put to death for his own sin." That's a clear difference in terms of personal responsibility for one's actions!

A Model Code

There are many instances in the Torah where a general law is given—for example, the penalty if one's ox causes damage—that also serves as a model for similar cases. It would be impossible to spell out laws to cover every possible contingency, but ways of dealing with a wide variety of situations have been derived from careful study of the laws that do appear in the Bible. In fact, the Torah continues to be consulted, along with additional Jewish legal treatises, in matters of modern concern.

VISIT
BEAUTIFUL
JERICHO!!

People and Places

Trying to start a scandal, a newspaper in Israel once accused the Israeli Prime Minister of being a secret "shellfish addict"—an addiction to which he allegedly succumbed on trips abroad. In Israel, those are fighting words!

Keeping Kosher

Some of the most interesting laws have to do with food. This is the basis of "keeping *kosher,*" which many Jewish people still do today. Certain animals are prohibited as food. Furthermore, if an animal's meat is consumed, it should not contain blood, and there are rules for the humane slaughtering of allowable beasts.

Even today, kosher butcher shops exist to prepare meat for human consumption according to Biblical laws. The dietary laws generally deal only with animal products. Vegetables and mineral products (like salt) are generally okay for all-around consumption.

These You May Eat

The rules governing which animals may be eaten are very specific.

> Whatever parts the hoof and is cloven-footed and chews the cud, among the animals, you may eat. (Leviticus 11:3)

This includes the ever-popular cows, goats, and sheep. Animals such as rock badgers, rabbits, and camels, which chew the cud but do not have split hooves, are forbidden. Pigs, which have split hooves but don't chew the cud, are forbidden. Don't eat them, and don't touch their carcasses.

> These you may eat, of all that are in the waters. Everything in the waters that has fins and scales, whether in the seas or in the rivers, you may eat ... But anything in the seas or the rivers that has not fins and scales, of the swarming creatures in the waters and of the living creatures that are in the waters, is an abomination to you. (Leviticus 11:9)

Some of the things to avoid include eels, catfish, lobsters, and shrimp.

Foul Fowl!

And stay away from these birds: eagles, osprey, kites, falcons, ostriches, hawks, sea gulls, owls, cormorants, ibises, nighthawks, water hens, pelicans, carrion vultures, storks, herons, hoopoes, and bats. Sure, today we call the bat a mammal, but they've got wings and they fly around, so they can very feasibly mix in with other big flying things.

Don't Eat Bugs

Don't eat winged insects that "go about on all fours." It's okay to eat those "which have legs above their feet, with which to leap on the earth." (Leviticus 11:20–21) This includes locusts, crickets, and grasshoppers. You should also stay away from weasels, mice, lizards, geckos, land crocodiles, chameleons and turtles, snails, and moles.

Logos

Kosher, or **kashrut,** means "clean" or "fit" according to Jewish law. It applies especially to food but to other things as well. The opposite of kosher is treif (pronounced *trayf*).

Don't Mix Them Up

A real mainstay of a kosher diet is avoiding eating dairy products at the same time as meat products. This is based on the law in Exodus that states "You shall not boil a kid in its mother's milk." (Exodus 34:26) Later Jewish law forbade all mixing of milk and meat to make sure this commandment wouldn't be violated.

Illuminations

Kosher quiz time! Cheeseburgers, pepperoni pizza, and a Reuben sandwich: not kosher! Mushroom pizza, tuna fish, and hot dogs (all-beef only): kosher, as long as they meet any other associated standards!

This one requires a bit of thinking, because it's not just a matter of avoiding specific foods, but also knowing about the ingredients and combinations of foods served at meals. A kosher kitchen will have separate bowls and utensils for dairy and meat foods, and even separate sinks and refrigerators!

Although it might sound like a real hassle to those not living the kosher lifestyle, its rigors usually prove meaningful for those who live it. The food can be great, and much of it is good for you. Some have argued that a kosher diet has health advantages.

For Orthodox Jews, these laws are all taken very seriously, whether or not medical science can demonstrate any health benefit. More liberal Jews, who tend to see their religion evolving with times, are less stringent.

Looking for kosher food? These are just some of the symbols to look for on many of the food products found in your supermarket. Some manufacturers actually have an in-house rabbi to make sure everything is kosher.

(After Ronald H. Isaacs, The Jewish Information Source Book, *London: Aronson, 1993, pp. 264–266)*

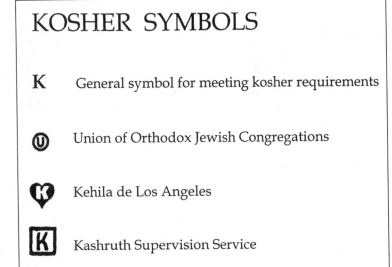

KOSHER SYMBOLS

K	General symbol for meeting kosher requirements
Ⓤ	Union of Orthodox Jewish Congregations
(K in heart)	Kehila de Los Angeles
[K]	Kashruth Supervision Service
(K in Hebrew letter)	Kosher Supervision Service

What's with the Pigs?

The reasons for Biblical food prohibitions have been widely discussed, and there are several possible explanations for them, some or all of which might be true. Here are a few things to think about:

Illuminations

There are people today who argue for new "eco-kosher" standards that will be even more stringent than the old rules when it comes to ingredients such as additives. They are also concerned about the ethics regarding who produces food and the processes they use.

- Avoiding certain foods is an exercise in self-control or maybe even a personal sacrifice in accordance with divine law.
- Certain things are set aside not because they are necessarily bad, but because obeying such prohibitions is an act of holiness that all similar believers share; some such prohibitions also separate believers from those who aren't.
- A classic explanation for prohibiting pigs and shellfish involves health issues. Pigs can carry several diseases that can be passed on to humans. Consume some bad shellfish, and you'll wish you were eating kosher. Trust me on that last one! (On the other hand, *any* animal product has the potential to bring about human distress under certain conditions.)
- It has been claimed that pigs are economically impractical, that the costs of raising them aren't worth the resources you have to invest. Also, unlike cattle, sheep, and goats, they are not easy to herd, especially if you're on the nomadic side. (Then again, pigs, like goats, have a reputation for eating all kinds of leftovers and aren't necessarily connoisseurs with expensive tastes.)
- Animals such as pigs and eels don't fit in with the normal system of classification, making them suspect. Pigs have split hooves but don't chew the cud. Eels swim but have no scales. They're weird animals that just don't match the others!
- God says don't eat pigs, so don't eat them. And while you're at it, quit asking so many questions!

When you think about it, though, cultural food preferences aren't all that strange. Americans, for the most part, don't eat dogs, cats, rats, horses, or insects. And raw meat or fish is not the norm. Some cultures are vegetarian by religious preference or otherwise. It's all in how you look at it.

The Search for Mount Sinai

Well, we've spent a lot of time talking about the Ten Commandments and the laws of God, but now how about a geographical question: Where is this mountain of God where Moses received the tablets? There have been a number of proposals. A favorite is Jebel Mousa, which is located in the Sinai Peninsula of Egypt.

In fact, in A.D. 327 this mountain was identified as the Biblical one by Helena, the mother of the Roman emperor Constantine, who was touring around the Holy Land in search of sacred sites. A chapel was built at the base, and today a large, beautiful Greek Orthodox monastery named St. Katherine's can be found there. Within its walls are an impressive library of old manuscripts and a scraggly shrub which some claim is a distant relative of the famous burning bush.

A Thousand Steps

A couple of trails beyond the monastery lead to the summit, and one path features thousands of steps carved out of stone which were the life's work of a dedicated monk. A mosque and small chapel can be found on the summit. Although Jebel Mousa is not the highest mountain in the immediate area, it is beautiful and impressive.

A view of Jebel Mousa in Egypt's Sinai Peninsula. Is this the mountain of Moses?

(Photo by author)

Myriad Mountains

While Jebel Mousa receives the bulk of tourists, other sites have been suggested, some based on various proposals about the route of the Exodus and the wanderings of the Israelites. They include …

- Other mountains on the Sinai Peninsula.
- Jebel el Lawz, a mountain in Saudi Arabia.
- Har Harkom, located in a remote section of Israel's Negev desert.
- The site of Petra, an extraordinarily beautiful area in southern Jordan known for its ancient Nabatean ruins.

Various theories come and go about what happened when, and where, but is knowing the location of the real Mount Sinai all that important? Some will say no: It's not where it is but what happened there that gives the story meaning. It's probably impossible to prove such a thing, but let's say that the location could be convincingly identified—what next? Build some more shrines?

An Invisible Epic

Given the epic proportions of the Exodus story, one might expect there would be some evidence of it. One would think that a group of hundreds of thousands of people wandering for 40 years would leave quite an impact on the landscape. Archaeologically, though, this is a real problem.

Under the right conditions, a single stone campfire circle can remain intact for many thousands of years, but there is as yet no physical trace of the Exodus. It's possible that the forces of nature have altered or destroyed the evidence, or that it lies buried. It's also possible that the route of the journey is still unknown and unexamined, and the true site of Mount Sinai remains to be found.

Revelations

The lack of archaeological evidence for the Exodus remains a puzzle. In North America, there is a similar example from the time of the early European explorers. A large expedition led by Hernando de Soto (1500–1542) left Spain for the New World in 1538 and explored much of the American Southeast during the following few years. Despite a veritable army of 600 men and a couple of hundred horses, barely a trace has yet to be found of their passing.

The Bare Minimum

According to some of the Biblical minimalists, it's a waste of time to look for such evidence, since they believe the whole story never happened. It's not real history, they say, but, along with the conquest of the Promised Land that followed, part of a national origins myth that was written down around the sixth century B.C.

But then again, who would construct a story in which their ancestors were slaves who, after being delivered by God, continually misbehaved? The book also has a reasonable amount of knowledge about Egypt that lends an air of authenticity.

Keeping What Matters

Ultimately, the meaning of the Exodus story, a tale of God's deliverance and the giving of the law, is what is of lasting importance. Wherever and whenever it might have happened, its impact, much of it positive, continues to persist into modern times.

The Least You Need to Know

- The miracles of the Exodus continued after the Israelites left Egypt.
- The Ten Commandments, received by Moses on Mount Sinai, have had a lasting impact on Western society. They and other Biblical laws continue to shape our values.
- It can be difficult to understand the meaning and intent behind the Biblical laws, but many believe in these laws and attempt to follow them faithfully.
- The location of the true Mount Sinai remains controversial, and at this time there is little archaeological evidence for the story of the Exodus.

Chapter 9

The Promised Land

In This Chapter

- The Hebrew tribes invade the Promised Land
- God's assistance turns the tide
- A royal house rises and falls
- A look at the archaeological evidence
- The ten lost tribes

After being divinely rescued from Egypt and receiving God's laws, not to mention wandering about the desert for 40 years, it was time for the roving Israelites to venture into a new land where they could finally settle down. It wouldn't be a matter of just walking in and putting down roots, though; there were lots of people already living there. In this chapter, we'll look at some of the stories, miracles, and archaeological controversies associated with this dramatic episode of Biblical history. It's a wild and wondrous tale featuring amazing people, places, and events!

The Land of Milk and Honey

After Moses received the Ten Commandments at Mount Sinai, the wandering Hebrew tribes prepared to enter the land of Canaan. This was essentially the same as the area of modern Israel along with the West Bank of the Jordan River—a land flowing with milk and honey and promised to them by God. As the Israelites stood poised at the edge of the Promised Land, God gave clear instructions as to what they were to accomplish:

> ... When you pass over the Jordan [River] into the land of Canaan, then you shall drive out all the inhabitants of the land from before you, and destroy all their figured stones, and destroy their molten idols, and demolish all their high places [altars]; and you shall take possession of the land and settle in it, for I have given the land to you to possess it. (Numbers 33:51–53)

Illuminations

According to Deuteronomy 34:5–6, God buried Moses in the land of Moab (modern Jordan) "but no man knows the place of his burial to this day."

The Israelites' great leader Moses would not be joining them. He died in the desert, but not before he caught a glimpse of the Promised Land from a high peak, Mount Nebo, in modern Jordan. (Deuteronomy 34)

Poised at the border of Canaan, the Israelites sent out spies to check it out. The spies returned with some good news and some bad news. The good news was that there was lots of food, and they wouldn't have to eat manna anymore. The bad news was that they were going to have to confront some huge people who were living there already.

Revelations

The Israelite spies investigating the Promised Land returned with reports of a bountiful "land of milk and honey" and brought back bunches of giant grapes as evidence. The people in that land were said to be oversized, as well. (More about giants in Chapter 21, "Some Strange Characters.")

Joshua Fights the Battle of Jericho

Under the command of a new leader, Joshua, whose book follows Deuteronomy, the attack on Canaan began. But first the Hebrews had to cross the River Jordan, which lay between them and their first target—the great city of Jericho. In an episode reminiscent of the Sea of Reeds, a dry place appeared in the river and the Israelite army was able to march across.

The walled city of Jericho was not captured in the traditional fashion. Instead, on God's instructions, the Israelite army marched around the walls six times, blowing trumpets all the while, over a period of six days. Then on the seventh day they did seven laps, blew the trumpets some more and yelled, and, according to the Bible, the walls came tumbling down. The Israelite army then went in and completely demolished the place.

The walls of Jericho come tumbling down.

(Illustration by Gustav Doré)

Acts of God?

The story contains two major miracles: the river drying up and the walls falling down. Some have sought to explain them as either God at work through nature or, on the other side, as fortuitous natural calamities that were believed to be miracles.

There are a couple of obvious candidates for natural phenomena that would cause such effects. An earthquake is a favorite candidate to explain the falling walls. A mudslide has been proposed to account for the Jordan River temporarily drying up, allowing the Israelites to cross.

The Longest Day

Visit
Beautiful
Jericho!!

People and Places

Rahab the prostitute and her family were the only survivors of the raid on Jericho. She protected the Israelite spies who reconnoitered the city earlier and then hung a red cord out her window so she might be later identified and spared.

After Jericho, Joshua and his army continued their program of conquest, and cities continued to fall. During an attack against the Amorites, the Bible records two more amazing miracles. As the enemy army was fleeing from the Israelites ...

> The Lord threw down great stones from heaven upon them ... and they died; there were more who died because of the hailstones than the men of Israel killed with the sword. (Joshua 10:11)

Now hail isn't all that odd a thing, and skeptics might say we have yet another case of the divine interpretation of a natural event. But then again, the Israelites apparently remained unscathed, so it appears that the hail was specifically targeted at the bad guys.

What happened next, though, is truly mind-boggling. Apparently running out of daylight to finish the work, Joshua commanded the sun and the moon to stay still:

> And the sun stood still, and the moon stayed, until the nation took vengeance on their enemies .... The sun stayed in the midst of heaven and did not hasten to go down for about a whole day. There has been no day like it before or since, when the Lord hearkened to the voice of a man; for the Lord fought for Israel. (Joshua 10:13–14)

Meet the Philistines

LOGOS

Logos

A geographical term for the region in the vicinity of the modern state of Israel is "Palestine," which is derived from the word "Philistine."

When the Israelites entered the Promised Land, the Bible tells us there were lots of people already living there for them to fight. Most prominent were the various Canaanite peoples who lived in much of what is now Israel, as well as a group of people named the Philistines, who lived along the southern coast in an area of prime agricultural land and international trade routes. There were five major Philistine cities, which were known for their metallurgy and olive oil production.

The exact origins of the Philistines are somewhat mysterious. They appear to be relative latecomers to the region, appearing perhaps around 1150 B.C. They seem to be the same as a group known as the Sea-Peoples, who began attacking the Egyptian coast about that time and may have been refugees or warlike colonists from the vicinity of Crete in the Mediterranean or mainland Greece. They were adept sailors, and their fighting skills are well attested in the Biblical stories.

Visit
Beautiful
Jericho!!

People and Places

The term "Philistine" today is used to refer to someone who is uncultured or brutish, but the label is hardly a fair one. Artifacts from recent excavations at such Philistine cities as Ashkelon and Ekron suggest that Philistines may have been more culturally sophisticated than their Canaanite neighbors.

Proving a Miracle

Although the Bible goes into considerable detail about the conquering of the Promised Land, there is a big debate about how much of this story is real history. In fact, as with the Exodus scenario, there are Bible scholars who claim that the conquest never occurred.

Take the site of Jericho, which, apart from what the Bible tells us, has the reputation of being one of the world's oldest cities. People were living there at least as early as around 8500 B.C. The city was walled during much of its history, and the evidence indicates that it was abandoned and later expanded and rebuilt several times.

The site of Jericho was excavated most notably by John Garstang (1876–1956) between 1930 and 1936 and Kathleen Kenyon (1906–1978) between 1952 and 1958. Garstang and Kenyon did find collapsed walls, but it isn't possible to prove who or what caused them to fall.

Furthermore, it is strongly argued that the timing is all wrong and that Jericho was already wrecked and abandoned by the time the Israelites got there. If the Exodus took place just after the time of Ramses II, the most popular date, then the place would have been destroyed a couple hundred years before the Israelites arrived.

Visit
Beautiful
Jericho!!

People and Places

British archaeologist Kathleen Kenyon was one of the most prominent female excavators of all time. She served as a lecturer in Palestinian archaeology at University College in London and, along with Sir Mortimer Wheeler, devised methods of excavating difficult sites that were widely adopted in Near Eastern archaeology. She was a tough and persistent leader, best known for her excavations at Jericho and in the city of Jerusalem.

A City Called Ai

There are similar problems with the second city said to have been conquered by the Israelites, a city called Ai. There is very little evidence of widescale destruction at the appropriate time, so what is going on? There are several possibilities.

One is that some of the ancient places, such as the city of Ai, have yet to be properly identified. This is not an unusual problem when we're dealing with archaeological remains. Some people have tried to identify sites by pure speculation (such as the traditional location of Mount Sinai), while others have tried to use geographical clues found in the Bible to come to such conclusions.

Occasionally, a place name might persist through the ages in the form of the surviving name of a nearby village or land feature, but even so, it can be hard to decide which nearby tell the name might relate to, if any. In short, it's often hard to positively identify sites that are known solely from the Bible.

Revelations

The miraculous activities at Jericho and elsewhere were not forgotten by the early Christians, who used them as an example of faith. In the New Testament Book of Hebrews we find:

> By faith the people crossed the Red Sea as if on dry land; but the Egyptians, when they attempted to do the same, were drowned. By faith the walls of Jericho fell down after they had been encircled for seven days. By faith Rahab the harlot did not perish with those who were disobedient, because she had given friendly welcome to the spies. (11:29–31)

Just a Story

There are a number of Biblical minimalists who firmly believe that the conquest of the Promised Land never happened. It's foolish to look for physical evidence of these events, they say, because they simply didn't happen. The archaeological evidence just doesn't support it.

They feel that the story, along with that of the Exodus, is part of a national epic saga, not unlike Homer's *Iliad,* that provides a heroic history for the Hebrew people. They believe that it, like Exodus, was first told, if not written down, during the sixth century B.C.

Examining the Evidence

But what would account for the fact that the Merneptah stele, which we discussed in Chapter 7, "Let My People Go!" mentions a people called Israel and that there is plenty of physical evidence of Israelites to be found in the Palestine region? The minimalists will answer that yes, the people were there, but they came not out of Egypt, but probably from within Canaan.

Some have suggested that the emergence of the Israelites was the result of a peaceful immigration or perhaps even a civil revolt. Small settlements began to appear on less-desirable land on the hilltops of Canaan at the appropriate time. It has also been suggested that a population crisis could have caused a split.

On the other hand, some of these hard questions might be resolved if these scholars gave some historical credence to the Biblical stories, and would accept an earlier date for the Exodus. As we saw in the last chapter, there have been all kinds of proposals for the who's and when's of the Exodus, and an earlier date might make some of the dates in Palestine, such as the fall of Jericho, fall more in line with what the Bible says.

We Three Kings

As the Israelites became successful in capturing territory, it was time to set down some roots. According to the Bible, the conquered land was to be divided among the Hebrew tribes. These tribes each had their own rulers, called "judges," before a united monarchy was established around 1030 B.C.

These "judges" were not judges in the sense of people presiding over trials, although they certainly did their share of conflict resolution. They were leaders who oversaw each tribe and made important political decisions during the time before the tribes came under the rule of a single king.

Visit
Beautiful
Jericho!!

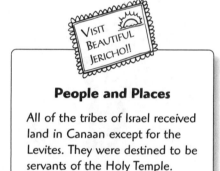

People and Places

All of the tribes of Israel received land in Canaan except for the Levites. They were destined to be servants of the Holy Temple.

The first king, Saul, was appointed by a priest named Samuel; Saul's story begins in 1 Samuel 9. Saul was followed by David, who established the official Hebrew capital at Jerusalem around 1005 B.C., and was in turn followed by Solomon. Each of these kings had a distinct personality, and each was very human, with plenty of personal flaws.

Saul: A Slow Start

Israel's first monarch, Saul, came from the tribe of Benjamin, and was chosen because the Hebrew tribes wanted a king to rule over them. Although Saul was apparently a good military leader, he turned out to be a disappointment to God. Being a bit paranoid, and wanting to know the future, Saul did something against God's will: He consulted the Witch of Endor to summon the spirit of the deceased priest Samuel to advise him. (1 Samuel 28)

Samuel duly appeared and gave Saul the bad news: He would die the next day. The prophecy came true when Saul committed suicide on the battlefield—something of a self-fulfilling prophesy. This put David in charge.

David the Giant Killer

David, a lowly shepherd boy from the tribe of Judah, first became prominent in the Bible when he answered a challenge to fight the Philistine giant, Goliath. David killed his fierce opponent with a well-placed rock to the forehead and then cut his head off.

His harp-playing skills subsequently made him a favorite in the court of Saul. David's military prowess against the Philistines, and God's preference for him, drove Saul to try to kill him. When David became king, he ruled from the city of Hebron for seven years before conquering Jerusalem and moving the capital there.

Some of the stories about David are unpleasant. For example, after secretly watching a soldier's gorgeous wife taking a bath and seducing her, he saw to it that her husband was assigned to the front battle lines where he was soon killed. David afterward took the widow as his wife.

Illuminations

In ancient Israel, the kings, and sometimes the priests, would be inaugurated into their office by being anointed with olive oil. The Hebrew term *Messiah,* which refers to a prophesized savior of the people literally means "the anointed one" (see Chapter 14, "Who Was Jesus?").

David wasn't always a popular ruler, and at one point his son Absalom usurped the throne, but only briefly. Overall, though, he seems to have been a powerful and shrewd ruler who unified and strengthened the kingdom and built a small empire in the region. David is credited with writing some of the beautiful poems found in the book of Psalms.

The Wisdom of Solomon

David's son Solomon succeeded David and developed the capital at Jerusalem by building an elaborate palace and a temple. His expertise in foreign affairs was well-known, and he had a reputation for being wise. The Bible says that God told Solomon that he could have anything he asked for, and Solomon requested wisdom. (1 Kings 3) He is said to have had an international collection of 700 wives, and his wealth was legendary.

The Queen of Sheba

There's a great story in the Bible about the Queen of Sheba, a woman of legendary beauty who had heard of the superb wisdom of Solomon. Intrigued, she paid the king a visit to ask some truly difficult questions.

The two exchanged expensive gifts and, according to Ethiopian tradition, perhaps a little genetic material as well. The location of Sheba is not known, but it was probably located in the area of modern-day Yemen on the Arabian peninsula, or perhaps in Ethiopia.

VISIT
BEAUTIFUL
JERICHO!!

People and Places

Wise King Solomon is often credited with contributing some of the sage advice found in the book of Proverbs. According to tradition, he is also the author of the Bible's best-known love poem, the Song of Solomon. Some say that he also wrote Ecclesiastes, a long reflection on the temporary nature of all goods and pleasures.

Some Historical Problems

We've already encountered the difficulties associated with finding archaeological evidence for various Bible stories, and the frustrating search for history isn't quite over. Although the Bible provides us with lots of detail about the lives and times of Saul, David, and Solomon, there is very little physical evidence of their existence.

A few critics equate King David with the mythical King Arthur, claiming that they both serve as cultural icons, and also that the historical reality of both is in question. That theory has recently suffered a major blow.

VISIT
BEAUTIFUL
JERICHO!!

People and Places

The last king of Ethiopia, Haile Salasie (1892–1975), bore the title "Lion of Judah" and claimed to have been a direct descendant of Solomon and the Queen of Sheba.

In 1993, at the site of Tel Dan in Israel, a fragment of stone was uncovered with an inscription referring to "the House of David." This is among the first tangible evidence of King David's existence, and it is still controversial.

Some have called it a fake, while other skeptics maintain that the name "David," written without vowels in Hebrew, could actually mean a couple of other things, including the word "beloved"—thus the inscription would mean "House of the Beloved." Nevertheless, the possibility remains that more and more clues will be found in the future. That's one reason archaeologists continue to dig!

Revelations

Scholars shouldn't be too quick to dismiss myths. For years, it was thought that the Norse stories about reaching "Vinland," the New World, had no basis in history. Then, in the early 1960s, a Norse settlement was discovered and excavated in Newfoundland, and the Vikings were vindicated!

Logos

Many of the names found in English Bibles are not quite the same as those found in the original Hebrew. Moses, for example, is **Moshe** in Hebrew, Solomon is **Shlomo,** and Isaac is **Yitzak.**

Ten Missing Tribes

After the death of Solomon, the central monarchy dissolved and the Israelites broke into two kingdoms. In the south, centered at Jerusalem, were the two tribes of Judah and Benjamin, and the other ten tribes of Israel were confederated in the north.

The ten tribes, though, would "disappear," so to speak, when the Assyrians invaded Palestine around 721 B.C. Although it is likely that they were marched back to Mesopotamia and incorporated into Assyrian society, there has been plenty of wild speculation about what else might have happened.

Theories multiplied when Europeans first began to explore the New World. Could some of the people found there be descendants of the lost tribes, they asked? Similarities in some customs and words became prime evidence.

The tribes were also occasionally invoked in the speculation about who built the huge artificial mounds found in North America. The Europeans were unwilling to believe that the ancestors of the local Indians had been capable of building them, so they imagined a mythical race of Moundbuilders, some of whom were thought to have been, perhaps, missing Israelites.

The speculation about the ultimate destination of the lost tribes didn't end with the New World. A wide variety of other places have been suggested, and continue to be. Some of them envision the tribes scattering—that is, one tribe ended up here, another there. Here are a few of their suggested destinations:

- Ireland; Sweden; the Netherlands
- Nigeria; Kenya
- Persia; Yemen
- North Africa; Ethiopia
- India

Illuminations

Take any two cultures on this planet, and you'll probably find some resemblances in the things they do, or maybe even a few identical words. It takes more than a handful of similarities to prove that the two are related!

Accumulating Evidence

While there is a distinct lack of concrete, objective physical proof for the accuracy of Biblical history through the reign of Solomon, the evidence starts accumulating after the time of the united monarchy. Names of rulers of the divided kingdom begin to appear in foreign texts, as do events reported in the Bible. A good example is that of the Assyrian attack on the fortified Israelite city of Lachish.

When the Assyrian king Sennacherib attacked Palestine, Lachish was one of the cities he assaulted, in 701 B.C. This is noted in the Old Testament (2 Kings 18:13), and most remarkably, the attack is featured on sculpted reliefs in the palace of Sennacherib in the Assyrian capital of Nineveh. The reliefs show the Assyrian use of siege machines against the city and the carrying away of booty. When the tell was excavated, archaeologists found plenty of evidence of this event.

A bulla with the name of Baruch the Scribe, an individual mentioned in the Bible as the scribe to the prophet Jeremiah. The inscription dates to the late seventh century B.C.

(P. Kyle McCarter, Ancient Inscriptions, *1996, p. 149)*

Naming Names

Perhaps even more interesting than foreign reports of Biblical events and personages are some discoveries made in the Promised Land itself. In the last few decades, clay

Logos

A **bulla** (plural **bullae**) is a clay seal bearing a stamp with an individual's name. They were typically used to seal documents.

seals called *bullae* have been found which actually record the names of specific individuals noted in the Bible. The seals, which date to the appropriate Biblical time periods, were used to make a stamp in clay, typically as official signatures on such things as sealed papyrus scrolls or letters.

The Story Continues

After fighting so hard for the Promised Land, the Israelites would lose their grip on it, regain it, and ultimately lose it again. As we saw in the preceding section, the ten northern tribes disappeared. Many members of the two surviving tribes, Judah and Benjamin, would be led away to slavery in Babylon, and allowed to return home only when the Persians defeated the Babylonians and become the latest winners in the ancient Near Eastern musical chairs of power.

The Greeks would follow to rule and fight over Palestine. The Jews would again emerge as an independent entity, but only until the Romans became the dominant regional power. Arabs, Crusaders, Turks, and the British are just some of the others who would control the Promised Land. It wasn't until A.D. 1948 that the Jewish people were once again formally reinstated in the land of their ancient heritage in the modern state of Israel.

The Least You Need to Know

- The Bible describes how God assisted the Israelites in conquering the territories he had promised them.
- The evidence for the Israelite conquest of the Promised Land is scanty, but miracles are notoriously difficult to prove archaeologically.
- Some scholars dispute that the conquest of the Promised Land ever took place.
- A Hebrew monarchy was eventually established to rule over the Israelites. Though short lived, it is well known, and Saul, David, and Solomon feature prominently in the Bible.
- The ten northern tribes of Israel disappeared after an attack by the Assyrians. Speculation abounds about all the places they may have ended up, but they were most likely absorbed into the Assyrian empire.

Part 4

Oh, Jerusalem!

After entering the Promised Land, the Israelites eventually established their capital at Jerusalem, a city which 3,000 years later still commands the world's attention on a regular basis. The city is holy to billions of people and contains sites precious to Jews, Christians, and Muslims.

There once stood the magnificent temple of YHVH, with its rich symbolic architecture and ornamentation. In the Temple's Holy of Holies sat the famous Ark of the Covenant, the famous lost chest that served as a kind of throne for the presence of God. In this part, we're going to explore the Temple, the Ark, and the glorious city of Jerusalem itself. The marvels and mysteries continue!

Chapter 10

The Temple of the One God

In This Chapter

- The Hebrews create a portable sanctuary
- Magnificent temples are built and destroyed
- Time brings changes in Jerusalem
- Judaism goes on

Many of the great religions of the world have major centers of worship. For Islam, it's Mecca; for the Jews, it's Jerusalem. There a temple built to divine specifications once stood; it served as the center of worship for almost a thousand years. It was destroyed, rebuilt, and ultimately destroyed again, never to be rebuilt.

These two temples were magnificent structures and perhaps deserve consideration as an eighth wonder of the ancient world. The fascinating history of the temples begins way back in the time of Moses and continues into modern times.

Make Me a Sanctuary

The Temple story really begins at Mount Sinai. There God instructed Moses to build a portable tent-like structure that would serve as a worship center for the migrating Israelites: "And let them make me a sanctuary, that I may dwell in their midst." (Exodus 25:8)

The building materials, including acacia wood, goat skins, gold, silver, and bronze, were provided by the people. The instructions for building the Tabernacle were quite specific. Here is just a small sample of the detail spelled out in Exodus 26, in this case, dealing with the curtains:

> Moreover you shall make the tabernacle with ten curtains of fine twined linen and blue and purple and scarlet stuff; with cherubim skillfully worked shall you make them. The length of each curtain shall be twenty-eight cubits, and the breadth of each curtain four cubits .... And you shall make loops of blue on the edge of the outmost curtain in the first set .... Fifty loops you shall make on the one curtain and fifty loops you shall make on the edge of the curtain that is on the second set .... (NIV)

Words of Wisdom

"There is something in us which demands, and finds satisfaction in, the act or at least the attitude of worship. But, since there is nothing in the visible creation which has a dignity corresponding to that attitude, we may be very sure that there is more in existence than our visible creation contains."

—Ronald A. Know, *Broadcast Minds* (1932)

The Holy of Holies

The end result was a rectangular structure about 145 feet long, 72 feet wide, 7 feet tall, and enclosed by curtains. Within was another compartment divided in two by a veil. Its innermost chamber was the sacred Holy of Holies, which contained nothing but the Ark of the Covenant, a special box containing the Tablets of Law. (It's so special, in fact, that it gets its own chapter, coming up next.)

In front of the veil hiding the Holy of Holies was an incense altar, a bread table, and a seven-branched candelabra, all made of precious materials. In the courtyard outside was a washing bowl and an altar for burnt offerings.

An old engraving showing the Tabernacle.

A Traveling Tabernacle

The tabernacle was sufficiently portable that it could be moved and set up as the Israelites wandered. Much of it could be carried on poles, and various groups were assigned responsibility for the different pieces. When it was erected, the Israelites camped around it in a specific order according to tribe.

It must have been quite an operation each time the Israelites moved and set up camp. When they eventually reached the Promised Land, the Tabernacle was set up for a long stretch of time at Gilgal, and the Ark would be removed and carried into battle. When David became king, it was time to make things permanent.

Logos

The glorious presence of God has been called the **Shekinah.** It was thought to be present in the Holy of Holies, and on occasion was noted in the form of a cloud descending on such places as the Tabernacle and Temple.

The Bible tells us that David purchased a high spot on Mount Moriah in Jerusalem that was used as a threshing floor by a man named Araunah. This was also the traditional site where Abraham took his son Isaac to be sacrificed. Here the Temple would be built. David, however, would not be the builder because, as God explained to him, he was "a man of war, and had shed blood." He did, however, pass the plans on to his successor, Solomon.

Build Me a Temple

When Solomon became king, he came into control of the not insubstantial empire built by David, his father. There was a peaceful political environment and sufficient wealth to build a splendid monument, and the work began.

Solomon was assisted by a Phoenician king, Hiram, who facilitated the harvesting of huge numbers of cypress and cedar logs from the forests of Lebanon. The logs were tied together like rafts and floated down the coast. According to 1 Kings, the amount of work involved in building the Temple was staggering:

Illuminations

God obviously is neither confined to nor in need of a tent, temple, or any other sort of structure. Such structures can, however, serve as a center of religious focus for humans.

> King Solomon raised a levy of forced labor out of all Israel; and the levy numbered thirty thousand men. And he sent them to Lebanon, ten thousand a month in relays; they would be a month in Lebanon and two months at home .... Solomon also had seventy thousand burden-bearers and eighty thousand hewers of stone in the hill country, besides Solomon's three thousand three

hundred chief officers who were over the work, who had charge of the people who carried on the work. At the king's command, they quarried out great, costly stones in order to lay the foundation of the house with dressed stones. (1 Kings 5:13–17)

Revelations

Certain secret societies trace their roots back to the builders of the holy Temple. The Masons, for example, believe that some of their ideas and philosophies have their origins with the talented stonemasons of Solomon's Temple. Other groups believe that the building secrets of Biblical times were maintained by the medieval craft guilds who built the magnificent cathedrals of the Middle Ages.

Angels and Flowers

Illuminations

The great cedar forests of Lebanon were well-known to ancient people. In 1954, a 4,600-year-old royal boat was found buried at the base of the Great Pyramid in Egypt. It was built of cedar that was probably imported from that region.

The dimensions of the temple were about 90 feet long, 30 feet wide, and 45 feet tall. The walls were decorated with images of flowers, angels, and palm trees. Gilded olivewood doors with the same decorative theme led to the inner sanctum. The Holy of Holies was built of cedar and the walls and floor were gilded in gold. Inside were two identical figures of angels made of olive wood overlaid with gold. Each stood 10 cubits (about 18 feet) high with a wingspan of 10 cubits.

A bronze specialist was brought from the Phoenician city of Tyre to lend a hand. He cast two elaborately decorated pillars, which he named Jachin and Boaz and set up in the vestibule of the Temple, and then produced an impressive array of ceremonial equipment. An enormous bronze tub was made, 10 cubits across and holding the equivalent of "two thousand baths." It stood on the backs of four pairs of three bronze oxen facing the cardinal directions. There were also 10 elaborate wheeled bronze stands to hold a bronze basin with a capacity of "forty baths."

Fine Furniture

Other temple furnishings were constructed from gold: an altar, a bread table, candelabras, incense dishes, lamp snuffers, fire pans, and sockets for the Temple's doors. The sheer wealth represented in the Temple is an important thing to remember. It would make it a prime target for foreign invaders seeking rich booty.

The whole Temple-building project was said to have taken seven years. Afterward, the temple was dedicated with prayers and a whole lot of offerings, and the Ark was installed in the Holy of Holies.

Making Sacrifices

Offering rituals were held daily at the Temple, presided over by priests of the proper lineage. On a typical morning, the fire was stoked and the altar was cleaned. The oil in the lamps was replenished and the incense lit. Twelve fresh loaves of bread were placed on their special table. The High Priest, bedecked in his special garments, could now proceed with the sacrifices.

There were a number of reasons for making a sacrifice, and the offerings for each one varied. They typically involved unblemished animals that were then sacrificed and burnt on the altar. There were nonanimal offerings, too, including barley and wheat, wine, olive oil, and precious substances such as frankincense. In many cases, a portion of the offering went to the priests.

An engraving from 1754 depicting Solomon's Temple in action.

Visit
Beautiful
Jericho!!

People and Places

The Temple was primarily staffed by members of the tribe of Levi. The priests were thought to be descendants of Aaron, and during certain time periods, the High Priest served as a political figure as well.

LOGOS

Logos

Yom Kippur, the Day of Atonement, is the most solemn day of the Jewish religious calendar. In celebrating this holiday today, Jews are to contemplate their shortcomings and regrets from the previous year and seek betterment in the year to come.

Here are a few of the occasions under which one might present an offering to God at the Temple:

- Sin offerings, to make one ritually clean after an offense.
- Guilt offerings, to atone for various offences against people, breaking of minor laws, and so on.
- Free-will offerings, for no special reason.
- As a thanks to God for special things.
- At the ordination of priests.
- As festival offerings.

On one day during the year, *Yom Kippur,* the High Priest would enter the Holy of Holies alone. A smoke screen of incense prevented a clear view of the Ark, and two sin offerings were presented in the form of sprinkled blood—one representing the High Priest, and the other for the people.

Instructions for the rituals performed in the Temple are provided in great detail in the Torah. Even the clothing to be worn by the priests is described, giving us an amazing picture of the goings-on at this magnificent structure.

A Quick History

After Solomon died, there was a split between the ten tribes of Israel in the north and the tribes of Judah and Benjamin in the south. The Temple was located in Judah, so for the most part, the northern division had to do without.

Instead they built various worship centers of their own, some of which were pagan. Even in the south, one of the kings, Menasseh, slipped into paganism and placed idols in the holy Temple. This episode, however, was short-lived.

In another incident, the Egyptian king Sheshonq I (called Shishak in the Bible) attacked Judah and "came against Jerusalem." Solomon's successor Rehoboam seems to have avoided destruction by paying off the Egyptian king. The tribute included Temple treasures.

The Temple Is Destroyed

When the Assyrians carried off the ten northern tribes (2 Kings 17), Jerusalem managed to survive, but as Assyrian power declined, the Babylonians grew in strength, and soon they were knocking on Jerusalem's door. In the year 586 B.C., under the leadership of Babylonian King Nebuchadnezzar, Jerusalem was conquered and the Temple was destroyed. (2 Kings 24–25)

Since the Temple was lined with gold-gilded wood, a thorough burning was probably useful in the looting process. Many of the portable objects were carried off whole. You can read about what might have happened to the Temple's most famous artifact, the Ark, in the next chapter.

Illuminations

Among the most curious objects noted in the Bible are two objects called the Urim and Thummim. These were apparently two little plaques that were kept in a pouch under the upper garment of the priest. They were used to answer yes and no questions and were perhaps thrown like dice.

The Temple Is Rebuilt

After about 50 years in Babylonian captivity, the Jews were freed by the Persian King Cyrus and allowed to return home. Cyrus also ordered the return of the Temple equipment that Nebuchadnezzar had carried away and placed in his own temples. The tally of items given in Ezra is impressive:

> … A thousand basins of gold, a thousand basins of silver, twenty-nine censers, thirty bowls of gold, two thousand four hundred and ten bowls of silver, and a thousand other vessels; all the vessels of gold and of silver were five thousand four hundred and sixty-nine. (Ezra 1:9–10)

Visit
Beautiful
Jericho!!

People and Places

A descendant of David named Zerubbabel deserves foremost credit for rebuilding the Temple after the Babylonian exile. He seems to have served as governor of the region of Judah, perhaps appointed by the Persians.

Back in Jerusalem, priests of the proper lineage were sought, donations were obtained, and the Temple rebuilding began. A foundation was laid, and wood was again brought down from Lebanon. There was opposition to the project by some of Judah's neighbors, though, and they successfully appealed to the Persian King Xerxes to have the work stopped.

The building resumed not long after Xerxes' successor, Darius, took the throne, and royal Persian money was used to assist in the project. The second Temple was by no means as splendorous as that of Solomon. For one thing, the Ark of the Covenant was gone. The Temple served its purpose, nonetheless, and the offerings and rituals continued.

Revelations

The Persian King Darius made a search of the royal archives to retrieve Cyrus's decree allowing the Jews to rebuild the Temple. After it was found, Darius resumed his commitment to the project and wrote: "Also, I make a decree that if anyone alters this edict, a beam shall be pulled out of his house, and he shall be impaled upon it, and his house shall be made a dunghill." (Ezra 6:11, RSV) Message? Don't mess with the Temple!

Politics as Usual

Some 200 years later, Alexander the Great conquered the Persian Empire (among others), and after he died, his empire was carved into several pieces, each ruled by his generals and their descendants. The area of Palestine fell first within the kingdom of Egypt, and then Syria.

Along with Alexander and his successors came *Hellenization,* the spread of Greek culture. In order to solidify control of the conquered territories, Greek religion, customs, and language were regularly imposed upon the diverse ethnic groups found in the various territories. Many people adapted and were assimilated into the Greek culture, including many Jews.

Logos

Hellenization is the process of spreading Greek culture. It was a policy regularly practiced by the Greek rulers of the territories conquered by Alexander the Great.

Adding Insult to Injury

Those Jews who remained true to their faith refused to succumb to the new culture, which did not conform to their belief in one God. Things really got out of control under the reign of the Hellenistic monarch Antiochus IV, which began in 175 B.C.

With the goal of homogenizing the people living in his territories, Antiochus forbade many of the essential Jewish customs, including circumcision, observance of the Sabbath, and the use of the Temple for Jewish worship and offerings.

Just to be nasty, pigs were sacrificed on ceremonial altars and a statue of Zeus was erected in the Temple. This was definitely not kosher! Jews were being forced to give up their religious practices and perform profane acts under penalty of death.

The Mighty Maccabees!

Given this intolerable situation, it's not surprising that there was a strong reaction. A Jewish rebellion began under the leadership of a man named Mattathias of the Hasmonean (or Maccabee) family. His son, Judah Maccabeus, would prove to be a great general.

The rebels engaged the Greek enemy on many occasions, using guerilla tactics in difficult terrain and hiding in the inhospitable desert. Several great battles were fought, and the Jewish army, with God's help, according to the Bible, was ultimately successful.

Their story is found in the two books called Maccabees, which are not included in all Bibles (see Chapter 17, "Alternative Scriptures and Fabulous Fakes").

Revelations

When officers of Antiochus approached Mattathias and asked him to serve as an example to others and engage in pagan worship, the Jewish leader was steadfast in his refusal:

> And Mattathias answered and said in a loud voice: "Even if all the nations that live under the rule of the king obey him, and have chosen to do his commandments, departing each one from the religion of his fathers, yet I and my sons and my brothers will live by the covenant of our fathers. Far be it from us to desert the law and the ordinances. We will not obey the king's words by turning aside from our religion to the right hand or the left." (1 Maccabees 2:19–22)

Come See the Lights

When Judas Maccabeus and his men finally liberated Jerusalem, they found that the Temple had been greatly desecrated and badly damaged. They set about cleaning up the mess and making repairs, including building a new altar. There were eight days of celebration and thanksgiving when the temple was rededicated.

Logos

Hanukkah is the annual Jewish holiday that commemorates the successful battle against the forces of Antiochus IV, who sought to destroy Jewish culture and religion.

According to Jewish tradition, a great seven-branched candlestick, or menorah, was still present in the Temple, but there was only enough untainted kosher oil remaining to last one day. A miracle occurred when this limited amount of oil burned and provided light for the whole eight days.

The story of this rebellion against oppression is celebrated annually in the Jewish holiday of *Hannukah.* The story of Antiochus IV and Judas Maccabeus is retold, and the liberation of the Jewish people and the Temple is remembered by the symbolic lighting of a menorah; eight candles are burned over eight nights to represent the miracle of the Temple oil.

Along with special food, gifts, and music, there is a game played with a spinning top called a dreidel. On each of the four sides are Hebrew letters which together stand for the phrase: "a great miracle happened there," referring not only to the lamp oil, but, more important, to the victory over oppression with God's help.

Revelations

Technically, Hanukkah is considered to be a minor Jewish holiday. Yet it has become one of the best-known, because it occurs annually during December, the month of the Christian Christmas celebration. As a result, it has taken on more public recognition, and, like Christmas, has suffered from a good bit of commercialization.

Under Roman Rule

After the victory over Antiochus, a dynasty of Hasmonean kings ruled in Jerusalem for several decades until the Romans appeared in their steady conquest of much of Alexander's old empire. Unlike Antiochus, the Romans let the Jews continue their religious practices as long as they didn't rebel. They also appointed a client-king to rule over Palestine and the Jews, a man known as Herod the Great.

Herod's personal reputation is pretty poor. He's generally considered to be a homicidal maniac, among other things, but he was nevertheless a great builder. With a penchant for architecture on a grand and elaborate scale, he built several palaces for himself, along with public buildings. His crowning achievement, though, was his remodeling of the Temple Mount.

Herod Remodels

Herod expanded the Temple Mount into a huge plaza faced with mammoth blocks of carved stone. On top, the old Temple of Solomon was essentially overwhelmed by Herod's new structure. Great staircases and gates were built leading up to the Temple, and the result must have been absolutely awesome.

So immense and dramatic were his construction activities that the results are often referred to as the Third Temple. Herod, being the Roman toady that he was, installed a big Roman eagle over the entrance to the Temple as a sign of his submission.

Visit
Beautiful
Jericho!!

People and Places

There was more than one King Herod. Don't confuse Herod the Great, who ruled from 37 to 4 B.C., with Herod Antipas, who ruled part of Palestine from 4 B.C. to A.D. 39, during the time of Jesus' ministry.

History Repeats Itself

As was the case a couple of centuries before, the Jews became disenchanted with their foreign oppressors, and a rebellion broke out against the Romans in A.D. 66. In A.D. 70, the Romans attacked Jerusalem and completely destroyed the Temple, for the third and final time.

The destruction was overseen by the Roman general Titus, who built a victory arch in Rome celebrating his conquest. The sculptured surface of the arch, which still stands today in Rome, includes a scene showing temple booty, including a great menorah, being hauled away.

It is seen as almost a mystical coincidence that the destruction of the Temple by both the Babylonians and the Romans reportedly occurred on the ninth day of the Jewish month of Av. As a result, this sad day is remembered annually in the Jewish religious calendar.

Illuminations

In addition to the dual destruction of the Temple, other tragic events in Jewish history occurred on the ninth of Av, including the final battle of Bar Kokhba's rebellion, the signing of the edict to expel the Jews from Spain in 1492, and the squashing of the Warsaw Ghetto rebellion. World War I also began on the ninth of Av.

Years of Change

In A.D. 130, the emperor Hadrian rebuilt Jerusalem and renamed it Aeoli Capitolina. A temple to the god Jupiter was erected on the Temple Mount. When Christianity became the official religion of the Roman Empire in the fourth century, the Temple Mount was used as a garbage dump by Christians, who could make a statement about Judaism and the pagan Romans at the same time.

In 635, a new era was initiated when the Arabs conquered Jerusalem. The Temple Mount thereafter became home to two impressive Islamic structures: the Dome of the Rock, and the El-Aksa Mosque. The former, built in 658, is topped by a huge dome, gilded in gold.

This structure was built over top of the large exposed rock that legend says was the place where Abraham brought his son to be sacrificed. It is also the place, according to Islamic tradition, from which the prophet Mohammed rode his horse on a nocturnal visit to Heaven.

Visit
Beautiful
Jericho!!

People and Places

Julian the Apostate (reigned A.D. 361–363) was an anti-Christian Roman emperor who wanted to resettle the Jews in Jerusalem and rebuild the Temple. Due to his extremely short reign, the task was never accomplished.

LOGOS

Logos

The famous Wailing or Western Wall is known in Hebrew as the **kotel.** It is the surviving western wall of the great platform of Herod's Temple. There is an old tradition in which personal prayers are written on pieces of paper and shoved into the cracks of the Wall. An organization in Israel will do this for you if you send them a fax.

What Remains?

Both the Dome of the Rock and the El-Aksa Mosque remain in place today on Herod's immense Temple Mount. There is very little, if anything, left of Solomon's temple. A portion of an old wall exists on the Temple Mount, alongside blocks from Herod's platform, that might be part of the original Temple.

Just a few years ago, an interesting little object showed up in an antiquities dealer's shop in France: an ivory pomegranate that once fit on the end of a staff. An inscription in old Hebrew letters reads, "belonging to the temple of Y ...." The inscription is incomplete, but it's likely that the "Y" is the first letter of the name *YHVH,* and might be all we have left of Solomon's Temple or its equipment.

There is likewise little or nothing to be seen of the rebuilt Second Temple. A couple of stone blocks here and there with a little writing have been found from King Herod's Third Temple. One inscription refers to a place of trumpeting and might have come from the spot where the priests blew their horns on special occasions. The other is a warning sign, in Greek, that warns non-Jews to stay out of the sacred area.

Read All About It

With so little left to study of these magnificent structures, we need to rely on the descriptions in the Bible to give us an idea of what the Temples looked like. A few other old texts also assist in our attempts to reconstruct the Temple in its various manifestations. The Jewish historian Josephus, in particular, describes the Temple Mount as it existed during the first century A.D., before its destruction.

The Search Continues

There have been several recent attempts to pinpoint the location of the ancient Temple on the Temple Mount as it remains today. There are those who say that the Dome of the Rock was built directly over the Holy of Holies, and the Ark once rested upon the rocky platform itself. There are others who insist it lays elsewhere. (For a little more Temple-talk, see Chapter 12, "City at the Center of the World.")

VISIT
BEAUTIFUL
JERICHO!!

People and Places

A magnificent detailed model of Herod's Temple Mount is a popular attraction at the Holy Land Hotel in Jerusalem.

No More Tears

Despite the destruction of the Temple, Judaism persisted, although it developed on a different path than it might have had the Temple survived. Instead of a centralized priesthood based in Jerusalem, Jewish rabbis and sages became community leaders and teachers of Torah as Jews spread throughout the world. This is still the case today. The western wall of the Temple Mount, however, became a sacred site of prayer. It is called the *kotel* and has become a place of pilgrimage for Jews worldwide.

Illuminations

The ivory pomegranate that might be associated with Solomon's Temple was dated to the appropriate period by the style of its inscription. It was purchased for $550,000 by the Israel Museum in Jerusalem, where it can be seen today.

This structure has long been referred to as the Wailing Wall, a mournful declaration of the Temple's loss, and for many years it was inaccessible to most Jews. In 1967, however, the Israelis captured East Jerusalem from Jordan, and the Wailing Wall was incorporated into the modern state of Israel. Although plenty of sorrow remains from the past, the wall is now often referred to as the Western Wall, and remains available for prayer today.

The sacred site of the Western Wall in Jerusalem, also known as the Wailing Wall, is a place of prayer.

(Photo courtesy of John Petersen)

The Least You Need to Know

- Both the movable Tabernacle and the later permanent temples in Jerusalem were built as places to worship the One God of the Hebrews.
- The Bible contains very specific instructions for the building of the Tabernacle and the Temple, and also includes specifications for their ritual equipment.
- Solomon's original Temple was built in the tenth century B.C. Its construction took seven years and employed thousands of skilled workers.
- Solomon's Temple was destroyed by the Babylonians in 586 B.C., rebuilt several decades later, enhanced by King Herod, and destroyed again by the Romans in A.D. 70.
- Very little survives of the Temples. The platform upon which they sat is now occupied by Islamic monuments.

Chapter 11

The Ark of the Covenant

In This Chapter

- God designs a very special box
- On the road with the Ark of the Covenant
- The ark disappears!
- The search for the lost ark and other Temple treasures

One of the most famous, and you could even say popular, Biblical artifacts of all time is a mysterious box that was constructed under God's specific orders. It was carried with the wandering Israelites as they made their way from Sinai, it helped them in battle and caused trouble for their enemies, and it was eventually kept in one of the most sacred and secret places in the world: the Holy of Holies of the Jerusalem Temple. And from there it disappeared!

This box is commonly known as the *Ark of the Covenant*. Its power and mystery are such that people have speculated about its whereabouts for centuries. In recent times, the ark achieved even greater celebrity status when it was featured in the adventure film *Raiders of the Lost Ark* (1981). In this chapter, we're going to take a look at this extraordinary object and its interesting history, and explore some ideas about what might have happened to it and where it might be now.

Follow Thy Directions

Logos

The **Ark of the Covenant,** also known as the Ark of the Testimony, was a wooden box constructed according to God's specifications. It contained the tablets of the law given to Moses, along with a couple of other important objects. It is not to be confused with Noah's Ark, a big boat that goes by a different Hebrew word.

As we saw in the last chapter, God gave Moses specific directions for building the portable tabernacle and its accompanying equipment. This included the most special object of them all, the Ark of the Covenant. Here are the building plans:

> They shall make an ark of acacia wood; two cubits and a half shall be its length, a cubit and a half its breadth, and a cubit and a half its height. And you shall overlay it with pure gold, within and without shall you overlay it, and you shall make upon it a molding of gold round about. And you shall cast four rings of gold for it and put them on its four feet, two rings on the one side of it, and two rings on the other side of it. You shall make poles of acacia wood, and overlay them with gold. And you shall put the poles into the rings on the sides of the ark, to carry the ark by them. The poles shall remain in the rings of the ark; they shall not be taken from it. (Exodus 25:10–15)

The Ark of the Covenant.

(Illustration by Chris Tyler)

The Mercy Seat

The instructions continue:

> Then you shall make a mercy seat of pure gold; two cubits and a half shall be its length, and a cubit and a half its breadth. And you shall make two cherubim of gold; of hammered work shall you make them, on the two ends of the mercy seat .... The cherubim shall spread out their wings above, overshadowing the mercy seat with their wings, their faces one to another; toward the mercy seat shall the faces of the cherubim be. And you shall put the mercy seat on top of the ark .... (Exodus 25:17–21)

VISIT
BEAUTIFUL
JERICHO!!

People and Places

Although he has become an archaeological frame of reference for millions of people, Indiana Jones is more of a treasure hunter than an archaeologist. Read my book, *The Complete Idiot's Guide to Lost Civilizations* (1999), for a true understanding of the difference!

In short, what is described is a gold-gilded wooden box that can be moved about on two poles. Its close-fitting lid, called the "mercy seat," featured two golden angels with outstretched wings. Inside were placed the tablets of law. A verse in the New Testament (Hebrews 9:4) indicates that it also contained a gold urn containing a piece of manna and Aaron's staff. A scroll containing the book of Deuteronomy was kept next to it.

Illuminations

One of the most unusual explanations for the configuration of the ark was put forth by Erich Van Daniken, author of *Chariots of the Gods?* (1969). Van Daniken claimed that the components of the ark would neatly serve as an electrified radio, allowing communication between Moses and his extraterrestrial handlers.

The Throne of God

The purpose of the ark is as follows:

> There I will meet you, and from above the mercy seat, from between the two cherubim that are upon the ark of the testimony, I will speak with you of all that I will give you in commandment for the people of Israel. (Exodus 25:22)

So it seems that the ark is a symbolic throne for God. Just as God himself isn't confined or contained within a building such as the Temple, neither is God restricted to a throne. Being in the presence of the ark, however, served as a sacred meeting point for an encounter with God. It also occasionally served as a visible reminder of God's power.

Hands Off!

The ark was not to be touched, and those who did paid the price. There's a perplexing story in the book of 2 Samuel that gives a harsh example of what could happen to those who came into direct contact with the box.

One day, the ark was being transported on the back of a cart, instead of on its poles. When the cart began to tip, a man named Uzzah reached out to keep the ark from tumbling to the ground. He was struck dead. (2 Samuel 6:6–7)

Why did this happen? Some might say that the very fact that the ark was being carried on the cart showed disobedience to God's word, and Uzzah's death brought this point dramatically home. In any case, the ark was nothing to mess around with. On an earlier occasion, curiosity seekers had tried to take a peek into the ark, and 70 people died as a result.

A Powerful Symbol

The ark visited a number of places while the Israelites moved about Canaan. When it wasn't residing in its place in the portable Tabernacle, the ark was often carried into battle. The waters of the Jordan parted when priests carrying the ark set foot in the river, and the ark was paraded around the city of Jericho before the city's walls fell.

The crossing of the Jordan is reminiscent of the parting of the Sea of Reeds in Exodus. Here's what Joshua told the people about the coming event:

> Behold, the ark of the covenant of the Lord of all the earth is to pass over before you into the Jordan. Now therefore take twelve men from the tribes of Israel, from each tribe a man. And when the soles of the feet of the priests who bear the ark of the Lord, the Lord of all the earth, shall rest in the waters of the Jordan, the waters of the Jordan shall be stopped from flowing, and the waters coming down from above shall stand in one heap. (Joshua 3:11–13)

For 14 years, the ark was stationed in the Tabernacle while it remained at the site of Gilgal, and afterward it spent many years at Shiloh. Its power became legendary. The foes of the Israelites were well aware of its reputation and feared it. But one time, the Philistines were able to capture the ark, and they thought it was a good thing.

Not for Everyone

After the Philistines captured the ark, they brought it back to their city of Ashdod and set it down in the Temple of their chief god, Dagon. Immediately, strange things began to happen. The statue of Dagon was found tipped over face first not once but twice, and the second time it was severely damaged. According to the story …

> This is why the priests of Dagon and all who enter the house of Dagon do not tread on the threshold of Dagon in Ashdod to this day. (1 Samuel 5:5)

The problems with Dagon were just the beginning. The people of Ashdod became afflicted with "tumors" and blamed it on the ark. They decided to send it away to another Philistine city, Gath, whereupon its unfortunate citizens were likewise stricken.

The Ark on Tour

Amazingly, considering all the trouble the ark gave them, the Philistines kept it for seven months, and then concluded that they had to get rid of it. After consultations with their priests, it was decided to put the ark on a cart attached to two cows and send it on its way.

Along with the ark, the Philistines sent a box containing a guilt offering: five golden images of their tumors and five golden mice, representing the five Philistine cities. It was hoped that the God of Israel would have mercy and relieve them of their miserable afflictions.

Illuminations

There has been a range of speculation about the nature of the tumors suffered by the Philistines because of their possession of the ark. Some think the tumors may have been associated with swellings from bubonic plague. Others have suggested hemorrhoids.

Home to the Hebrews

The cows departed with their precious cargo, without any human to guide them, and you can bet the Philistines were hoping that they wouldn't turn around and bring the ark back! Amazingly, the cows made a beeline for the Israelite town of Beth Shemesh. Needless to say, the Israelites were thrilled to have the ark back, and promptly sacrificed the two cows.

It was not long afterward that the curiosity-seekers were struck dead when they tried to have a look inside the famous box. The ark was transferred thereafter to a house in the town of Kiriath Jearim, where it remained for 20 years.

Dancing in the Street

After David established his capital in Jerusalem, he decided to have the ark moved there. It was on this journey that the incident with Uzzah occurred. David was furious about what had happened to the man, and parked the ark in a house along the route for three months.

Eventually the trip to Jerusalem continued. David became so excited when the ark finally entered his city that he danced wildly—naked! The ark was set down in a tent, and when Solomon's Temple was completed, it was transferred to the Holy of Holies.

Where'd It Go?

Visit
Beautiful
Jericho!!

People and Places

David's wife Michal, the daughter of King Saul, was apparently so utterly disgusted with her husband's ecstatic behavior that she harshly criticized him. The two had no children together afterward.

The last the ark is heard of, it is in its rightful place in the Temple at Jerusalem, where it is ceremoniously visited once a year by the High Priest. The Babylonians destroyed this Temple in 586 B.C., and from then on, the whereabouts of the ark are unknown.

The ark apparently was not available to be restored to its place when the Temple was rebuilt, which leaves us with a few possibilities:

- It was destroyed along with Solomon's Temple.
- It was taken to Babylon and dismantled or destroyed there.
- It survived the destruction of the Temple and remains hidden to this day.

A trip to Babylon seems unlikely. Given the history of the ark, one would expect tales of great doom to accompany its removal. It is not mentioned in the inventory of Temple implements that were given back when the exiled Jews returned home. There are, however, a lot of people who think it still exists. Let's look at a few of the theories.

Under the Mount

Illuminations

Because of the possibility that the ark (or pieces of it) might be buried in the Temple Mount, or the possibility that one might step on the site of the Holy of Holies, Orthodox Jewish law forbids Jews from visiting the top of the Temple Mount today.

Some Jewish texts suggest that the ark and other temple objects might be hidden in chambers under the Temple Mount, or even directly under the Holy of Holies. In 1981, a couple of prominent rabbis began digging tunnels under the Mount. Just as they glimpsed the ark in a hidden chamber, they say, their activities were discovered by Muslim Arabs, and a ruckus broke out. Their excavation was shut down and sealed shut.

Did these rabbis actually see the ark? It's hard to be sure. They were certainly enthusiastic about it. On closer examination, it seems more likely that they felt that they were on the path of discovery before their work was halted. There is one way to find out, of course, but it would be difficult to do so without incurring the wrath of those above who control the Temple Mount. So far, excavations have been forbidden.

Mount Nebo

The apocryphal book 2 Maccabees (2:4–6) records that the prophet Jeremiah saved the ark from the Babylonian destruction:

> It was also in writing that the prophet, having received an oracle, ordered that the tent and the ark should follow with him, and that he went out to the mountain where Moses had gone up and had seen the inheritance of God. And Jeremiah came and found a cave, and he brought there the tent and the ark and the altar of incense, and he sealed up the entrance. Some of those who followed him came up to mark the way, but could not find it.

There are a couple of candidates for this mountain. It could have been Mount Sinai, wherever that is, or, more likely, Mount Nebo, where Moses was shown the Promised Land before he died.

In the early 1980s, an American claimed to have found the ark in a tunnel in Mount Nebo. He produced some photos that showed part of an odd golden object, but upon analysis, it appears to be of modern manufacture. The discovery site seems to be in a well-known tunnel under a church, and the report lacks serious credibility.

Revelations

The movie *Raiders of the Lost Ark* suggests a dramatic cinematic answer to the ark's whereabouts: hidden somewhere in a big old U.S. government warehouse. Fascinating idea, but keep in mind, it's all fiction.

In Ethiopia?

There's an old Ethiopian legend that says that the real ark was carried to Ethiopia by Menassa, the alleged son of Solomon and the Queen of Sheba. According to the story, a duplicate was left in its place in the Holy of Holies in the Temple, and the original ended up in the Ethiopian city of Axum.

Some say that it is still there, well-guarded in a local Christian church, and indeed, once a year, a covered box is removed and paraded around. It seems unlikely that this is the real ark, however. It's probably an old artifact made by the Christians themselves a long time ago. This is true, some say, but it's just a substitute for the real one, which is always kept hidden inside.

Look over Here!

A few other locations for the ark have been advocated, Ireland being perhaps the most far-out. Or how about the Vatican, a favorite of conspiracy theorists? Some of the looted Temple treasures did make it to Rome, where they are commemorated by the Arch of Titus, but the ark seems to have been long gone or hidden by then. In Israel, people have searched at various places near the Dead Sea with no luck.

Ark Hunting

Just as some are intent upon finding Noah's Ark, many people have gone in search of the Ark of the Covenant. Among the more unusual was a fellow named Ron Wyatt. Wyatt claimed that he had found the ark while excavating below an area thought by some to be the hill where Jesus was crucified. Wyatt claimed to have found a labyrinth of tunnels in which was a room containing the lost ark. The blood of Jesus, he claimed, had dripped through cracks in the ceiling above onto the lid of the ark.

Illuminations

Ron Wyatt had blood samples analyzed which he believed belonged to Jesus. He claimed that his initial analysis revealed an abnormal number of chromosomes in the DNA. I remain very skeptical.

As an archaeologist, I find many parts of this story difficult to believe, although I have not personally examined the site or other physical evidence. Ron Wyatt, though, seems to have made a career out of finding the most extraordinary of Biblical artifacts, including Noah's Ark at the foot of Mount Ararat in Turkey, the real Mount Sinai in Saudi Arabia, and even chariot wheels in the Red Sea. Wyatt died in 1999, and if even one of his supposed discoveries is proven to be authentic, he has made a place in history. Enough said.

A Real Treasure Map?

In 1952, a provocative discovery was made in a cave at Qumran near the Dead Sea, in what was then Jordan. It was a scroll bearing some strange texts—technically, in fact, one of the Dead Sea Scrolls (which we'll explore in Chapter 16, "Scrolls in the Desert"). Unlike the other scrolls found in the area, however, this one was made of two rolled strips of copper. When spread out, the scroll would have been almost nine feet long. The text inscribed on the copper is in an odd form of Hebrew, but what it says is even more striking.

The Copper Scroll

The Copper Scroll seems to be a list of 64 hiding places for various treasures. Most of the treasure is in the form of gold and silver, and estimates for the total amount listed range between 58 and 174 tons!

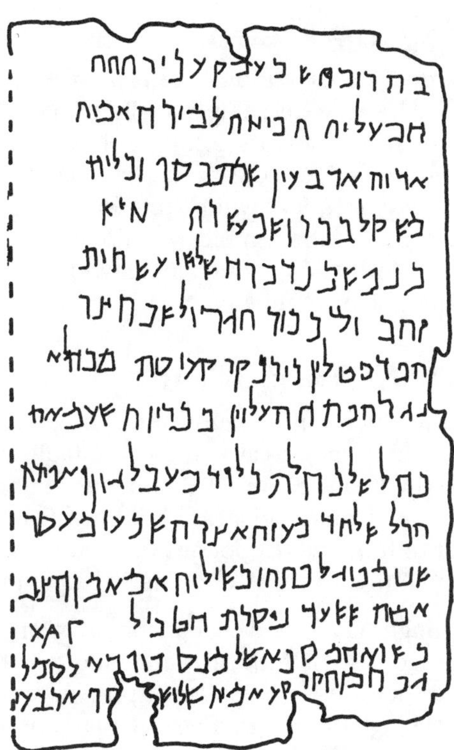

A sample of the mystery text of the Copper Scroll.

(After John Allegro, The Treasure of the Copper Scroll, *1960, p. 32)*

Apart from being difficult to read, the text is difficult to interpret. Is this a real list of treasures, or is it some sort of mystical document? The fact that it's written on metal suggests that its maker was hoping it would survive for a while.

Buried Treasure

It has been theorized that the treasure listed might have come from the Temple in Jerusalem, hidden to protect it from the Romans, who destroyed the Temple in A.D. 70. Another idea is that it is the treasure of the community that once existed in the vicinity of the cave, perhaps a group known as the Essenes.

Although the scroll lists a location for each of the buried amounts, none is known to have been discovered. Intriguingly, location number 64 is said to contain another, perhaps more detailed scroll.

Illuminations

And now for something truly different. There is a theory out there that the ark contained an extraterrestrial manna-making machine. Go figure.

VISIT
BEAUTIFUL
JERICHO!!

People and Places

Beware of people claiming that they were the inspiration for the fictional archaeologist Indiana Jones. Jones is the creation of producers George Lucas and Phillip Kaufman, along with director Steven Spielberg, who were inspired by the cliff-hanging tales featured in old movie matinee serials. Indiana was the name of George Lucas's dog, and the character's last name was originally Smith.

Digging Deep

One of the most curious recent players in the search for lost Temple treasures is a fellow name Vendyl Jones. For many years, Mr. Jones has engaged in a search for various objects and materials which, upon discovery, he hopes will help to bring about the restoration of the Temple. (See the next chapter for more information about people who want to rebuild the Jerusalem Temple.)

What's That Smell?

Inspired by interpretations of the enigmatic Copper Scroll, Jones has excavated most notably in locations near the Dead Sea. In 1992, Jones announced that one of his excavations in a cave had revealed a buried deposit of hundreds of pounds of a red substance that he claimed to be a cache of hidden Temple incense.

Although he asserted that a laboratory analysis was not inconsistent with his claim, another study indicated that it was probably nothing more than red dirt. A little juglet found in a nearby cave was also proclaimed to contain anointing oil from the Temple.

Sacred Cows

At the top of Jones's list of most desirable discoveries are the ashes of the red heifers, which were especially pure cows who were sacrificed and burned, and their ashes mixed with water for purification rituals. The discovery of these ashes might enable modern-day priests to be purified as part of the preparation for the Temple restoration.

It is difficult to evaluate Vendyl Jones's work, because few if any scientific publications have published his work to thoroughly explain what he is doing, how he is doing it, and what he has found. Few professional archaeologists have heard of him, although he seems to have a popular following in certain religious circles.

Jones seems to have an archaeological agenda that is less than scientific, but that doesn't necessarily mean it's without value. If and when he does find anything of real interest, I hope that professional archaeologists will have access to the data and give it a look. Who knows? Maybe through sheer enthusiasm and determination he'll find something that will dazzle us all!

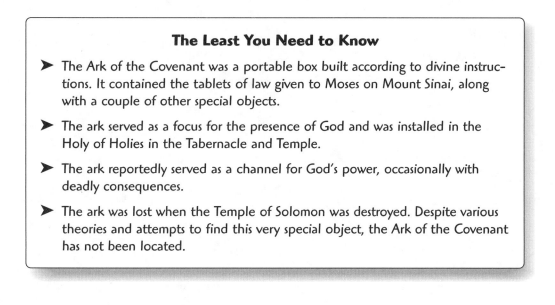

The Least You Need to Know

- The Ark of the Covenant was a portable box built according to divine instructions. It contained the tablets of law given to Moses on Mount Sinai, along with a couple of other special objects.
- The ark served as a focus for the presence of God and was installed in the Holy of Holies in the Tabernacle and Temple.
- The ark reportedly served as a channel for God's power, occasionally with deadly consequences.
- The ark was lost when the Temple of Solomon was destroyed. Despite various theories and attempts to find this very special object, the Ark of the Covenant has not been located.

Chapter 12

City at the Center of the World

In This Chapter

- Jerusalem: a special and holy city
- Archaeological discoveries
- Battles, wars, and conflicts
- An ancient city reaches into the present and future

It is a city revered by three of the world's great religions. It has been the site of some of history's greatest triumphs and tragedies. It is a city over which people have been fighting for thousands of years, and they continue to do so.

It is a city with a physical presence and a spiritual aura, a timeless city where the past, present, and future seem to converge. It is Jerusalem, the ancient City of David, the capital of the modern State of Israel, and to some, a future world capital to be overseen by God himself in a new age.

A Thrice-Sacred City

To Jews, Jerusalem was the original capital of the Hebrew tribes, united together in the Promised Land under the protection and authority of God. The Holy Temple was built there as a center of worship to the one God, YHVH, and was twice destroyed.

As we discussed earlier, a section of wall from the platform of Herod's Temple at the base of the old Temple Mount today serves as the holiest site in Judaism. While Jews have been scattered over the centuries, Jerusalem has remained the spiritual homeland, and with the establishment of the modern state of Israel in the twentieth century, its ancient status has been renewed.

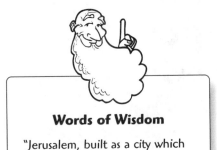

Words of Wisdom

"Jerusalem, built as a city which is bound firmly together, to which the tribes go up, the tribes of the Lord, as was decreed for Israel, to give thanks to the name of the Lord. There thrones for judgment were set, the thrones of the house of David. Pray for the peace of Jerusalem! May they prosper who love you!"
—David, Psalms 122:3–6

Jerusalem plays a vital part in the story of Jesus, and to Christians, it is the place where Jesus preached, performed miracles, and died. Churches and monuments were built at every possible site that could be identified with the Savior, and the city has been the destination of Christian pilgrimages for nearly 2,000 years. Great battles pitting Christians against Muslims and Jews were fought there in an effort to defend these holy places.

For Muslims, Jerusalem is the third most sacred city, after Mecca and Medina. The golden Dome of the Rock, built on the platform where the Holy Temple once stood, covers a rock that bears a traditional history relating it both to Abraham and Mohammed.

Oh, Jerusalem!

As someone who is scientifically trained and who tries to be objective, I must nevertheless admit that there's some sort of intangible special feeling about Jerusalem. It's difficult to put into words. It's almost as if its walls are bursting with its tortured and triumphant history. Or perhaps it's the city's religiously cosmopolitan atmosphere, where Jews, Christians, and Muslims of all kinds, from all over the world, come together. It is a wonderful, haunting, and mysterious place.

Logos

The name **Jerusalem** is thought by many to be a combination of the words for "city" and "peace." Some say it refers to two cities of peace: a physical city and a spiritual one.

What's in a Name?

The name *Jerusalem* is interesting. In Hebrew, the name is *Yerushalayem,* which many say is a combination of the words for "city" and "peace." The ending of the word for "peace," *shalom,* is somewhat provocative, because it uses a dual grammatical ending, suggesting a double city. Some have interpreted the name to imply that Jerusalem is actually two cities: a physical city and a spiritual city. Some say that the latter is yet to come.

The Center of the World

On some old maps, Jerusalem is pictured as the center of the world, and from a limited European standpoint, it might be pictured as a place where three continents come together: Europe, Africa, and Asia. Geographically, the whole region of Palestine, in which Jerusalem sits, was a crossroads between cultures for millennia.

Humans were living in the region for tens of thousands of years before cities appeared. In the age of great civilizations, the area produced its own thriving population centers, and served as a trampling ground for empire-builders on either side, including the Egyptians, Assyrians, and Babylonians.

A map from 1580 showing Jerusalem as the center of the world.

An Ancient Crossroads

Jerusalem lies on elevated land that stretches from north to south across the center of the Palestine region, about 35 miles from the Mediterranean coast. In ancient times, the city itself was situated at a convenient crossroads, with hilly flanks that made it easier to defend.

The areas surrounding the city provided suitable land for growing crops and trees and for grazing livestock. Very important to the city's ability to survive was an adequate and reliable water supply. This necessity was provided by the Gihon Spring, situated in a valley to the city's east.

City of Old

Archaeologists have found evidence of people living in Jerusalem as far back as 3000 B.C. A city was definitely there around 1800 B.C., and it is mentioned in the written correspondence of neighboring civilizations. In the time of King David, about 1000 B.C., the city was in the hands of a group of Canaanite people called the Jebusites.

Revelations

One of the earliest mentions of Jerusalem in an ancient text was found on the pieces of a broken bowl from Egypt dating to about 1800 B.C. In a kind of magical cursing, the names of enemies were written on bowls and other objects and then smashed. The ruler of Jerusalem and his retainers are mentioned, along with a lot of other folks who had irritated the Egyptians.

David Conquers a City

As we have seen, the land promised to the Hebrews was already occupied by other peoples, and the same was true of Jerusalem. It was something of a fortress, in fact, with its hilly location and fortified walls. How did David conquer such a place? I'm glad you asked. The Bible talks about a water shaft that the Hebrews ascended in order to attack the city. What could that be all about?

One compelling idea is that the Israelite soldiers were able to infiltrate the Jebusite stronghold from the inside. A little way upslope from the outlet of the Gihon spring is a deep natural sink hole in the limestone that drops down into the subterranean water. This sink hole is called Warren's Shaft, after the English explorer who investigated it in the nineteenth century.

Warren's Shaft

Earlier residents of Jerusalem had built an underground tunnel from behind the city wall leading into Warren's Shaft. That way, if the city were under attack, which wasn't an uncommon thing in those days, people could still visit the spring and obtain water by dropping a bucket down the shaft.

Could Warren's Shaft have been the ticket to conquering Jebusite Jerusalem? Might David's soldiers have accomplished the difficult rock-climbing feet of clandestinely ascending the shaft as a route to invasion? It's a fascinating question, and like many questions in the Bible, it will be difficult to prove without additional archaeological data or information from ancient texts.

Illuminations

2 Samuel 5:9 mentions that David "built the city [of Jerusalem] round about from the Millo inward." It's not clear exactly what the Millo was, but some think it might refer to a big stepstone structure that has been discovered in Jerusalem, which might have served as an ancient retaining wall.

A United Capitol

However they did it, the Israelites were victorious, and Jerusalem became the united capital of the Israelite tribes, gaining even more prestige when the sacred Ark of the Covenant was brought into town. Jerusalem was expanded, and the remains of David's city have been excavated on the modern eastern slopes.

After ruling from the city for 37 years, David died. A visitor to Jerusalem today will find a structure traditionally referred to as David's tomb. He's not inside, though. This tomb is relatively recent, dating to about the fourth century A.D.

Although it was customary to bury people outside the city walls, it's possible that an exception was made for David and a few other royals. Some rock-cut tombs within the confines of David's city walls have been found, and perhaps it was here that he was laid to rest. Tombs placed in special locations tend to belong to very special individuals.

VISIT BEAUTIFUL JERICHO!!

People and Places

The Assyrians were masters of brutal warfare. Their highly organized army was expert at siege tactics and terrorism. With a penchant for burning, pillaging, and scarring the earth, their reputation was sufficient to cause many people to flee or surrender. At home, they prospered from the booty and maintained an artistic and literate civilization.

Holding the Fort

Jerusalem continued to prosper even after the Israelite Kingdom was divided and the ten northern tribes were led away by the Assyrians. It, too, was a target of the Assyrians, but the city survived the assault and its population actually grew, due to an influx of refugees from the north.

The city was spared thanks to the efforts of King Hezekiah (reigned 715–687 B.C.). The Bible tells how he prayed to God for help and the next morning found 185,000 dead Assyrians outside the walls. He also prepared the city by building a 20-foot-thick wall to withstand a brutal assault. But his most famous accomplishment was an enduring marvel.

Water for the People

Hezekiah was well aware of the tactics of the Assyrians, who were more than willing to cut off food supplies and water to the cities they aimed to conquer. Dead or weakened people don't put up much of a fight. To ensure that water would be available to the city of Jerusalem, Hezekiah initiated an amazing building project: a tunnel was carved from the Gihon Spring to provide water within the expanded city's walls.

The tunnel stretches for about one third of a mile, and two crews worked simultaneously from each end to meet in the middle. The route of Hezekiah's tunnel is by no means straight—in fact, it curves quite a bit. In addition, the tunnel maintains an appropriately gentle slope to keep the water moving. The real mystery is how the two teams were able to meet up at all.

Do Some Wading

One solution to the puzzle might be that the tunnel diggers were following a natural geological fault or crack in the rock. In any case, an ancient inscription found at one end of the tunnel recorded the triumphant meeting of the two teams. They could apparently hear each other as they approached.

If you're not too claustrophobic, and you don't mind getting wet, you can have a real adventure in Hezekiah's tunnel. With a good flashlight, it's possible to slosh your way from one end to the other. The water is cool, clear, and refreshing, and it makes for an exciting activity on a hot day.

Revelations

The famous Siloam Inscription (named for the pool at one end of the tunnel) records the meeting of the miners who created Hezekiah's tunnel. It's not to be found in Jerusalem, however. It was chipped away from the rock, sold to an antiquities dealer, and eventually taken to Turkey, where it now resides in a museum in Istanbul.

The Babylonians Prevail

Although the people of Jerusalem were spared when the Assyrians attacked, they weren't so lucky with the Babylonians. As we saw when we talked about the Temple, the Babylonians were extremely successful in their assault on the city, which took place in 586 B.C.

Not only was Solomon's Temple destroyed, but archaeologists can confirm that much of the city was burned as well. Many of the Israelites, including elite Jewish families, were led into captivity in Babylon, where they would remain until the Persians took control of the ancient world.

Archaeological Remains

An interesting archaeological discovery was made in 1979 when Israeli archaeologist Gabriel Barkay was investigating some old stone tombs outside the city walls. Underneath a collapsed ceiling, he found an amazing collection of human bones and artifacts. About a hundred people were buried there, along with around a thousand objects, including pottery and jewelry.

What's surprising is that some of the pottery dates to the time period just after the Jews were said to have been taken away into captivity. The grave appears to have belonged to members of the wealthy Jewish elite, and it shows that not all of them left. They apparently continued a good life in the aftermath of the fall of Jerusalem.

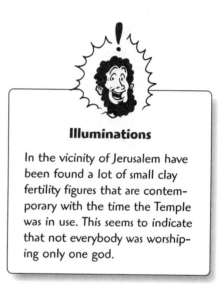

Illuminations

In the vicinity of Jerusalem have been found a lot of small clay fertility figures that are contemporary with the time the Temple was in use. This seems to indicate that not everybody was worshiping only one god.

The Lord Bless Thee and Keep Thee

Perhaps the most remarkable objects recovered from Barkay's excavation were two amulets, each consisting of a rolled silver strip. When they were painstakingly unrolled, the strips revealed two versions of the priestly blessing from Numbers 6:24–26:

> The Lord bless thee, and keep thee; The Lord make his face shine upon thee, and be gracious unto thee; The Lord lift up his countenance upon thee, and give thee peace. (KJV)

The discovery of an ancient text of any kind from this part of the world is exciting, especially something relating to the Bible, but these are extra special. The two amulets date to around 650 B.C. and are the oldest known Biblical texts!

The Greeks and Romans Arrive

In the last chapter, we discussed how the Temple was rebuilt after the return of the Jewish captives from Babylon. Another city wall was also built at this time. And a couple centuries later, when the Greeks came to dominate Jerusalem, they brought along some of their culture, including a bit of architectural influence.

Some impressive tombs carved into the rock just outside the walls have elements that look as if they were borrowed from Greek temples. And we already saw how during Roman times, King Herod made dramatic changes to the city, including his spectacular remodeling of the second Temple.

Building and Burning

The time of the Romans was also the time of Jesus of Nazareth, and Jerusalem is famous for its role in his life. There are many sites and monuments relating to Jesus to be found there, and we'll talk about some of those in future chapters.

The Romans destroyed the Temple in A.D. 70 during the Jewish revolt. Another serious revolt took place against the Romans in the years A.D. 132 through 135. The rebels were led by a charismatic man named Simon Bar-Kokhba. Although successful in winning a number of skirmishes against the Romans, Bar-Kokhba's warriors were ultimately defeated. Thereafter, Jews were banned from Jerusalem.

Revelations

Caves which served as the hideouts of the Bar-Kokhba rebels have been discovered in cliffs in the Judean desert. One in particular contained letters and other artifacts preserved from that period. Ominously, the remains of a Roman camp have been found on top of this particular cave. Starving out the enemy was a common Roman military practice.

Building Again

In A.D. 130, during the reign of the emperor Hadrian, Jerusalem was rebuilt and renamed Aeoli Capitolina. A temple of the Roman god Jupiter was built on the Temple Mount. In just a couple hundred years, Christianity would become the official religion of the Roman empire, Jews would return, and Jerusalem would receive visitors from Europe seeking holy artifacts and hoping to locate sites mentioned in the Bible.

Fighting for God and Glory

During the first two millennia A.D., Jerusalem would be controlled by many different powers. The Arabs invaded Palestine in A.D. 635 and brought with them the new religion of Islam. In Jerusalem they built the Dome of the Rock and the Al-Aksa Mosque on the Temple Mount, along with many other structures.

Jerusalem became an Islamic city and, as fellow "peoples of the Book," Jews and Christians were permitted to live in relative peace with their Muslim neighbors and rulers. Things were stirring in Europe, however, that would transform the holy city into a wild battleground.

The walled city of Jerusalem with the golden rotunda of the Dome of the Rock.

(Photo courtesy of John Petersen)

"Liberating" the Holy Land

Beginning in A.D. 1096, Christian armies formed in Europe to engage in eight major campaigns to "free" the Holy Land from non-Christian *infidels*. A request by a Christian emperor to send assistance to fight against the Turks in Palestine inspired Pope Urban II (1088–1099) to issue a call to arms.

Logos

Infidel is a pejorative term for someone who doesn't maintain the same religious beliefs as you do.

In the speech that inspired the First Crusade, the Pope reported that Christians were being killed and holy sites in Jerusalem and elsewhere in the Holy Land were being desecrated and destroyed. He promised those who died in their defense automatic forgiveness for their sins.

Huge armies left Europe, and in 1099, Jerusalem was taken by the Crusaders after a horrible slaughter of its inhabitants. Little Crusader kingdoms were set up in the region. The Muslims were not at all happy about this and fought to win back the territory.

More Blood Shed

A Second Crusade was called in 1147 through 1149, and was a big failure. A Third Crusade (1189–1192) began after the great Islamic leader, Saladin, captured Jerusalem in 1187. The results of this Crusade were mixed, and the armies went home without recapturing Jerusalem. Christian pilgrims, however, were still permitted to visit the Holy City.

Five more Crusades took place between 1204 and 1291, and Jerusalem changed hands a couple of times in the process. The city would ultimately return to the Muslims. The Crusades were not just about religion, but also about greed, commerce, and power. Untold thousands died in the process, and not a whole lot was accomplished.

People and Places

Before the First Crusade began, a fanatical rag-tag peasant army, led by Peter the Hermit, rampaged through Europe on their way to Jerusalem, harassing Jews along the way. They never made it. Along with another general, Walter the Penniless, these motley crusaders were eventually slaughtered by the Turks in Asia Minor.

A City Divided

Palestine was incorporated into the Turkish Ottoman Empire in 1516 and remained there until Jerusalem was captured by the British during World War I. Palestine became a British Mandate in 1922.

Tensions rose during the next couple of decades due to an influx of Jewish immigrants, which the local Arab population found threatening. With more and more Jewish refugees hoping to move to their ancestral homeland, especially after the profound tragedy of the Nazi Holocaust, British policy was unable to keep the peace.

War and Peace

The United Nations partitioned Palestine into a Jewish state and an Arab state. Jerusalem was to be an international city. The Arabs never agreed to this plan, and when the state of Israel was declared on May 14, 1948, war broke out. The Jewish settlements in Jerusalem were cut off by Arab forces, but the Israelis eventually prevailed. Jerusalem, which was declared the capital of a new country known as Israel, was left divided.

The western sections were under Israeli control, and the ancient walled Old City, containing the Temple Mount, was in the hands of the Jordanians. In 1967, another war broke out, and the Israelis captured the Old City, along with other territories belonging to Jordan, Egypt, and Syria. Another war between Israel and several Arab states was fought in 1973, which Israel again survived.

Illuminations

Want to step back into time? A trip through the Hasidic neighborhood of Mea Sharim in Jerusalem is like a visit to an eastern European Jewish shtetl of 200 years ago. The rules are posted at the entrance: Dress modestly, and observe the Sabbath.

The Palestinian Question

The Arab people who now live in, or who fled from, the areas captured by Israel in the wars have organized themselves under the name "Palestinians." A good many don't accept the original United Nations division of the land and have engaged in a long-term struggle with the State of Israel. Some have called for the utter dismantling of Israel, to be replaced by a secular, modern state of Palestine.

Israel has already made many concessions and returned some of the territories captured during the wars. But one of the biggest bones of contention in this Biblical region is the ultimate status of the city of Jerusalem.

VISIT
BEAUTIFUL
JERICHO!!

People and Places

The status of the city of Jerusalem remains internationally controversial. Many countries attempt to stay out of the dispute by placing their embassies in the modern Israeli city of Tel Aviv.

The Palestinians would like to make Jerusalem the capital of what they hope will be a Palestinian state. They wish to regain control over the eastern part of the city, the part captured in 1967, which includes not only the sacred Western Wall and the Temple Mount, but also many Jewish homes and establishments built in the last 30 years in the walled Old City's Jewish Quarter.

As of this writing, the negotiations are continuing, and you can bet that the status of the city of Jerusalem will be one of the most difficult of the many issues to be settled.

Rebuilding the Temple

If the political situation between the Palestinians and the Israelis isn't enough, there are also attempts—some serious and some downright odd—to restore the city of Jerusalem as the center of the Jewish worship of YHVH. To the idea's proponents, this means rebuilding the Temple and resuming its activities.

Much of this belief is tied into the notion that rebuilding the Temple will usher in the age of the Messiah, a heavenly savior who will heal the world and bring peace. To Jews, he has yet to come; to Christians, the Messiah was Jesus, and he is expected to return.

Illuminations

Ranters claiming to be reincarnated Biblical prophets and self-styled Messiahs are not uncommon on the streets of Jerusalem. In fact, psychologists have a name for it: the Jerusalem Syndrome.

People of both faiths can be found in the small campaign to rebuild the Temple. Some Temple paraphernalia has been built, genealogies have been scoured to locate individuals eligible for the priesthood, and a cornerstone has allegedly been cut.

A Dangerous Idea

Why is this restoration not a good idea? First of all, the Temple Mount is now occupied by Islamic monuments, including the Dome of the Rock. Since physics tells us that two things can't occupy the same place at the same time, then something has to go if the Temple is to be rebuilt.

The destruction or removal of these precious Islamic monuments would be an assault upon all of the world's Muslims, just like blowing up the Vatican in Rome would be an assault on the world's Christians. The Israeli government certainly doesn't want to create an epic battle. But consider these scary incidents:

- In 1982, a Jewish radical was arrested for attempting to blow up the Dome of the Rock.
- In 1984, another attempt to destroy Islamic monuments on the Temple Mount was thwarted. Several people were apprehended with many pounds of explosives and hand grenades.
- In 1990, tensions over the Temple Mount erupted into a riot in which 22 Arabs were killed.
- In 1996, a sealed-off tunnel running alongside the Temple Mount was opened to pedestrians. It caused a big riot.

So why not just locate the Temple elsewhere on the Mount? A few Temple advocates have tried to demonstrate that the original site of the structure was not where the Dome of the Rock now sits, but off to the side. That being the case, both monuments could sit on the same platform. Others, though, insist that the Holy of Holies was located on the legendary rock protected by that golden dome.

Words of Wisdom

"Pray for the peace of Jerusalem! 'May they prosper those who love you! Peace be within your walls, and security within your towers!' For my brethren and companions' sake I will say, 'Peace be within you!' For the sake of the house of the Lord our God, I will seek your good."
—David, Psalms 122:6–9

Leaving Well-Enough Alone

Apart from the political implications, it would be fair to say that a good many Jews today have no interest in returning to the old days of animal sacrifices and such. Judaism has successfully survived, evolved, and flourished over the centuries without the Temple. And as far as Christians are concerned, most believe that the need for Temple sacrifices was negated with the death and resurrection of Jesus. If there is to be a Second Coming, it will happen in its own good time, with or without the Temple.

A Visit to the City

Jerusalem is a wonderful city today. The narrow streets and stone walls of the Old City exist side by side with a vibrant modern city. Jewish people flock to the Western Wall daily while Muslims pray at the mosques above. Thousands of Christians wander the city in awe of the sites where Jesus spent much time.

Jerusalem is also home to the Israel Museum, which exhibits a superb collection of artifacts from Biblical times. The sites, sounds, and smells of Jerusalem are unforgettable. The city's enchanting qualities cannot be fully described, certainly not in this book. They are best experienced firsthand!

Illuminations

Stop the presses! New archaeological discoveries in Jerusalem and elsewhere are always capable of changing or enhancing many of the ideas we have about the past. Keep current by reading some of the magazines listed in Appendix B, "Biblos," such as *Biblical Archaeology Review*.

The Least You Need to Know

- The ancient and modern city of Jerusalem is held sacred by Jews, Christians, and Muslims.
- Jerusalem served as the capital of the Israelites in ancient times and serves as the capital of the modern state of Israel today. It has changed hands numerous times over the years.
- Archaeological discoveries have shed interesting light on the history of this amazing city, but much remains to be discovered.
- The city remains controversial to this day, and plays a central role in the conflict between Israel and the Palestinians.

Part 5

Jesus

It's been about 2,000 years since Jesus of Nazareth walked the byways of Palestine, and the world has never been the same. The life of Jesus as reported in the New Testament was punctuated by wise commentary and many miracles. The long-term impact of this rabbi and social critic survives today in hundreds of variations.

The religion that emerged from the life and teachings of Jesus of Nazareth often developed despite persecution. Who is this man for whom many of his followers were willing to die? Was he the promised Messiah whose coming was predicted by the Old Testament prophets, or even God on earth? The vast majority of Christian believers say yes to both questions, and some claim that the wonders and miracles continue to this day. In the next three chapters, we'll take a look at the extraordinary life of Jesus, and at some of his dedicated followers as well.

Chapter 13

A Miraculous Life

In This Chapter

- The miraculous birth of a baby boy
- Jesus: the early years and the missing years
- On the road with Jesus
- Life, death, and hope

How does one begin to talk about Jesus of Nazareth? Perhaps you could mention that over a billion people today claim to be his followers. Or that he is respected by at least a billion more people of other faiths. Most everything about his life is profound and mysterious, and two thousand years after he walked the earth, his influence continues to grow. In this chapter, we'll take a look at the birth, life, and death of this amazing figure.

The Gospel Truth

The "official" story of Jesus is found in the Christian portion of the Bible, the New Testament. Parts of his life and teachings are described in the first few books of the New Testament, and the rest consists of commentaries about his teaching. The first four books are referred to as the Gospels. As I mentioned in Chapter 1, "Introducing the Book of Mysteries," there is some controversy about who wrote them.

The first three, Matthew, Mark, and Luke, are very similar, suggesting that they may have shared a common source or sources. Whereas these three books all have some of the characteristics of a historical narrative, the fourth Gospel, that of John, is quite different in its approach and spiritual tone. After these first four books, Jesus makes a brief appearance in the Book of Acts, and that's it for his physical presence for the rest of the Bible.

Logos

The word **Gospel** is from the Greek word for "good news," and to Christians, the life and teachings of Jesus are considered to be good news for everybody.

The Virgin Birth

One thing that characterizes the life of Jesus is the sheer quantity of miracles involved, in everything from his birth to his death. In fact, the miracles and supernatural events start even before he's born. The angel Gabriel announces to Mary, a virgin, that she will miraculously give birth.

This kind of news is generally unsettling, especially to Mary's fiancé, Joseph. Fortunately, he, too, received a heavenly visitor to assure him that his wife-to-be wasn't messing around. So the main characters were reassured, but it still must have been a bit of a scandal in the neighborhood.

Angels and Wise Men

The story of Jesus' birth finds Joseph and Mary traveling to Bethlehem to register for a census. When they can't get a room at the local hotel, Mary gives birth in a stable, and the baby's first cradle is a manger.

More heavenly visitors make their appearance as angels tell some nearby shepherds to go and pay their respects to the newborn baby. A group of wise men also arrive from somewhere in the East, seeking the baby Jesus to present him with precious gifts. They claimed to be following a star which guided them to Bethlehem.

Illuminations

The name of the town of Bethlehem, where Jesus was born, is composed of two Hebrew words, "Bet" and "Lechem," which mean "House of Bread."

Star of Wonder

There's been plenty of speculation about this divine signal that is said to have guided the wise men on their journey. Some have suggested it was a comet or an especially bright star. Or it could have been a dying supernova, which would have produced a temporarily bright stellar phenomenon.

Others have suggested that a meteor shower was involved, or perhaps the planet Venus. Other theories involve the aurora borealis (northern lights), or maybe two or more planets in conjunction that would produce a bright glowing effect. Or perhaps it was a combination of two or more of the above.

And what of these wise men? It's been suggested that they were astrologers from Mesopotamia or Persia. As such, they would have been students of the sky who constantly searched the heavens for signs and portents. In any event, they managed to find the stable in Bethlehem and deliver their gifts of gold, frankincense, and myrrh.

Visit
Beautiful
Jericho!!

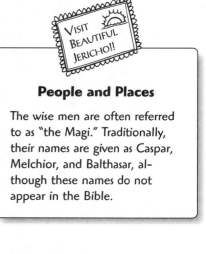

People and Places

The wise men are often referred to as "the Magi." Traditionally, their names are given as Caspar, Melchior, and Balthasar, although these names do not appear in the Bible.

The Divine Birthday

So when was Jesus born? We're not exactly sure, but it seems clear that he was born out of sync with our modern calendar. The Gospel of Luke tells us that Jesus was born while the Jewish king Herod the Great was still alive, which gives us an important clue.

Since Herod is known to have died in 4 B.C., the birth of Jesus must have taken place in that year, or prior to it. A Roman census is mentioned in Luke, and some have argued that this event took place in 6 or 7 B.C. All of this, of course, leads to the odd situation of Jesus having been born perhaps four years before his official calendar "birthday."

LOGOS

Logos

The name Jesus in Hebrew is **Yeshua** and is the same name as **Joshua.** The English name "Jesus" is derived from the Greek via Latin.

The calendar universally used today was developed in A.D. 525, when a monk named Dionysius Exiguus (known as "Little Dennis" to us English speakers) was asked by Pope St. John I to reform the calendar then in use. The new calendar would begin its annual count from what they considered the most significant event in human history, the birth of Jesus. So the "zero" point was the birth of Jesus, and the count continues to this day.

Thus, for example, the year 1999 is considered to be 1,999 years since the birth of Jesus. We now know that Little Dennis's calculations were off by at least four years, so if any of you were expecting the return of Jesus or other special events to occur 2,000 years after his birth, it already came and went. More on that in Chapter 22, "Revelation: The End?"

The newborn baby Jesus in the manger, with his parents and assorted onlookers.

(Illustration by Gustave Doré)

Herod Strikes Out

In any event, we know King Herod was still around when Jesus was born because, according to the Gospel of Matthew, the wise men approached him to ask where they might locate the newborn king of the Jews. This, of course, immediately riled the egotistical and homicidal Herod, who decided to locate the baby Jesus and have him killed before he could compete for the throne.

He asked the wise men to let him know where this special baby could be found, using the excuse that he wanted to join them in honoring him. Warned about Herod's plans in a dream, however, the wise men found Jesus, presented their gifts to him, and left without informing Herod. Herod, determined to have the baby destroyed, went on a killing rampage, ordering the deaths of all male children two years old or younger in the vicinity of Bethlehem.

Travels in Egypt

An angel appeared to Joseph in a dream, telling him to take his family and escape to Egypt. The details of their travels are not described in the Bible. In Egypt, however, there are rich traditions that trace the path of the Holy Family on a journey that may have lasted three years.

VISIT
BEAUTIFUL
JERICHO!!

People and Places

The children killed by Herod are often referred to as the "Holy Innocents." Given that Bethlehem wasn't such a large town, the number of victims is thought to be somewhere between 6 and 25. The Holy Innocents are noteworthy as the only ones to have died not for Jesus (as with martyrs), but instead of him. Their story is found in Matthew 2:16–18.

Miracles in the Desert

There are lots of interesting stories about the baby Jesus performing a variety of miracles in Egypt, including healing people, calming wild animals, and producing springs of fresh water. On at least a couple of occasions, the legends say, he was able to cause trees to bend over so that their delicious fruit could be picked.

Today, one can find churches located up and down the Nile and elsewhere in Egypt at places where Jesus and his family are thought to have spent time or where miracles supposedly occurred.

Revelations

The Copts are members of the oldest orthodox Christian group found in Egypt. The Coptic church was founded by St. Mark and flourishes today as a minority in an overwhelmingly Islamic country. Coptic churches and monasteries are plentiful in Egypt. Much of their liturgy and other sacred texts is written in Coptic, the last surviving remnant of the ancient Egyptian language.

A Mysterious Childhood

Jesus and his parents returned from Egypt at the death of Herod and settled in the town of Nazareth in the Galilee region. There's really not a whole lot to say about his childhood. His father was a carpenter, and he had brothers and sisters.

Visit
Beautiful
Jericho!!

People and Places

Jesus had four brothers—James, Joseph, Judas, and Simon. James became one of his 12 disciples. The names of his sisters are not recorded in the Bible.

Illuminations

Jesus probably spoke two languages, possibly three. The standard language of the region during his lifetime was Aramaic, introduced long before as the international language of the Assyrian empire. The Scriptures, in which he was well versed, were written in Hebrew. He may also have spoken Greek, which was widely used in the region as a result of the Hellenization brought by earlier Greek rulers.

He had a traditional Jewish upbringing, including being circumcised on the eighth day after his birth. There are stories about his early years that don't appear in the Bible, but these have been rejected as unauthoritative by the compilers of the New Testament. (See Chapter 17, "Alternate Scriptures and Fabulous Fakes," for a look at some of them.)

In My Father's House

As far as the Bible is concerned, we next find Jesus at age 12 accompanying his parents to Jerusalem to celebrate the Passover. On the way home, they notice that he's missing and return to Jerusalem to search for him. When he's eventually found, he's at the Temple, dazzling the scholars.

When his worried parents reprimand him, he answers, "Did you not know that I must be in my Father's house?" (Luke 2:49) He went home with his parents and was a good boy, although they must have had quite a time raising such a child.

The Missing Years

After the story about the Temple, the Bible provides no details regarding the life and whereabouts of Jesus from age 12 to perhaps around age 30, when he began his ministry. Given the profound impact of what we know of his life, it's not surprising that all manner of theories have appeared to explain what was going on during the undocumented years.

Some say that he dutifully worked with Dad in the carpenter's shop. Others suggest that he was on a spiritual quest, perhaps living an ascetic life in the desert with a group of monk-like Jews known as the Essenes. Other ideas place him farther afield, studying mysticism in India or interning with Buddhists in the Far East and on excursions in Tibet, Persia, and Greece. We don't really know, and there is no evidence to firmly indicate that he ever left Palestine.

The Ministry Begins

Jesus' ministry is thought to have begun when he was around 30 years old, and may have lasted up to three years before his execution. It begins with an encounter with an interesting fellow named John the Baptist. John apparently had his own ministry going, in which he preached that people should repent of their sins. John presided over a ceremony of symbolic purification in water, or baptism.

John the Baptist seems to have been a bit of a wild man. The Bible describes him as living in the desert, wearing clothes of camel hair and eating locusts and honey. The book of Luke tells of his somewhat miraculous birth to an elderly couple, forewarned by the angel Gabriel. As a traveling minister and prophet, John foretold the coming of someone greater than himself.

A Dip in the River

A baptism by John in the Jordan River seems to have been the formal beginning of Jesus' career as recorded in the Gospels. When he emerged from his baptism, Jesus received a divine ordination:

> And when he came up out of the water, immediately he saw the heavens opened and the Spirit descending upon him like a dove; and a voice came from heaven, "Thou art my beloved Son; with thee I am well pleased." (Mark 1:10–11)

Revelations

John the Baptist met a sorry end. He had been imprisoned by King Herod Antipas for condemning the king's marriage to his brother's ex-wife. The wife's daughter, named Salome, danced for the king and so pleased him that he granted her a wish. She asked for the head of John the Baptist on a platter. The king complied, and John was killed.

The Wandering Rabbi

As Jesus toured about, he collected a dozen close followers, or disciples. It isn't the place of this book to go into depth about all of Jesus' teachings; there are scores and scores of other volumes that address those. In summary, however, he taught love and compassion and the commonality of flawed humanity. He was also a great advocate of forgiveness.

He fraternized with societal outcasts and taught that it wasn't enough just to go through the motions of following God's law—it was necessary to live the spirit of the law as well. Like John the Baptist, he preached about the need for repentance and lived his life as an example for others to follow.

Words of Wisdom

Jesus was once asked what was the greatest commandment. This is how he answered:

> "... You shall love the Lord your God with all your heart, and with all your soul, and with all your mind. This is the great and first commandment. And a second is like it, You shall love your neighbor as yourself. On these two commandments depend all the law and the prophets."
>
> —Matthew 22:37–40

Miracle upon Miracle

Although the message of Jesus is the true focus of the Gospels, the ministry of Jesus is heavily punctuated by accounts of many miracles. The miracles were seen as a clear demonstration that he was no ordinary man and also served to impress potential followers who were either directly affected or who looked on in awe. Let's take a look at some of these astounding events.

The Original Miracle Cure

The Gospels record that Jesus performed a number of physical healings. The specific nature of some of the afflictions is not clear, although others, such as leprosy, are well known. Various individuals were cured, including an official's son who was healed of an unknown life-threatening illness, his disciple Peter's mother-in-law, who was cured of a fever, and a woman who had been suffering from internal bleeding for years.

Most dramatic were the restoration of sight to several blind men, including one who was blind from birth, and the healing of a number of lepers, cripples, and a paralytic. Jesus also healed several people afflicted with demonic possession. During his arrest, he restored the ear of a Roman soldier which had been lopped off by the sword of an overly rambunctious disciple.

Revelations

Leprosy was a much-dreaded contagious disease in Biblical times. The disease attacks the nerves under the skin and can result in great disfigurement. Lepers were widely shunned, and the willingness of Jesus to assist these people was extraordinary in his day. Leprosy, often called "Hansen's disease," today affects up to five million people in the world, and is finally curable.

Walking on Water

Several miraculous events surely defy the laws of nature. In the Gospel of Matthew, the disciples are in the Sea of Galilee in rough conditions when they spot Jesus walking on the water. The disciples thought they were seeing a ghost, so Jesus invited one of them, Peter, to come on out. Peter, too, walked across the water toward Jesus until he lost faith and sank. Jesus pulled him out, though.

Loaves and Fishes

There are two stories in which Jesus is able to create food. In both cases, there were crowds following him who brought with them their blind, sick, and injured. Feeling compassion for them, Jesus fed them with what little food the disciples could scare up. In the first instance, 5,000 men, plus women and children, were miraculously fed with five loaves of bread and two fish. In the second case, with seven loaves and a few fish, over 4,000 enjoyed a meal. Following both events, there were several baskets of food left over.

Water into Wine

Lest you think that Jesus was all serious, there is the tale of him being invited to a wedding in the village of Cana. When the wine ran out, Jesus saved the party. Six large jars of water were miraculously turned into an adult beverage. And it was first-class wine, too! (Read that story in John 2:1–11.)

Second Chances

On two occasions, Jesus raised people from the dead. One was the recently deceased daughter of a community leader. When he went to the house where the girl lay, he declared to the mourning crowd that she was only sleeping. They all scoffed until Jesus took the dead girl by the hand and she got up.

A close friend of Jesus named Lazarus was the other beneficiary. He had been dead for four days and was wrapped up in cloth and closed in a burial cave. Jesus called to Lazarus and he came on out. Needless to say, this caused quite a stir, as did most of Jesus' miracles.

Words of Wisdom

"Many, as has been well said, ran after Christ, not for the miracles, but for the loaves."

—John Lubbock, *The Pleasures of Life* (1887)

Illuminations

A recent trend among American Christian teenagers is to wear clothing or jewelry emblazoned with the letters WWJD. The letters stand for the phrase, "What would Jesus do?" It serves them as a reminder of Jesus as a role model for life's choices.

Words of Wisdom

"Jesus would have asserted his freedom and critically examined his status quo from the principle of love, and in so doing he would meet the same fate in the sixteenth century or even in the twentieth century as he did in his own."

—Mason Olds, "A Developmental Interpretation of Jesus," *Religious Humanism* (Spring 1991)

Signs and Wonders

Although healing was the most common of Jesus' miracles, there are a few sundry events that are likewise interesting. One day, he took a few of his disciples up on a mountain. There he became "transfigured," glowing white, and was seen chatting with Moses and the prophet Elijah. A voice came forth from a cloud announcing, "This is my beloved Son, with whom I am well pleased; listen to him." (Matthew 17:1–8) It was the voice of God.

Jesus also had an interesting way of paying taxes. On one occasion, he told his disciple Peter to go out fishing. The first fish he caught would have a shekel in its mouth which could be used to pay the tax man. Equally unusual was the time he became perturbed at a fruitless fig tree and cursed it. The tree immediately withered.

Making Waves

Jesus did a number of things which infuriated some Jewish authorities. Some of the more pious ones reacted to him hanging out with the riff-raff, and some were offended by his apparent breaking of traditional laws, such as when he healed people on the Sabbath. It didn't help matters that Jesus could have a sharp tongue and disdained hypocrites.

Even though Jesus taught his followers to turn the other cheek, he occasionally engaged in a little righteous indignation, especially when confronted with the corruption or hypocrisy of the religious leaders of the time. In one story, he went to the Temple courtyards and encountered people trying to profit from the Temple by selling goods for sacrifice and trading various forms of currency. Jesus made a whip out of cords and drove them away.

Jesus was also seen as applying new standards to traditional Jewish law. He taught, for example, that not only was it wrong to murder someone, but it was likewise wrong to contemplate such a thing. In a sense, it was an internalization of the law, in that it required that the spirit of the law be respected as much as the letter of the law.

Final Days

There are some questions as to the length of Jesus' ministry. The first three Gospels suggest a year to a year and a half, while John seems to indicate three. Whatever it might have been, the ultimate impact was enormous and lasting. Although the majority of the Jews and others living in Palestine at the time seem to have been unaffected by Jesus, his teachings, spread by disciples and missionaries, would come to have a powerful effect that continues to this day.

The Gospels tell us much about the last days of Jesus. He and his disciples traveled to Jerusalem for the Passover. At what was likely a Passover seder meal (now popularly known as the Last Supper), Jesus informed his disciples that his time was short, although he had been dropping hints about his departure for some time. Later, he went to pray and was arrested by the Romans. He was identified for them by one of his own disciples, Judas.

Good Friday

The Jewish authorities were concerned that Jesus' followers might stir up too much trouble and cause the Romans to crack down on them, so they had Jesus arrested for allegedly organizing and engaging in anti-Roman activities. The religious leaders were also irked by what they considered to be blasphemy on the part of Jesus (see Chapter 14, "Who Was Jesus?" for details).

VISIT
BEAUTIFUL
JERICHO!!

People and Places

The disciple who betrayed Jesus was known as Judas Iscariot. Judas apparently sold out Jesus for the price of 30 pieces of silver. Wrought with guilt, he afterward hung himself.

Even though Jesus didn't offer much of a defense, the Romans found no reason to have him executed. They turned him over to the Jewish king of Galilee, Herod Antipas, who returned him to the Roman officials. Although he was found innocent, it was expedient to have him executed, and he was, on a Friday.

Jesus was executed using a most cruel and painful Roman form of torture: crucifixion. Crucifixion involved the suspension of the condemned person from a cross-bar affixed to a vertical post. The individual's arms were spread out and the hands were tied to the bar, and the feet to the post. In its most brutal form, as practiced on Jesus, nails were driven though the hands or wrists and feet to assist in pinning the condemned to the structure.

The crucifixion of Jesus.

(Illustration by Gustave Doré)

The Crucifixion

How did he die? There have been medical studies to suggest that crucifixion causes eventual asphyxiation, an inability to breathe. Others have disputed this and suggest shock caused by the Romans' penchant for breaking the legs of the condemned on the cross (although the Gospels don't report that Jesus' legs were broken).

It's plausible that some people might have survived for days before succumbing to dehydration and exposure. As for the nails through the hands, some grisly medical research has shown that nails driven through hands cannot support a body's weight. Few dispute that the wrists are capable of it, however.

Revelations

In the 1970s, a Jewish tomb was found in Jerusalem with a stone box containing the bones of a young man crucified during the first century A.D. Interestingly, two bones of the foot were found pierced through with a large nail. A fragment of wood was attached to the back as if ripped off when the body was torn free from the cross. One of the victim's lower leg bones appeared to have been shattered by a hard blow. This discovery provides one of the few pieces of physical evidence for the brutal Roman practice of crucifixion.

Short Stay in the Tomb

According to the Gospels, at the moment of Jesus' death, some amazing things happened. The sky darkened, there was an earthquake, and the great veil in the Holy of Holies in the Jerusalem Temple ripped. Even more spooky were reports that dead people came out of their graves and began walking around.

Jesus was removed from the cross and taken to a respectable tomb donated by a man named Joseph of Arimathea. The rock-cut tomb was closed with a heavy stone and placed under guard. The disciples and relatives of Jesus were thoroughly distraught. A few days later, the Gospels tell us, visitors to the tomb were surprised to find the guards gone and the stone rolled away from the entrance. An angel at the tomb reported that Jesus had risen from the dead.

The Ascension

Even those who had witnessed the various miracles Jesus performed during his lifetime found it difficult to believe that he was no longer dead, but it is said that he appeared on a number of occasions to his surprised and overjoyed disciples. After 40 days of sporadic visits, Jesus was seen to ascend into heaven, and he promised that someday he would return.

Illuminations

The day of the Sabbath was moved by the early Christians from Friday to Sunday, to celebrate and commemorate the traditional day of the resurrection.

The Ultimate Sacrifice

The death and resurrection of Jesus are of the utmost importance to Christian theology. Jesus is seen to represent an unblemished (in this case, sinless) sacrificial lamb. Like the lambs sacrificed once a year during Yom Kippur to atone for the people's sins, Jesus, as the Son of God (if not God Himself), took on the burden of the sins of humanity.

This ultimate sacrifice is seen as eternal as long as there are those willing to believe and ask God for forgiveness. The resurrection demonstrates the unique status of Jesus and gives hope to believers that they, too, will experience a resurrected life in heaven after death.

The Least You Need to Know

- Jesus was born in a town called Bethlehem to a virgin named Mary. The exact year is in dispute.
- Despite speculation, no one is sure what Jesus was doing for much of his life.
- The ministry of Jesus is characterized by a variety of miracles and righteous teachings emphasizing love, compassion, and a genuine adherence to the spirit of God's law.
- According to the Gospels, Jesus was crucified, died, and was resurrected. This forms the basis of Christian theology.

Chapter 14

Who Was Jesus?

In This Chapter

- Jesus: a real man and his times
- Who is the Messiah?
- What was Jesus' true message?
- Who killed Jesus?

The story of the life of Jesus is an amazing and miraculous one indeed. But did this all really happen, and if so, what does it mean? Who was this man named Jesus and what was he really trying to say? These questions were asked during his own time, and continue to be asked 2,000 years later. In this chapter, we'll take a look at the historical context of Jesus' life and times and some different ways of interpreting the events surrounding him.

The Historical Jesus

First of all, lest there be any concerns that we're dealing with a King Arthur, Achilles, or similar mythological character, an individual named Jesus did actually exist in Palestine during the first century A.D. For those skeptical about the reliability of the New Testament, there are outside sources which also attest to his existence.

Visit
Beautiful
Jericho!!

People and Places

Flavius Josephus (ca. A.D. 37–100) was a Jew living in Palestine during the first century A.D. He participated in a revolt against the Romans, was captured, and later became a Roman translator and historian. Two of his principle works, *The Jewish Wars* and *The Antiquities of the Jews,* provide valuable insights into the history of his times.

Words of Wisdom

"The truth is, it is not Jesus as historically known, but Jesus spiritually arisen within men, that is significant for our time, and can help it."

—Albert Schweitzer, *The Quest of the Historical Jesus* (1906)

The best-known mention of Jesus is found in the writings of the Jewish historian Josephus. In his record of Jewish history, *Jewish Antiquities* (18:63–64), he writes:

> At this time there was a wise man who was called Jesus. And his conduct was good, and (he) was known to be virtuous. And many people from among the Jews and the other nations became his disciples. Pilate condemned him to be crucified and to die. And those who had become his disciples did not abandon his discipleship. They reported that he had appeared to them three days after his crucifixion and that he was alive; accordingly, he was perhaps the Messiah concerning whom the prophets have recounted wonders. And the Christian community named after him has survived to this day.

This famous statement by Josephus is somewhat controversial. Other translations have been made which have him demonstrating "surprising feats" and boldly asserting that "He was the Messiah" who had been "restored to life." There has been some obvious Christian editing in this version, as there is no evidence that Josephus was a believer and thus he would not be expected to make such bold statements.

Life and Times

The life and teachings of Jesus are best studied in the context of his time—that is, Jesus as a Jew living in Palestine under Roman rule during the first century A.D. Taken out of this cultural, political, religious, and temporal milieu, the story of Jesus can be confusing. Let's take a brief look at the players in his time.

The Romans held sway in Palestine after Pompey incorporated the region into the Roman Empire in 63 B.C. At the time of the birth of Jesus, a Jewish king, Herod the Great, was allowed to rule Palestine. The territory was divided among his sons upon his death.

Herod Agrippa ruled the area of Galilee that included Nazareth, the hometown of Jesus. Eventually, a Roman procurator, or governor, was assigned jurisdiction over the region that included Jerusalem. Pontius Pilate served in this capacity during the latter years of Jesus' career.

Rendering unto Caesar

As was common throughout the Empire, taxes were collected from the various Roman subjects—a situation not well-appreciated everywhere. The Romans were generally lenient toward people of other beliefs, including the Jews, allowing them to keep their temples and practice their religion as long as political stability remained intact.

Threats to Roman control, however, were generally met with great brutality by troops stationed throughout the Empire. Rebellions could be expected to end in massacres and executions.

> Visit Beautiful Jericho!!
>
> **People and Places**
>
> Pontius Pilate was the Roman governor of Palestine from A.D. 26 to 36, during the ministries of both John the Baptist and Jesus. Although not much is known about his life and career, Jewish sources describe him as a cruel and insensitive man.

Worshipping YHVH

The Judaism of the first century A.D. was not unified. Although the Temple, spectacularly enlarged by Herod, continued to house the daily rituals, there were several Jewish religious and political factions, often at odds with each other. A volatile mixture of politics and religion was sure to complicate matters on many occasions, and certainly greatly affected the life, and death, of Jesus.

Pharisees

The Pharisees were the dominant group and promoted traditional religious practices. Although they insisted that the details of Jewish law be fulfilled, they were somewhat flexible in its interpretation. The Pharisees believed in the coming of a Messiah, life after death, heaven and resurrection, and a final Judgement Day.

Jesus and the religion that developed from his life incorporated many of these beliefs, with Jesus seen as the Messiah. The New Testament, though, is highly critical of the Pharisees, who are often presented as pious hypocrites making public displays of their righteousness.

Sadducees

In opposition to the Pharisees were the Sadducees. This group believed in a very rigid interpretation of religious law. And all of the business about heaven and resurrection? Forget about it! It's not surprising that they were often antagonists of the Pharisees. Many were apparently priests and judges. They essentially disappeared after the Roman destruction of Jerusalem in A.D. 70.

Essenes

Yet another Jewish faction was the Essenes. Not much is known about these people, who seem to be a marginal fringe-group. They reportedly lived in remote communes where they practiced agriculture and studied Jewish religious texts. Their beliefs were kept somewhat secret, but it seems clear that they wanted to separate themselves from the mainstream of religious practice that was centered in Jerusalem at the time. It is possible that the ruins found at Qumran near the site of the discovery of the Dead Sea Scrolls are the remains of an Essene community.

Jesus preaching.

(Illustration by Gustave Doré)

Zealots

There was also a political group known as the Zealots, whose goal was to rid Palestine of the Romans. They eventually attempted to overthrow their oppressors, and lost.

Where Did Jesus Fit In?

Where does Jesus belong among all these different factions? Some scholars see many of his teachings falling in line with the beliefs of the Pharisees. Others, though, suggest that he might have been an Essene, as John the Baptist might have been. One of the disciples of Jesus, a man named Simon, was a Zealot. Although Jesus sought justice, he promoted a more passive approach than the violent methods advocated by the Zealots.

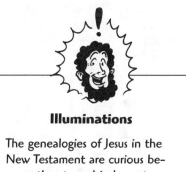

Logos

The **Messiah** is an awaited savior sent from God to deliver His people from oppression and to restore the world. Prophecies predicting his coming are found in the Old Testament. Christians believe that this Messiah is Jesus.

Is This the Messiah?

Judaism has long had a tradition that at some time in history, when things are really bad, God will send a deliverer, a savior who will right wrong and establish a Godly kingdom. Some of the prophets of the Old Testament spoke of such an individual, or *Messiah,* and longed for the day of his coming. To Christians, this Messiah was none other than Jesus.

There are descriptions of the coming Messiah in the Old Testament, and Christians believe that Jesus matches the picture from his birth to his resurrection. The Messiah was expected to be a descendant of David, and there are genealogies in the New Testament that make an effort to trace the lineage of Jesus back to this royal ancestor. But is he really the Messiah?

His followers seemed to believe so, and Jesus is reported to have implied it on several occasions. Skeptics, however, will say that some of the verses describing the Messiah were taken out of context, or even mistranslated when applied to Jesus. More importantly, the Jews of his time, as is still the case today, do not believe that Jesus fulfilled the requirements of the anticipated Deliverer.

Illuminations

The genealogies of Jesus in the New Testament are curious because they trace his descent through the male line. If the father of Jesus was God, or the spirit of God, then is it useful to trace his heritage through the husband of his mother Mary, who was not his biological father?

Not What They Had in Mind

The heavily taxed and Roman-dominated Jews of first-century Palestine were looking for a physical strongman-leader, a charismatic and powerful king who would relieve them of their oppression. This was their expectation of the Messiah. Instead, peaceful Jesus came along, speaking in abstractions about a heavenly kingdom.

His followers saw hope and redemption in the meaning of his death and resurrection, but this was not what many were seeking at the time. Jesus himself promised that he would come again, and the scenarios for this return call for physical restoration and judgment of the kind that the Jews expect.

Some Would-Be Messiahs

Speaking of the Messiah, a lot of people probably don't know that a number of other individuals were proclaimed the Messiah, or have presented themselves as such, even to this day. Here are a few of the more famous:

Logos

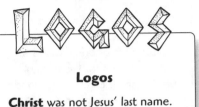

Christ was not Jesus' last name. The word Christ is derived from the Greek word *christos*, which is a translation of the Hebrew term *mashiach*, or "Messiah." Thus, Christians will often refer to Jesus as Jesus [the] Christ, Christ Jesus, or just plain Christ.

- **Molcho,** a.k.a. **Diego Pines** (ca. 1500–1532), circumcised himself, adopted a Hebrew name, and thought he was the Messiah. Although protected at first by Pope Clement VII, he was later burned at the stake.
- **Shabbetai Tzevi** (1621–1676) was probably the most prominent of the pseudo-Messiahs. He had a huge popular Jewish following, and at one point enacted a marriage ceremony between himself and the Torah. His messianic aspirations were severely weakened when he was imprisoned by the Turks and converted to Islam.
- **Jacob Frank** (1726–1791) believed himself to be a reincarnation of Shabbetai Tzevi. Frank preached that it was necessary to get all of the evil out of your system, so orgies and such became standard practice. After being regularly thrown out of Jewish communities, Frank and his followers began a Christian-like cult which persisted into the early nineteenth century.
- More recently, some members of the Lubavitch Hassidic sect of Orthodox Judaism declared their inspirational and aging rabbi, **Menachem Schneerson** (born 1902), to be the Messiah. He died in 1994, and his messianic status has dwindled. He is still, however, highly revered by the Lubavitcher Hassidim.

Man or God?

Being the Messiah is one thing, but was, and is, Jesus also God? Jesus implied it indirectly, and some see it spelled out in the opening lines of the Gospel of John, which are in some ways as profound as those of Genesis:

> In the beginning was the Word, and the Word was with God, and the Word was God.

Christian interpreters today generally believe that the "Word" was Jesus, who was one and the same with God.

Jesus occasionally referred to himself as Son of Man or Son of God. Literalist believers will say yes, he was the son of God born of a human mother. Some will say that we are all children of God, and such titles were not uncommon in the culture of Jesus' day.

Visit
Beautiful
Jericho!!

People and Places

In Islam, Jesus is known as Isa. Muslims believe in the virgin birth and the miracles, but they do not believe that Jesus died. A substitute died on the cross instead, they say, and Jesus was taken to heaven.

The Controversy

Figuring out exactly who Jesus was, or is, has been a question that has never completely gone away. It was certainly an issue in the first few centuries A.D. Among the ideas floating around about the nature of Jesus was that of Arius. Arius, basing his belief on scriptural verses where Jesus emphasizes the difference between himself and the divine Father, argued that Jesus was not literally "God" in the way the Father was.

Arius believed that Jesus was a creature, like all humans. As Arius put it, "there was a time when he was not," meaning that Jesus had not existed for all eternity like the Father. Jesus did have a special place as the highest created being, however. Arius had many followers, including influential bishops, and at times Arianism had the upper hand in the power struggle with those who believed that Jesus was indeed God.

The Creed

That changed in A.D. 325, however, when the Christian Roman emperor Constantine held a conference in Nicaea, located in modern-day Turkey. One of its primary goals was to gather the Christian leaders together to reach some definitive conclusions about the nature of Jesus. The Arianist controversy was one of the inspirations for these proceedings.

As a result, a creed was later established outlining the Christian beliefs that would be considered official, or "orthodox." This creed is called the Nicene Creed, and once it was adopted, those who subscribed to other beliefs were considered heretics and treated accordingly. Here is the Creed:

> We believe in one God, the Father, the Almighty, maker of heaven and earth, of all that is, seen and unseen.
>
> We believe in one Lord, Jesus Christ, the only Son of God, eternally begotten of the Father. God from God, Light from Light, begotten, not made, of one Being with the Father.

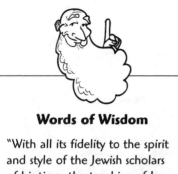

Words of Wisdom

"With all its fidelity to the spirit and style of the Jewish scholars of his time, the teaching of Jesus did nevertheless pass beyond the boundary, to stand in a place of its own. Had it not done so it most probably would not have created a world religion."

—Sholem Asch, *What I Believe* (1941)

Through him all things were made. For us and our salvation he came down from heaven; by the power of the Holy Spirit he became incarnate from the virgin Mary, and was made man. For our sake he was crucified under Pontius Pilate; he suffered death and was buried. On the third day he rose again in accordance with the Scriptures; he ascended into heaven and is seated on the right hand of the Father. He will come again in glory to judge the living and the dead, and his kingdom will have no end.

We believe in the Holy Spirit, the Lord, the giver of life, who proceeds from the Father and the Son. With the Father and the Son he is worshiped and glorified. He has spoken through the prophets. We believe in one holy catholic and apostolic Church. We acknowledge one Baptism for the forgiveness of sin. We look for the resurrection of the dead, and the life of the world to come.

The Creed defines Jesus as one person of the Godhead (he was "not made," as the Arians had affirmed), and also codifies the concept of a Trinity which sees God, Jesus, and the spirit of God which works through humans (the "Holy Spirit") as three personifications of the same one God.

The Truth as We See It

All of the questions about the nature of Jesus might be a little easier to answer if we had more to go on. Unfortunately, we have no writings by Jesus himself. Instead, we have the collected testimonies of witnesses and the writings of some of his early followers, as found in the New Testament.

As a result, today there are hundreds of different churches, each of whom thinks it has the most accurate interpretation of Jesus' message. It's sort of a shame that Jesus didn't leave a rule book that would have made it all clear. There are a number of issues the various branches of Christianity see differently. Let's take a look at two of the most basic ones.

Bread and Wine

During his last meal with his disciples, Jesus shared bread and wine with them:

> And he took bread, and when he had given thanks he broke it and gave it to them, saying, "This is my body which is given for you. Do this in remembrance of me." And likewise the cup after supper, saying, "This cup which is poured out for you is the new covenant in my blood." (Luke 22:19–20)

These famous words have been interpreted in several different ways. In the Roman Catholic Church, the bread and wine presented during religious services are thought to turn literally into the body and blood of Jesus through a holy mystery called transubstantiation.

Lutherans and many other Protestant groups, however, don't believe in a literal physical transformation, but rather believe that God is present symbolically in the bread and wine passed out to parishioners. Still others believe that this rite of the last supper is essentially a perpetual memorial service.

Jesus and his disciples at the Last Supper.

(Illustration by Gustave Doré)

Getting Wet

Baptism, too, has a wide range of interpretations. You may recall that John the Baptist advocated a ritual bath to accompany the repentance of sin. Today, there are arguments over whether people should be fully dunked in water, or if a mere symbolic sprinkling will do.

Further questions address whether it is appropriate to baptize babies, or only people old enough to understand the ritual's meaning. And do all Christians need to be baptized to be born again, with dire afterlife consequences for those who do not? There is, of course, a wide range of answers.

Who Killed Jesus?

Another issue that has provided some controversy in the past is the question of who is ultimately responsible for the death of Jesus. Rash conclusions on this subject on several occasions produced some truly tragic consequences. Certain groups, even today, have maintained that the Jews were behind his death, and if Jesus was God, this reasoning goes, then the Jews killed God. This sort of thinking has inspired the persecution of Jews on numerous occasions. Let's go back and look at the actual story.

Jesus made the Jewish authorities of his day very nervous for several reasons. Jesus was critical of some of the contemporary religious practices and seemed to bend some of the formal laws. And in the secular realm, in trying to maintain a delicate political balance with the Romans, the authorities were afraid that Jesus' growing number of followers might appear intimidating, especially when people were suggesting that he might be the Messiah, a king to save the people from oppression. The Roman response to rebellion was brutal and well known.

Revelations

In 1990, contractors came across a tomb in Jerusalem dating to around the time of Jesus. The tomb contained several stone boxes containing bones. One held the remains of a man about 60 years old whose name is identified on the box as Joseph, son of Caiaphas. Some believe that this could be the burial place of the very High Priest who presided over the trial of Jesus.

Pilate Washes His Hands

Jesus was passed around between the Roman governor Pontius Pilate and the Jewish puppet-king Herod Antipas. Pilate seemed to be somewhat sympathetic to Jesus, but he finally gave in to the Jewish mob's cry for his execution, and, as he said, washed his hands of the whole thing.

Regardless of who was responsible, if Jesus hadn't died, then much of Christian theology becomes meaningless. The rich symbolism behind his death and resurrection would be neutralized. Jesus had to die to fulfill his destiny.

A Foregone Conclusion?

A puzzling notion comes up when one considers the idea that Jesus seemed to know how things were going to play out in all this. There are a number of stories in the Bible that indicate he was aware of his upcoming execution and other events. That being the case, we are confronted with the tricky theological idea of predestination.

Were the characters in the life of Jesus, such as Judas, condemned to act out their roles in a predetermined destiny? Or does God, in his omnipotence, see far into the future or know the weaknesses of individuals whose actions are predicted by prophets hundreds of years in advance? What does this imply about free will?

Illuminations

Over the last couple of millennia, there have been those who blamed the death of Jesus on the Jews. Ignoring the fact that Pontius Pilate, the Roman governor, had the final say in the matter, they have held millions of people responsible for the actions of an unruly Jewish mob. They conveniently forget that Jesus was Jewish, as were his disciples and most of his earliest followers.

Still Looking for the Truth

Perhaps the most controversial attempt to make sense of the historical Jesus is the work of a group known as the Jesus Seminar. Founded in 1985 by New Testament professor Robert Funk, the Seminar aims to study the Gospels to find out what Jesus may or may not have actually said or done. Their conclusions are startling.

According to the Jesus Seminar, only about 20 percent of the sayings attributed to Jesus were likely said by him. The rest were fabricated, borrowed, embellished, or otherwise interpreted by others. And a lot of the other stuff never happened either, they say, including the virgin birth, his performance of miracles, and his resurrection.

As you can imagine, their conclusions have provoked some anger. Their methods are even more provocative. The Jesus Seminar consists of a collection of about 200 Biblical scholars who study a Gospel saying or incident and then vote using colored beads to indicate whether or not they think it

Illuminations

Some critics of the Gospel stories doubt that the Resurrection actually happened. Common themes include conspiracies involving the theft of his body from the tomb by his disciples, or the idea that Jesus, though injured, survived the crucifixion.

is authentic. A red bead, for example, is a vote that Jesus undoubtedly said something, or a black bead is cast to indicate a belief that he did not.

Critics are appalled at the apparent arrogance and sloppiness of such an approach. For one thing, this approach isn't about reasoned scholarly consensus but about voting, and the publicized vote results don't show the range of views. For example, if half the scholars are convinced that a saying must be from Jesus, and half that it couldn't possibly be, the averaged result would be a "maybe"—this says nothing about the real views of the scholars or the reasons why they draw their conclusions.

Moreover, not all of the Seminar's members are particularly distinguished scholars in their own right, and many come from a small number of institutions that have trained scholars in a particular way—in other words, they don't represent the cross-section of New Testament scholarship they claim to speak for.

Revelations

Some of the Jesus Seminar's results have been published in a book entitled *The Five Gospels: The Search for the Authentic Words of Jesus* (1997). The so-called fifth gospel is a collection of sayings of Jesus called the *Gospel of Thomas* that is not included in the New Testament (which, remember, only has four gospels). See more about such books in Chapter 17, "Alternative Scriptures and Fabulous Fakes."

Words of Wisdom

"In every decade we instruct Christ as to what He was and is, instead of allowing ourselves to be instructed by Him."

—Amos N. Wilder, *Theology and Modern Literature* (1958)

Whatever the shortcomings of the Jesus Seminar, however, it has helped to teach people that the New Testament didn't just drop from the sky as a complete revelation. It resulted from a human process of collecting and editing, and the differences among the Gospels are interesting and important to study.

Various Views

What do non-Christians have to say about all this? Well, there are many people who do not believe that Jesus is God, or even the Messiah. To Muslims, Jesus is one in a line of great prophets leading up to the last and greatest, Mohammed. Jews, as we saw earlier, do not feel that Jesus met the criteria for the Messiah they were waiting for.

The often ugly and abusive treatment of Jews by some Christians has left Christianity with a questionable reputation for some. But is the Jesus who preached peace to be held responsible for the excesses of those who commit abuses in his name? That is certainly unfair, but given the long history of often-difficult Christian-Jewish relations, it is understandable why a suspicion remains.

What would Jesus have to say today about the religion that was created around him? Would he laugh, cry, nod his head in approval, or shake it in disbelief? I would venture that it would be a combination of all of those reactions.

Who was, or is, Jesus? That is something that every individual must decide for himself. The celebrated Christian writer C. S. Lewis proposed three of several possibilities: Jesus was either Lord, liar, or fool. Lewis presented arguments to eliminate the latter two possibilities, and if we find the first of them at all convincing, then it's worthy of paying attention to.

In the end, whoever Jesus was, it's hard to deny that his ethical teachings stood out and have continued to inspire huge numbers of people over the last 2,000 years.

Illuminations

While Jewish people today wait for the first coming of the Messiah, Christians await his return. It will be interesting to see if it's the same guy.

The Least You Need to Know

- Whatever else you might believe about who Jesus is or was, he was a real person, and he lived during the first century A.D.
- Christians believe that Jesus was the Messiah as prophesied in the Old Testament.
- Jews do not believe Jesus is the prophesied Messiah. Although there have been many pretenders to the title over the centuries, Jewish people continue to await the Messiah's coming.
- Jesus is best understood in the historical, cultural, religious, and political context of his time.
- Many of the statements attributed to Jesus were sufficiently abstract that almost 2,000 years later, we're still trying to figure them out.

Chapter 15

Spreading the Word

In This Chapter

- The spread of Christianity
- Those who followed Jesus
- Mary, the mother of Jesus
- Visions and inspirations

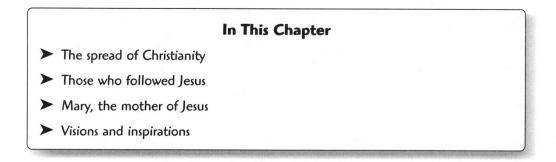

The death and resurrection of Jesus was just the beginning. The New Testament books that follow the Gospels record the spread of the message of Jesus and provide the foundation for the development of the Christian faith and its organized forms which persist to this day. Although Jesus and his followers were Jews living in Palestine, the faith would quickly spread elsewhere. What would become known as Christianity developed as a universal religion available to anyone who would accept it.

Wonders and Miracles

The book which immediately follows the Gospels is called the book of Acts, or the Acts of the Apostles, and in my opinion, it is one of the most amazing books of the New Testament. Miracles and incredible events abound. Jesus has departed, and his followers are left to make sense of it all and spread the word.

Not long after Jesus ascended into heaven, his followers got active. With Peter as their leader, there were now about 120 of them, including a new disciple who was chosen to replace Judas the traitor. On the Jewish festival of Pentecost, the disciples were gathered and amazing things began to happen:

> And suddenly a sound came from heaven like the rush of a mighty wind, and it filled all the house where they were sitting. And there appeared to them tongues as of fire, distributed and resting on each one of them. And they were all filled with the Holy Spirit and began to speak in other tongues, as the Spirit gave them utterance. (Acts 2:2–4)

This was quite startling to the cosmopolitan crowds of Jerusalem, who heard preaching in their own diverse languages coming from this group of apparently ordinary men.

Illuminations

When the disciples of Jesus began to speak in different languages, some of the observers accused them of being drunk. Peter, though, assured them that it was much too early in the day for that to be the case, and referred to Old Testament prophecies about the Holy Spirit to answer the scoffers.

The Miracles Continue

The speaking in tongues, along with Peter's dramatic teaching on the subject of repentance, resulted in 3,000 converts on that very day. And the miracles didn't stop with verbal communication abilities. The disciples were able to heal people by invoking the name of Jesus. Peter was even able to raise a fellow Christian, Tabitha, from the dead.

Not surprisingly, these sorts of activities didn't please the established religious authorities, and the disciples found themselves in jail from time to time. On one occasion in Jerusalem, an angel let them out of a locked prison, after which they were found preaching at the Temple.

Gifts of the Spirit

The manifestations of the Holy Spirit within people—"gifts," as they are often called—came in various forms. Certain churches today call themselves Pentecostal in reference to the day, Pentecost, in which the Spirit-filled disciples preached in different languages. Here are a few of the various manifestations of the Spirit:

- Healing
- Speaking in tongues
- Interpreting someone who is speaking in tongues
- Prophecy
- Wisdom

Members of Pentecostal churches pray to be filled with the Holy Spirit, as the disciples were. Spontaneous outbursts of unintelligible speech are not uncommon in such congregations, often followed by an interpretation by another member.

Skeptical linguists might question whether the sounds that come out are actually part of some sort of coherent identifiable language. In response, some who speak in tongues claim that they are either speaking a dead unknown language from the past, or a heavenly language which makes perfect poetic sense to the angels and God.

Bad Boy Turned Good

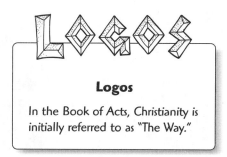

Logos

In the Book of Acts, Christianity is initially referred to as "The Way."

Many converts were made as a result of the miracles that followed Jesus' death. One of the most unlikely candidates to be a follower of Jesus was a man named Saul, who came from Tarsus in Asia Minor. Saul was a highly educated and observant Jew who looked at these renegade Christians as blasphemers against his own religion.

Intolerant of these radicals, Saul actively persecuted Christians when the opportunity arose, and even sought permission from the high priest in Jerusalem to capture any he might find in Damascus, where he was heading.

A Funny Thing Happened on the Way to Damascus

Saul got a big surprise on his way to Damascus when he was hit with a big heavenly light and heard the voice of Jesus: "Saul, Saul, why do you persecute me?" He was thereafter blind for three days, after which he regained his sight and converted to Christianity.

One can only imagine the fear and skepticism that must have arisen among the Christians on hearing that Saul was now one of them. Saul changed his name to Paul, began preaching in the synagogues of Damascus, and even had to be smuggled out of the city so he himself wouldn't receive the treatment he had formerly dished out!

Spreading the Word

Paul went on to become the premier spreader of the Gospel to the non-Jewish world. He traveled far and wide and preached in such far-flung places as Arabia, Syria, Cyprus, Asia Minor, Macedonia, and Rome itself. In his wake were left many new congregations of believers. Much of the New Testament consists of letters written (or supposedly written) by Paul to various newly established Christian communities who required spiritual guidance and support.

It is recorded that Paul, too, performed a few miracles, including healings and exorcisms, and he himself suffered no effects after he was bitten by a dangerous snake while on the island of Malta. During a late-night lecture, a young man seated at a window fell asleep and tumbled three floors to his death. Paul was able to bring him back to life.

The conversion of Saul of Tarsus.

(Illustration by Gustave Doré)

How Jewish Are You?

With its roots in Judaism, a big question for the early developers of the new Christian church was how Jewish Christians should be. After all, the teachings of Jesus were rooted in the Hebrew Bible, whose prophecies served to legitimize Jesus as the Messiah among his followers.

Visit
Beautiful
Jericho!!

People and Places

Like the majority of the original disciples, Paul did not live to a ripe old age. He was apparently beheaded in Rome.

Among Jewish converts, it wasn't too much of an issue, but to the outside world, like the Romans, Greeks, and assorted other pagans, such issues as kosher food and circumcision were big obstacles to conversion. The message of Jesus might be appealing, but some of the "baggage" that might come with it was not necessarily so.

Kosher No More

The kosher issue is dealt with in Acts 10:9–16, which describes how Peter fell into a trance and had a vision in which a giant sheet descended from heaven containing all kinds of food, including reptiles and other Biblically unclean beasts. A voice accompanying the vision revealed that all foods were now clean, thus opening the door of Christianity to all of those pig-chomping, shellfish-eating goyim, wherever they might be.

It's the Thought That Counts

Circumcision, too, had to be addressed. It is probably fair to say that however appealing the Christian message was, the idea of such a physical initiation among the grown men of the non-Jewish world was not. Like many of the teachings of Jesus, Christians decided that circumcision was to be understood as a spiritual demand, not a physical one.

It was decided that it was more important to be circumcised in one's heart than in one's body. That is, the covenant between God and an individual was personal rather than physical. One could be physically circumcised as a cultural reflection of Abraham's original covenant, but the actual spiritual relationship with God was the matter of overwhelming substance.

The First Martyrs

The followers of Jesus tended to be an outspoken lot, unafraid to address their detractors. The religious authorities in Jerusalem, in particular, were not amused by these bold upstarts who had few qualms about chastising even the most senior of officials. Imprisonments and beatings took place, and it wasn't very long before the Christians had their first martyr (after Jesus).

A man named Stephen, who boldly proclaimed his faith before the authorities, was thrown out of town and stoned to death as an accused blasphemer. This would start a trend of sorts, and many of the early followers of Jesus met unpleasant deaths.

Words of Wisdom

Paul addressed the circumcision issue with the following words:

> "For neither circumcision counts for anything nor uncircumcision, but keeping the commandments of God."
>
> —1 Corinthians 8:19

A Bad End

Let's take a look at what reportedly happened to Jesus' beloved original 12 disciples. Most of their stories are not found in the Bible, but are part of the Christian tradition.

- **Peter.** Crucified upside down.
- **James.** Beheaded.
- **Philip.** Crucified.
- **Matthew.** Stabbed.
- **James** (the brother of Jesus). Beaten, stoned, and clubbed.
- **Andrew.** Crucified.
- **Jude** (a.k.a. Thadeus). Crucified.
- **Bartholomew.** Crucified.
- **Thomas.** Stabbed.
- **Simon.** Crucified.
- **Judas.** Hung himself after betraying Jesus.
- **Matthias** (Judas's replacement). Stoned and beheaded.

The only disciple who enjoyed a natural death was John, a favorite of Jesus. One story says he was tossed into a pot of boiling oil but miraculously was unharmed. He was thereafter exiled to an island.

Revelations

Apologists for the Christian faith will often cite the painful deaths of the original disciples as evidence of the reality of Jesus and his miracles. Why would firsthand witnesses and followers of Jesus be willing to die for their beliefs unless they were absolutely convinced of what they saw and heard? Skeptics reply that martyrs can be found in many religions besides Christianity.

Roman Sport

The persecution of Christians became quite a sport in the Roman world in certain times and places. Some of the Roman emperors, such as Caligula and Nero, found ready victims among those who refused to bow down to the official gods of the state. Many Christians were publicly executed in arenas full of cheering crowds. Burning at the stake and being fed to wild animals were not unusual forms of execution.

Building the Church

Despite the persecutions, the message of Jesus spread far and wide, and many churches were established. Mark, the supposed author of the Gospel of Mark, is credited with establishing the Christian church in Egypt. The disciple Peter is considered to be the original patriarch of the church founded in Rome. As such, he was the first pope of the Roman Catholic Church, the largest Christian group in the world.

The Roman empire that once tortured and executed the followers of Jesus became formally Christian in the fourth century A.D. In the centuries that have followed, Christianity has visited every continent and is practiced by at least a few people, if not many, in nearly every country in the world.

Visit
Beautiful
Jericho!!

People and Places

The Roman emperor Nero (reigned A.D. 54–68), whom most historians agree was genuinely insane, is said to have blamed the Christians for a massive fire that broke out in Rome during his reign. Needless to say, the Christians were merely a ready excuse, and many were painfully executed as a result.

The Saints Come Marching In

With nearly two thousand years of Christianity behind us, you can imagine the long and complex history of the faith as it spread and developed in various places around the world. Some of its members were extraordinary, and a relative few of these have been accorded the title of *saint* by the Roman Catholic and some Orthodox churches. These special individuals stood out by being martyred for their beliefs or by exhibiting a special kind of holiness that was demonstrated by their ability to perform miracles.

LOGOS

Logos

Jesus used a pun to commission his disciple Peter to be the head of his followers. In Greek, Peter's name, *petros,* means "rock," and Jesus said, referring to him, "On this rock I will build my church."

There are hundreds of recognized saints, and several churches, including the Roman Catholic, have feast days to honor them. These saints are considered role models worthy of veneration and, in the firm belief that they are in heaven and friends of Jesus, prayers are often offered to them in hopes that they will intercede with God on behalf of the one praying.

Something for Everyone

Many of the saints are recognized as "patrons" of various occupations, conditions, and even nationalities. Archaeologists, for example, can look up to Saint Damasus, while astronauts are a special interest of Dominic. Beekeepers have Ambrose, cab drivers, Fiacre, and flight attendants, Bona. If you're a shoemaker, you might want to have a chat with Saints Crispin and Crispinian, and mountain climbers can consult with St. Bernard of Montjoux. There is even a patron saint for coin collectors, Eligius!

Illuminations

In Christian circles, the term "saints" can be used to describe all Christian believers collectively, as in the expression "the communion of saints." The more widely used meaning refers to a special status accorded to those who have led an extremely exemplary and honorable Christian life.

Have you lost something? Perhaps you could notify Anthony of Padua. Saint John of God is affiliated with heart patients, Ubald with dog bites, and Gregory the Wonderworker with earthquakes. If you're a Norwegian, St. Olaf is a favorite, and Casimir is popular with Lithuanian young people.

So You Want to Be a Saint?

Many of the hundreds of saints received that designation during the first thousand years of Christianity. There wasn't any official apparatus in place to confirm them, other than popular agreement that these individuals by their deeds were indeed special. Some individuals might even have been purely mythical. It wasn't until the tenth century that the Church officially got involved in the process of deciding who was a saint.

Since 1983, this process has become extremely rigid, and involves a lengthy and detailed judicial procedure that none but an elite few can pass. Not only must the prospective saint have led an exemplary life, but there must be clear evidence that miracles have been performed by intercession after a candidate's death. A declaration by the Pope himself is required to recognize the saint as a holy person in heaven, universally worthy of veneration.

Revelations

Roman Catholics and others who venerate saints have often been accused of worshiping these special people. Catholics disagree, saying that saints in heaven are being addressed in an attempt to have them intercede with God on behalf of the individuals praying.

A Very Special Mother

Of all the special people venerated by Christians, Mary the mother of Jesus holds a very special place. Mary is viewed as the one woman on earth chosen by God to give birth to and raise the Messiah. And if you believe that Jesus is a manifestation of God, then for some people Mary is, in a sense, the mother of God.

Mary, the mother of Jesus.

(Illustration by Gustave Doré)

To many, Mary was not only a virgin spiritually impregnated, but remained a virgin before, during, and after the birth of Jesus, even though she apparently gave birth to other children. Because of her exalted position, it is not surprising at all that Mary has held a special place in the hearts of many believers.

She is seen as a role model of motherly virtues, including compassion and mercy, and prayers to Mary are routine among Catholics. The prayer referred to as the "Hail Mary" summarizes the role of the Virgin:

> Hail Mary, full of grace! The Lord is with thee; blessed art thou among women, and blessed is the fruit of thy womb, Jesus. Holy Mary, Mother of God, pray for us sinners, now and at the hour of our death.

Mary Sightings

The Blessed Virgin Mary, as she is often called, is believed to hold a very special place in heaven, listening to prayers and consulting with God. On occasion, however, it is said that she has made a few personal appearances on earth to inspire and deliver messages. The Catholic Church recognizes several of these "Marian apparitions" as authentic. Let's take a look at some of the most famous from the last half-millennium.

Illuminations

There is no known tomb of Mary, the mother of Jesus. It is traditionally believed that she was brought both body and soul to heaven.

A First Visit to the New World

In December 1531, Mary is said to have appeared outside Mexico City to an Aztec Indian with the Christian name of Juan Diego. She requested that a small house be built for her on top of a hill sacred to the Aztec mother goddess and sent Juan Diego to the bishop with her request.

The bishop required more proof, and it eventually came in the form of an image of the Virgin which miraculously appeared on the inside of Juan Diego's cloak. A church built to "Our Lady of Guadalupe" was constructed on the requested spot, and the cloak remains there to this day. This miracle led to the conversion of the Mexican nation.

A Good Place to Have a Drink

In February 1858, a young French girl named Bernadette Soubirous was out gathering firewood with her friends when she saw a beautiful apparition of Mary in a cloud, glowing in the mouth of a small cave. Mary shared some secrets with the girl, and a spring emerged from the cave.

A small chapel was built on the site, and the water from the spring is believed by many to possess miraculous powers to cure many physical afflictions. Today, millions of pilgrims have made the trip to the shrine at Lourdes in the foothills of the Pyrenees Mountains, and a good number of amazing healings have been reported.

Bernadette herself was declared a saint. You can see a popularized form of this story in the black-and-white classic movie, *Song of Bernadette*. And yes, that's Vincent Price as the skeptic who eventually converts to the faith at the shrine.

Visit
Beautiful
Jericho!!

People and Places

Saint Bernadette Soubirous (1844–1879) was the girl who saw the vision of Mary at Lourdes. Although the spring which flows from the Lourdes grotto is said to have miraculous healing powers, Bernadette herself died at the early age of 35 from a painful disease.

Holy Secrets

Three young Portuguese children are said to have experienced six visitations by Mary near the town of Fatima during 1917. Mary, who appeared in radiant white garments, told the kids to recite the Rosary prayers and revealed to them three secrets. During the last visit, the children were accompanied by a skeptical crowd who were treated to an awe-inspiring sign as the sun danced in the sky. Mary as seen at Fatima is often called "Our Lady of the Rosary."

Revelations

The first two secrets of Fatima have been revealed and tell about devotion to Mary and the conversion of Russia to Christianity. The third has supposedly remained a mystery. Some say that the popes have cried when they've read it and have had the message concealed. Guesses as to the nature of the message range from a prediction of world catastrophe to mere recommendations that one should keep the faith.

Recent Sightings

The town of Medjugorje in the region of Bosnia-Herzegovina in the former Yugoslavia has recently played host to more revelations from Mary. Beginning on June 24, 1981, Mary is said to have appeared to six young people with messages of hope, faith, and peace. All of the six visionaries are still alive, and some continue to see Mary on a regular basis. Thus far, the Catholic church has yet to formally endorse these sightings and revelations.

Logos

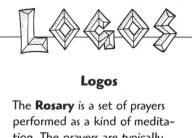

The **Rosary** is a set of prayers performed as a kind of meditation. The prayers are typically counted off with a set of strung beads.

Seeing Wonders

Images of Mary and Jesus have appeared in the most unlikely places. There have been sightings throughout history and all over the world. When they occur, they tend to inspire large throngs of people to take a good look.

The image of Mary has been seen in the bark of an oak tree in Watsonville, California. Images of Jesus, too, are occasionally discerned in such unlikely sources as rust stains on a soybean oil tank or a burnt tortilla, or in photographs of clouds.

Spiritual Inkblots

Many of these appear to be totally random phenomena, perhaps like some sort of pious Rorschach test where believers primed to see such things will discover these images and point them out to others. Even if such things are not to be classified as miracles, the fact that they might serve to inspire people in positive ways is not necessarily a bad thing.

Illuminations

Skeptics have a difficult time believing in the stigmata phenomenon. Some have concluded that the wounds are either originally self-inflicted or that they are psychosomatic.

Stigmata

Among the most unusual supernatural Christian phenomena are stigmata, spontaneous wounds which appear mysteriously on the body of a believer and mimic the wounds suffered by Jesus during the crucifixion. St. Francis of Assisi is said to have manifested these wounds, and about a dozen cases have been pronounced authentic by the Catholic church.

One of the most famous modern cases is that of Padre Pio, a beloved Italian Catholic priest. Bleeding wounds appeared on his hands and feet and also in his side. This began in 1918 and persisted for a full 50 years, until his death in 1968.

Living the Life

While saints, martyrs, and the witnesses of miracles often seem to have had their roles wished upon them, many other Christians sought out their spiritual encounters in various ways. There were the dedicated inhabitants of monasteries and nunneries, who committed themselves to lives of service, and then there were others whose lives of devotion were often served alone.

These folks were called hermits, and their preferred place to live was often a cave in the desert. There they could live an austere life of contemplation. Some relied on neighboring communities for food and supplies, while others seem to have been fairly self-sufficient. Some of these hermits developed loyal followings, and some eventually drifted out of the life to join like-minded people in monastic orders.

Revelations

Hermits are devout Christians who seek to come closer to God through simple and isolated living and personal deprivation. John the Baptist is thought to have been a hermit, and Jesus even spent a little time in the desert by himself after his baptism by John. Although hermits could be found in much of the Middle East and even here and there in Europe, the deserts of Egypt were a hot-bed, so to speak, for such people.

Spiritual Extremes

Hermits and other contemplative soloists not only lived the hard life, but sought it out. Fasting and braving the elements were par for the course. There were a few, however, who took things to the extreme.

Some locked themselves into rooms for years (recluses) or stood outside for long periods of time (stationaries). Perhaps the most bizarre were the stylites, individuals who lived on top of poles or pillars. Some of these would even offer a little sage advice to passersby, who might offer a little food in return.

Some people have had themselves temporarily crucified on crosses in order to experience the pain of Jesus. There have been others who have carried heavy wooden crosses for hundreds if not thousands of miles as a personal spiritual experience or as a means of attracting attention to and sharing their deeply held beliefs.

Drop the Serpent

At the end of the Gospel of Mark, the resurrected Jesus gives these instructions to his disciples:

> He who believes and is baptized will be saved; but he who does not believe will be condemned. And these signs will accompany those who believe: In my name they will cast out demons; they will speak in new tongues; they will pick up serpents, and if they drink any deadly thing, it will not hurt them; they will lay their hands on the sick, and they will recover. (16:16–18)

Visit
Beautiful
Jericho!!

People and Places

According to *The Guinness Book of World Records* (2000 edition), Arthur Blessitt of Florida holds the record for the longest distance walked. Since 1969, Arthur has walked 33,463 miles in 278 countries. Even more impressive, he travels carrying a 12-foot wooden cross weighing 40 pounds as a symbol of his Christian faith. Thirty years after beginning, he is still on the road.

This business with the snakes and the poison has been taken to some real extremes by a small number of people. There are a few churches that actually take Jesus at his word and handle poisonous rattlesnakes and drink small amounts of poison as a demonstration of faith. A surprising number actually survive the experience, even multiple times, while a few took the challenge and lost.

I may be wrong, but it seems to me that Jesus probably didn't expect anyone to tempt fate in such a way or make a ritual out of it! And, although we've looked at some pretty exotic and extreme behavior in this chapter, keep in mind that the average modern Christian is neither living in a cave nor sitting on a tall pole. Millions of ordinary Christian believers go to church every Sunday without any snakes, and that typically doesn't make the news.

The Least You Need to Know

- The disciples of Jesus carried on his ministry after his death by spreading the word and performing miracles.
- Most of the disciples of Jesus, and many of his early followers, died for their beliefs.
- A select group of extraordinarily dedicated Christians have been designated as saints over the last 2,000 years and continue to be held in very high regard.
- Mary, the mother of Jesus, holds a special place in the hearts of believers, and reports of Marian apparitions continue.
- While the majority of Christians live rather tame lives, there have been those who have sought to come closer to God through isolation and various forms of self-denial.

Part 6

Lost Books and Sacred Artifacts

Apart from its stories and messages, the Bible physically consists of words written or printed on paper. Before the invention of the printing press, the books of the Bible were recorded by hand and copied over and over again. The original documents are unknown, and even early copies of the books of the Bible are in short supply. Discoveries of such documents, therefore, are indeed exciting and important. In this part, we'll take a look at some wonderful discoveries, including the Dead Sea Scrolls.

In addition, a wealth of other manuscripts related to the Biblical canon were contenders (and some even pretenders) for inclusion but didn't make the cut. We'll look at several of them, and also take a look at some mysterious numbers that some say reveal mystical knowledge. Finally, we'll examine some of the interesting artifacts related to the Bible, including the famous Holy Grail and the bones of saints.

Chapter 16

Scrolls in the Desert

In This Chapter

- The famous Dead Sea Scrolls
- Scroll mysteries and intrigue
- Unlocking the secrets of the scrolls
- The discovery of other rare manuscripts

As influential and well-published as the Bible is, the fact remains that we have no original manuscripts for any of its books. All are copies and probably copies of copies. Given this situation, one can easily understand why the discovery of old Biblical manuscripts is so important. Such discoveries not only shed light on the Biblical text itself, but also often on the culture and times surrounding it.

In this chapter we're going to look at some amazing Bible manuscripts, including the famous Dead Sea Scrolls. Each new discovery of manuscripts from Biblical times commands the attention of the world's scholars, eager to see what new surprises might come forth from the texts, or what old revelations might be confirmed. These are exciting stories!

A Magnificent, Mysterious Discovery

In 1947, one of the most sensational archaeological discoveries of all time was revealed: the oldest known copies of books of the Old Testament, along with hundreds of other ancient documents dating from the first couple of centuries B.C. to shortly after the time of Jesus.

Illuminations

When it comes to rating discoveries, the Dead Sea Scrolls usually places somewhere near the top. In the November/December 1999 issue of *Discovering Archaeology,* the Scrolls made the list of the top ten greatest archaeological discoveries of the twentieth century. Others include the tomb of Tutankhamun, the cave paintings at Lascaux in France, and the armies of ceramic soldiers found buried in China.

The discovery had the potential to revolutionize what was known about the Bible at this very crucial time in religious history, when the Christian religion was first being established. Despite the importance of these documents, however, the exact circumstances of their discovery still remains a bit sketchy, and until recently, much of their content was likewise mysterious.

The documents, which would become known as the Dead Sea Scrolls, were found in desert caves near the eastern shore of the Dead Sea in what was then a part of Jordan. The traditional story of the discovery involves a young shepherd boy of the Ta'amireh Bedouin tribe, who was looking for a lost sheep (or maybe a goat).

As the story has it, he tossed a stone into a cave and heard breaking pottery. Closer examination revealed some large pots containing old rolled-up scrolls wrapped in linen. The year seems to have been early 1947, although earlier dates have also been suggested.

Secret Dealings

Visit
Beautiful
Jericho!!

People and Places

The young Bedouin who found the Dead Sea Scrolls was named Mohammed Ahmad el-Hamed, also known as "edh Dhib." Attempts to locate and interview edh Dhib have proven him elusive, however, with several people claiming to be the man.

Regardless of the exact details of discovery, seven intact scrolls made their way to Bethlehem in the spring of 1947. The Bedouins, not sure exactly what they had found, sold them cheap. Three were obtained by an Arab man named Faidi Salahi, who contacted Eleazer Sukenik, a Jewish scholar at Hebrew University in West Jerusalem.

This was a dangerous proposition, as the Arab and Jewish sections of the city were divided, and the two initially met on opposite sides of a barbwire fence. Sukenik recognized the potential importance of the scrolls, which included a complete copy of the book of Isaiah.

In an extraordinary coincidence of timing, Sukenik journeyed to Bethlehem on November 29, 1947, and obtained the first scrolls just hours before the United Nations voted for the partition of Palestine into Arab and Jewish territories. Conflict broke out the next day, and the state of Israel was formally declared the following year.

Revelations

The timing of the scrolls' discovery has struck some people as something of a miracle. It's an amazing coincidence, they say, that scrolls that were hidden as the Jews were being defeated by the Romans were now being revealed again during the birth of the modern Jewish state.

The other four scrolls from the original find were obtained by an antiquities dealer known as Kando. Kando contacted the local Syrian archbishop, Mar Samuel, who set out to sell them to raise money for his church. The archbishop even took them on tour to the United States, where his attempts to sell the scrolls failed. Mar Samuel eventually sold the scrolls for $250,000, to the Israelis.

The Search Is On

Once the remarkable discovery of the scrolls was revealed, there was a keen interest in finding their source and, of course, locating more documents if they existed. The cave that contained the original seven scrolls was located in an area near the Dead Sea called Qumran. Hundreds of caves in the vicinity were investigated, and eleven were ultimately found to contain ancient manuscripts.

Most of the documents were written on parchment, and a few on papyrus. The mysterious Copper Scroll mentioned in Chapter 11, "The Ark of the Covenant," was found in Cave 3. Overall, Hebrew and Aramaic were the predominant languages represented, although 19 fragments written in Greek were discovered in Cave 11.

Cave 11 also contained three intact scrolls, including copies of the Biblical books of Leviticus and Psalms. The real treasure-trove, though, was Cave 4, in which were found fragments of more than 500 documents in varying stages of preservation.

Illuminations

Mar Samuel's ad in the *Wall Street Journal* read as follows:

> *The Four Dead Sea Scrolls.* Biblical Manuscripts, dating back to at least 200 B.C., are for sale. This would be an ideal gift to an educational or religious institution by an individual or group.

Cave 4 was discovered and "excavated" by the Bedouins while archaeologists worked unaware nearby. When the scholars finally realized what was going on, much of the cave had already been cleared of thousands of fragments. With Kando the antiquities dealer as the middleman, the fragments were purchased with money from the Jordanian government and other sources, at a price of one Jordanian dinar (about $2.80) per square centimeter of written surface. The fragments were deposited in the Palestine Archaeological Museum in East Jerusalem, which was under Jordainian control at the time.

An Amazing Treasure-Trove

When all of the scrolls had been recovered, over 25,000 scroll fragments were found, representing all or part of approximately 800 documents. Over 200 of these documents were copies of books in the Old Testament.

The book of Psalms was well represented, with 39 copies, and Isaiah and the books of the Torah were also quite popular. Oddly, only a few examples of the so-called historical books of the Bible, such Joshua, Judges, Kings, and Chronicles, were found. The rest were mostly non-Biblical books or hitherto unknown documents relating to a communal Jewish religious sect.

The content and style of the scrolls indicate that they date approximately between the years 250 B.C. and A.D. 68. Radiocarbon dating was also done, and it appears to roughly agree with those dates, with an estimate of A.D. 35, plus or minus 200 years.

VISIT
BEAUTIFUL
JERICHO!!

People and Places

The Dead Sea is an inland body of water between Jordan, the West Bank territories, and Israel. It is the lowest spot on earth. The Dead Sea contains extremely high concentrations of salts and other minerals, and bathers find it both therapeutic and virtually impossible to sink in!

Mystery Writers

With the discovery of secret caches of ancient documents in the desert, the big questions on everyone's mind were who wrote them and why they were hidden. Archaeologists took note of old ruins found in the vicinity of the caves as a possible source for clues. These ruins, at Qumran, were initially excavated by Father Roland de Vaux and G. Lankester Harding between 1951 and 1956.

Father de Vaux, a Catholic priest, concluded that the Qumran settlement belonged to the Essenes, a little-known Jewish group. He identified a room with long tables as a "scriptorium" in which scrolls were written. A few ink wells provided additional evidence that things were being written there.

Some cisterns with steps resembling Jewish ritual baths supported the Essene hypothesis. Furthermore, many of the Dead Sea Scrolls themselves were documents belonging to a separatist Jewish community who lived out in the desert away from the despised mainstream action in Jerusalem.

Although the Essene theory is fairly convincing, others have suggested that the settlement is quite the opposite. The ruins have also been interpreted as Roman, or even as a luxury retreat for the wealthy citizens of Jerusalem. If this is the case, then what is the connection with the scrolls? Is it possible that the scrolls have nothing whatsoever to do with the nearby Qumran settlement?

Some of the caves at Qumran, where the Dead Sea Scrolls were found. Cave 4 is one of the larger ones in the picture.

(Photo courtesy of John Petersen)

Hiding from Rome?

Although likely, the connection between the caves and the Qumran settlement has yet to be absolutely confirmed. The latest of the manuscripts seem to be from around A.D. 68, about the time the Romans are thought to have destroyed Qumran. If Qumran was an Essene settlement, perhaps the caves were enlisted as secret repositories for their sacred documents as the Romans advanced.

It has also been suggested that the caves served as a hiding place for documents from Jerusalem, which itself was destroyed by the Romans a couple of years later. The strange Copper Scroll might even be a treasure map, some say, that shows the way to the lost wealth of the Temple.

Illuminations

After over 40 years, the data from the excavations at Qumran in the 1950s has yet to be formally published and made available to interested scholars. This lack of data makes it very difficult to argue for one interpretation or another.

Sorting Out the Scrolls

The original international team assigned to study the scroll fragments was appointed in 1953 by Father Roland de Vaux, the president of the Palestine Archaeological Museum in East Jerusalem, and one of the excavators of Qumran. The team at the time consisted of seven outstanding Biblical scholars, several of whom were Catholic priests.

Working in the museum, the team identified, matched, and catalogued the thousands of fragments. The task was long and tedious and required a good eye and an intimate knowledge of ancient writing and the Bible. Much of the task was completed by 1960, and by then, all of the original seven intact scrolls in Israeli hands had been published.

Revelations

There were no Jews on the original scroll team. One important reason was that most of the scrolls were housed in, and the property of, the Arab state of Jordan, a country that at the time was quite antagonistic toward Israel.

Visit
Beautiful
Jericho!!

People and Places

Several of the intact scrolls can be viewed today in a beautiful museum in Jerusalem named The Shrine of the Book. The exterior of the museum is in the shape of a lid from the cave pottery.

Changing Hands

In June 1967, Israel fought a war with its Arab neighbors. After a fierce six-day battle, Israel prevailed and took possession of several strategic neighboring territories, including East Jerusalem, which was part of Jordan. Included in the capture was the Palestine Archaeological Museum (now called the Rockefeller Museum), where the Dead Sea Scroll fragments were housed.

Thus, the vast majority of the scrolls came into Israeli possession, where they remain today. (The Copper Scroll is housed in Amman, Jordan.) During the war, a further intact scroll was confiscated from Kando, the antiquities dealer in Jerusalem. It was found hidden in a shoebox under his floor.

The Great Conspiracy

Apart from the major published scrolls, hundreds of other documents remained inaccessible. The original members of the scroll team, who had divided up the texts amongst themselves, held tight to their assignments, although some of their students inherited the exclusive "rights" to some of the manuscripts. Given the sheer quantity of documents from the Dead Sea caves, relatively few were accessible to scholars outside of an exclusive clique for almost four decades after their discovery!

This situation generated anger among scholars interested in what the scrolls might provide for their research, and it also stimulated a number of conspiracy theories among the public. Might the scrolls have something shattering to say about Judaism or Christianity? Do they reveal something secret about Jesus? Is the pope, the government, or some other authority hiding the truth?

A facsimile of one of the Dead Sea Scroll fragments.

(After John C. Trever, Scrolls from Qumran Cave 1, *1952, p. 154)*

Breaking the Monopoly

With all of the interest in the scrolls, their lack of accessibility became intolerable, and in the early 1990s the monopoly was finally broken. Several bold and fascinating things caused this to happen.

Back in the 1950s, when the scrolls were being sorted out, an index was made of the individual words in the different texts, including a note as to which word came before and which after. A few copies of this index became available in 1988, and a couple of enterprising scholars got to work.

Using a computer, Professor Ben Zion Wacholder and his student Martin Abegg of Hebrew Union College-Jewish Institute of Religion were able to use the index to reassemble the text of many of the Dead Sea documents.

In the meantime, Hershel Shanks, editor of the popular magazine *Biblical Archaeology Review,* began a campaign to expose the monopoly and demand the release of the scroll data. Shanks also had obtained many photos of the scroll fragments, and he began to publish them in 1991.

Free at Last!

Photographs of all of the Dead Sea scroll materials had been taken early on, and several sets of these photos had been placed in secure institutions around the world in case anything might happen to the original documents. The receiving institutions were under contract to show the photographs to no one. Due to some odd circumstances, though, one repository, the Huntington Library in Pasadena, California, ended up with a set of photos without the contract.

With pressure building for the materials' release, the Library rediscovered their set of photos and decided on its own to make them accessible to anyone who wanted a look. Although there were a few legal threats here and there, the monopoly had been broken, and today, you and I can examine these priceless documents. (But you'd better be able to read Hebrew and Aramaic if you want to make any sense of them on your own!)

Nothing Shocking

The availability of the Dead Sea Scrolls served to squash the more rash of the conspiracy rumors. Jesus is not specifically mentioned in any of them, and there really is nothing devastating in them that will ruffle anyone's religious sensibilities.

With the Dead Sea texts now available to anyone who cares to have a look, numerous researchers have been studying their contents, and hundreds of scholarly articles are appearing. The scroll team is now headed by an Israeli, and Jewish scholarship is well-represented.

Revelations

The Dead Sea Scrolls aren't the only archaeological materials to be unavailable to scholars and the public. In what has been called archaeology's deep, dirty secret, hundreds of important excavations worldwide remain unpublished after decades, and the results are thus unavailable to those who might be interested. Most of this seems to stem from a lack of time, money, or enthusiasm, and not from any conspiracy. The data from the famous tomb of King Tutankhamun, for example, is still not fully published, even though the tomb was discovered in 1922!

What Do They Mean?

The Dead Sea Scrolls are important in many ways. They include the oldest copies of the Old Testament books and therefore offer an opportunity to see how the texts may have been altered through time. Although there are a few differences here and there, the scrolls confirm the general accuracy of the Biblical texts as passed down through the following generations.

The scrolls also enhance our understanding of a time that was crucial for the development of Judaism and the Christianity that arose from it. One thing the scrolls reveal is that the Judaism of their time was considerably more diverse than previously thought.

Since they date to around the time of Jesus, the scrolls provide insights into the cultural, political, and intellectual environment of his time. They also provide a glimpse of Jewish thought and practice before it changed forever with the destruction by the Romans of the Temple in Jerusalem in A.D. 70.

VISIT
BEAUTIFUL
JERICHO!!

People and Places

Hershel Shanks, editor of *Biblical Archaeology Review,* is largely responsible for breaking the monopoly of the Dead Sea Scrolls. Shanks, a former lawyer who turned his love of Biblical archaeology into a remarkable publishing venture, used his magazine to put public pressure on the members of the scroll team to make the manuscripts accessible.

There have long been rumors that other intact scrolls from the Dead Sea area exist. If or when such scrolls might turn up is anyone's guess. They would be welcomed by all scholars, and I suspect the price would be quite a bit higher than what the Bedouins asked for the first scrolls!

Other Great Discoveries

The Dead Sea Scrolls aren't the only Biblical manuscripts around, although they are certainly the most famous. During the eighteenth and nineteenth centuries, there was a renewed interest in the discovery and study of early Bible documents. Several scholars and collectors visited the Middle East and returned with wonderful treasures: old manuscripts written in languages such as Greek, Arabic, Coptic, Syriac, Aramaic, and Hebrew.

Illuminations

Constantine Tischendorf used his royal Russian contacts to obtain the *Codex Siniaticus,* and the manuscript was originally housed in St. Petersburg. Under the Soviet regime, the Codex was offered to the British Museum in the 1930s for the then very hefty sum of £100,000.

The texts were often retrieved from caches found in old monasteries or from enterprising antiquities dealers. Constantine Tischendorf (1815–1874) was one such collector. As an expert in the early New Testament, he searched Europe and parts of the Middle East in his quest for the oldest Biblical documents he could find.

The Oldest Bible

In 1844, Tischendorf discovered a treasure-trove while examining the material in the library of the famous St. Katherine's monastery at the foot of Mount Sinai (Jebel Mousa) in Egypt. One day he noticed a batch of papers in a basket next to a fireplace. They were pages from an ancient book, and they were being systematically burned.

Tischendorf immediately recognized from the script that these were pages from a very old Bible and asked if he could have the rest. After several years of negotiation, he was able to retrieve the bulk of the manuscript; it proved to be the earliest known copy of the Bible to include the complete New Testament. This manuscript is called the *Codex Siniaticus* after the location of its discovery. The Codex dates to the fourth century A.D. and can be found today in the British Museum.

A Forgotten Treasure

In Jewish tradition, Hebrew Bible scrolls and books were, and often still are, written by hand with great care. Retired religious documents, especially those which mention the name of God, are not merely discarded, but are treated with great respect, as befits sacred objects. In many cases, such documents were accumulated and then eventually given a respectful burial. Some old synagogues included a special room called a *geniza* in which such documents could be collected.

The Ben Ezra synagogue in Cairo is today the oldest intact Jewish house of worship in Egypt, the building having served as such since the seventh century A.D. Its geniza was located through a small obscure door that led to a room packed with old dusty documents of various sorts. Not only were there bits and pieces of Bible texts, but tens of thousands of legal and personal documents, parts of the Talmud, and more.

The Cairo Geniza had been visited by a few scholars who reported its incredible contents, but it was a brilliant Jewish scholar, Solomon Schechter (1847–1915), who was responsible for preserving and studying this treasure trove. He was able to arrange for the purchase of the contents of the Geniza, and numerous bags were filled with documents and shipped to Britain. Today, this incredible collection of manuscripts is housed at Cambridge University.

Logos

A **geniza** is a temporary repository for sacred Jewish documents until they can be properly buried or otherwise disposed of.

Precious Garbage

Bernard Grenfell (1869–1926) and Arthur Hunt (1871–1934) were two of the most successful searchers for ancient documents. These Oxford scholars had an interesting approach. The Greeks had widely colonized Egypt after its conquest by Alexander the Great in 332 B.C., so they decided to go to Egypt and excavate the garbage dumps of the old Greek towns.

Their efforts paid off, and a huge quantity of mostly fragmentary papyrus documents was recovered. These bits and pieces of paper included everyday domestic transactions and letters that shed a lot of light on the daily affairs of the time. But they also found scraps of old Greek literary texts, some of which were hitherto unknown, and some Biblical material. Of special interest was a piece of a document recording some apocryphal sayings of Jesus and some bits of the Gospel of Matthew.

A Window on the Past

There are many documents and books from ancient times that we know about because they are mentioned or quoted in other texts, but we've never seen. Some books just get lost the way any artifacts do, with the passing of time. Others were deliberately repressed or burned because they were considered impious or threatening. Luckily, some of them are occasionally rediscovered.

The discovery and study of ancient manuscripts is always exciting. A written document allows us to look at the lives and thoughts of the past in a way that few potsherds and other artifacts can. What will the next discovery be? I, and thousands of other eager scholars, can hardly wait to find out!

The Least You Need to Know

- The Dead Sea Scrolls rate as one of the most important archaeological discoveries ever made.
- The contents of the scrolls were kept from the public for decades until scholarly pressure broke the monopoly.
- The Dead Sea Scrolls provide us with the earliest copies of some of the books of the Bible, and give us a glimpse of Jewish beliefs at a crucial time in religious history.
- Valuable Biblical manuscripts are occasionally still discovered, often under very unusual circumstances.

Chapter 17

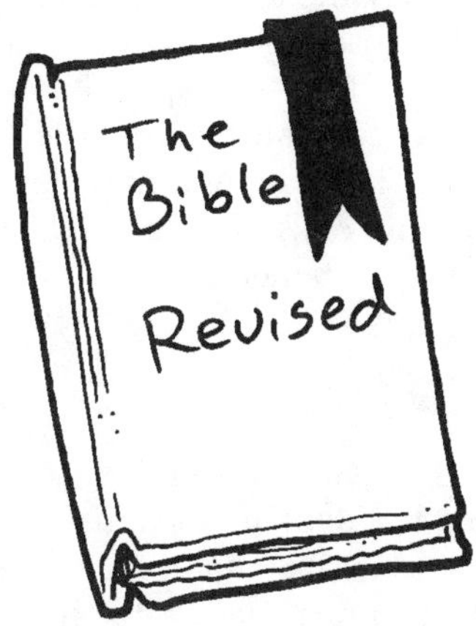

Alternative Scriptures and Fabulous Fakes

In This Chapter

- The Apocrypha: books that aren't in everybody's Bible
- Odd books that didn't make it into anybody's Bible
- Other versions of the truth—the Mormon and Gnostic writings
- Some fabulous fakes and forgeries

The Bible we read today by no means represents the total realm of old Jewish and Christian religious books. Indeed, the Bible is the result of a long and thoughtful process of sorting through numerous possibilities. There are dozens of books that didn't make it into the Bible, and even today, some Bibles have a few books that others don't.

A lot of the books that didn't make the cut were rejected with good reason. In this chapter, we're going to take a look at some of the controversial, scandalous, and even bogus books, most of which have by no means gained universal credibility. Additionally, we'll take a look at some of the Bible's missing books.

What's Wrong with the Apocrypha?

Pick up a modern Roman Catholic Bible and a Protestant one and take a look at the table of contents. The Catholic Bible has more books inside—books with names like Maccabees and Tobit. What's that all about? Doesn't everyone agree on what goes in the Bible?

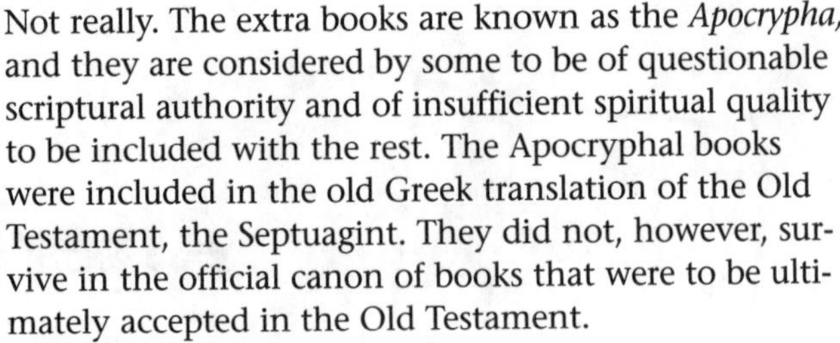

Not really. The extra books are known as the *Apocrypha,* and they are considered by some to be of questionable scriptural authority and of insufficient spiritual quality to be included with the rest. The Apocryphal books were included in the old Greek translation of the Old Testament, the Septuagint. They did not, however, survive in the official canon of books that were to be ultimately accepted in the Old Testament.

Logos

Apocrypha literally means "things that are hidden," and generally refers to those books of the Bible that are not universally accepted. It's not a particularly accurate term, because neither the books themselves nor their contents are really hidden. The term is more commonly used today to mean a story of which the accuracy or reality is in question.

Making the Cut

When Jerome translated the Bible into Latin (see Chapter 1, "Introducing the Book of Mysteries"), he included these extra books with some hesitation about the appropriateness of including them with the rest. In 1546, however, during the Council of Trent, the Catholic church proclaimed most of these books as bona fide members of the Old Testament, and condemned those who thought otherwise.

Words of Wisdom

In his translation of the Bible into German (1534), Martin Luther introduced the Apocrypha as follows:

> "Apocrypha"—that is books which are not held equal to the sacred Scriptures, and nevertheless are useful and good to read."

Reforming the Bible

As some Christians began to split away from the Roman Catholic Church in the sixteenth and seventeenth centuries, Bibles began to appear that omitted the Apocryphal books. Some were placed as appendices to the traditional Hebrew canon of books, while some printers saved money by not printing them at all.

What are the books of the Apocrypha? Here is a list:

- 1 and 2 Esdras
- Book of Tobit
- Book of Judith
- The Wisdom of Solomon
- Ecclesiasticus, also known as the Wisdom of Ben Sirah
- Book of Baruch
- The Letter of Jeremiah
- Additions to the Book of Daniel, including the Prayer of Azariah, the Song of the Three Young Men, Susanna, and the story of Bel and the Dragon
- The Prayer of Manasseh
- 1 and 2 Maccabees

Additionally, some Eastern Orthodox churches accept other books, including the third and fourth books of Maccabees and an extra Psalm, number 151. The latter celebrates the slaying of the Philistine giant, Goliath, by the young David.

Some Very Odd Manuscripts

While the books of the Apocrypha found in Catholic Bibles contain some pretty good history and some well-cherished inspirational material, there are numerous other books that didn't make the cut in anyone's Bible. Among them are the so-called *pseudepigrapha,* books someone wrote and then attributed to a distinguished character in the Bible.

There are books supposedly written by such Old Testament figures as Enoch, Abraham, Moses, and even Adam and Eve, and Gospels allegedly written by the likes of the disciples James and Thomas. Many of them are quite odd. Some were probably written to fill in historical gaps such as the unknown years in the life of Jesus, or perhaps to give credibility to a favorite political or religious idea.

A Holy Terror

From what we can gather from the New Testament Gospels, Jesus was a nice Jewish boy who loved his parents and was probably a model citizen. If we believe the theological notion that he was sinless, then he was a very good boy indeed. Other rejected "gospels," however, paint a picture of a less-than-perfect little boy who could use his divine powers on a whim.

Logos

Pseudepigrapha are books which claim to be have been written by notable people of the Bible. Most of these books were written during the first centuries B.C. and A.D. and are generally not accepted as scriptural in quality.

One of the most shocking of the extra-Biblical books is called the Infancy Gospel of Thomas (not to be confused with the better-known Gospel of Thomas). Here we find some alleged incidents from the childhood of Jesus that portray him as a dangerous, smart-alecky little brat. Jesus not only plays in the mud and forms little birds out of clay, but he can turn them into real birds that fly.

On two occasions, the young fellow gets perturbed with playmates, who are then struck dead. On another occasion, Jesus is playing on the roof with his friends when one of them falls off and is killed. When the adults blame Jesus, the playmate comes back to life to tell them it wasn't Jesus' fault. Needless to say, the parents of Nazareth were more than a little concerned.

According to this Gospel, Jesus was also quite a terror in the classroom, where he regularly insulted and lectured his teachers. It wasn't until he found a teacher who would acknowledge his prodigious superiority that he finally settled down as a student.

Virgin for Life

Another piece of pseudepigrapha, called the Infancy Gospel of James, is really more about Mary than about Jesus. In an effort to enhance her reputation for purity, Mary is described as having been raised in the Holy Temple, and her husband Joseph essentially won her in a lottery.

In this story, Mary remained a virgin her entire life. (Jesus' siblings must have been from a previous marriage by Joseph.) Even the midwife who delivered Jesus is brought into it, and in graphic detail she examines Mary after she has given birth and pronounces her to be, still, a virgin.

Illuminations

Coptic is the last vestige of the Ancient Egyptian language and is written in a modified form of the Greek alphabet. It is no longer actively spoken, but it remains the liturgical language of the Christian orthodox Coptic church of Egypt.

The Gnostics Add Some Mystery

In 1945, some Egyptian peasants were digging for fertilizer a few miles from the town of Nag Hammadi when they uncovered a large ancient jar. When the lid was removed, 13 leather-bound books (codices) were found inside, written in the Coptic language and script.

While a few of the papyrus pages ended up as fuel for fires, the manuscripts began gradually making their way to Cairo through the hands of various parties, including antiquities dealers. Altogether, there were 52 documents representing 48 different written works.

Logos

Gnosticism, as practiced by Gnostics, taught that the inherently evil material world could be transcended by secret spiritual knowledge, or **gnosis.**

A Cosmic Struggle

In 1947, scholars began to recognize what these documents were: the writings of a religious movement known as Gnosticism, which was contemporary with the early formative years of Christianity. The Gnostics believed that the world was involved in a cosmic struggle between good and evil.

The creator-god portrayed in the Old Testament was seen as evil, as were his creations. The material world was thus basically bad, but it could be transcended by reaching the superior spiritual realm. To do so, one needed to possess *gnosis,* or secret knowledge.

The Gnostic writings include Jesus as a regular character, a messenger of light who bears gnosis. Among the most notable writings in the codices is a virtually complete copy of the Gospel of Thomas, fragments of which had been found written in Greek elsewhere in Egypt.

Say What?

The Gospel of Thomas contains 114 purported sayings of Jesus, like the Gospels found in the New Testament, though unlike the New Testament Gospels, there is no obvious story to connect them all—in fact, their order seems pretty random. Although a number of the sayings are readily recognizable from their appearance in the traditional four Gospels, this book contains a number of statements with a distinctly Gnostic spin to them. Go figure these out, for example:

> **No. 105:** He who knows the father and the mother will be called the son of a harlot.
>
> **No. 114:** Simon Peter said to them, "Let Mary leave us, for women are not worthy of life." Jesus said, "I myself shall lead her in order to make her male, so that she too may become a living spirit resembling you males. For every woman who will make herself male will enter the kingdom of heaven."
>
> —Gospel of Thomas quotes from John Dart, *The Jesus of Heresy and History,* 1988, pp. 191–192

The Gospel of Thomas was probably produced by Gnostics who edited a pre-existing collection of the sayings of Jesus, inserting their special additions here and there. Some scholars have suggested that what we have here is actually a fifth Gospel that should take its place with the rest.

There are some problems with this view, however. First, as noted, the Gospel of Thomas is really more a collection of sayings than a story or account. Second, most of the sayings of Jesus in the book appear to be in a much later form than those of the Gospels, so for people of faith who turn to the Gospels as a way to approach the historical Jesus and his teachings, the book isn't of much use.

Finally, while Jesus as portrayed in the Gospels is not only about peace and love, it's a stretch to try to integrate his message there with a view that creation is evil and women are lower forms of human life!

Jesus Has the Last Laugh

Another book in the codices, the Apocalypse of Peter, presents another Gnostic, and somewhat disturbing, portrait of Jesus. In this book, Peter has a vision in which Jesus is laughing at the sight of his own Crucifixion. What's so doggoned funny?

As Jesus explains the vision, it's because he has shed his body and they're essentially nailing a substitute, in the form of his earthly body, to the cross. This idea flies in the face of mainstream Christian theology, however, which emphasizes Jesus' suffering as a way to redeem the world.

An example of some of the Coptic text found in the Nag Hammadi codices.

(After Stephen Emmel, ed., Nag Hammadi Codex III, *5, 1984, p.40)*

ⲡⲇⲓⲁⲗⲟⲅⲟⲥ ⲙ̄ⲡⲥⲱⲧⲏⲣ
ⲡⲥⲏⲣ ⲡⲉϫⲁϥ ⲛ̄ⲛⲉϥⲙⲁⲑⲏⲧⲏⲥ
ϫⲉⲏⲇⲏ ⲁⲡⲉⲟⲩⲟⲉⲓϣ ϣⲱⲡⲉ ⲛⲉ
ⲥⲛⲏⲟⲩ ϫⲉⲕⲁⲁⲥ ⲉⲛⲁⲕⲱ ⲛ̄ⲥⲱⲛ
ⲙ̄ⲡⲉⲛϩⲓⲥⲉ ⲛ̄ⲧⲛ̄ⲁϩⲉ ⲉⲣⲁⲧⲛ̄ ϩⲛ̄
ⲧⲁⲛⲁⲡⲁⲩⲥⲓⲥ ⲡⲉⲧⲛⲁⲱϩⲉ ⲅⲁⲣ ⲉ
ⲣⲁⲧϥ̄ ϩⲛ̄ⲧⲁⲛⲁⲡⲁⲩⲥⲓⲥ ϥⲛⲁⲙ̄ⲧⲟⲛ
ⲙ̄ⲙⲟϥ ⲛ̄ϣⲁⲉⲛⲉϩ ⲁⲛⲟⲕ ⲇⲉ
ϫⲱ ⲙ̄ⲙⲟⲥ ⲛⲏⲧⲛ̄ ϫⲉϣⲱⲡⲉ ⲛ̄
ⲧ̄ⲡⲉ ⲛ̄ⲟⲩⲟⲉⲓϣ ⲛⲓⲙ
ⲟ̄ⲩⲟⲉⲓϣ ϫ
ⲙ̄ⲙⲟⲥ ⲛⲏⲧⲛ̄
ⲣ̄ϩⲟⲧⲉ ϩⲏ
ⲉⲣⲱⲧⲛ̄
ϫⲉ ⲧⲟⲣⲅⲏ ⲟⲩϩⲟⲧⲉ ⲧ
ⲕⲓⲙ ⲉⲧⲟⲣⲅⲏ ⲟⲩⲣ
ⲁⲗⲗⲁ ϩⲱⲥ ⲁⲧⲉⲧⲛ̄ⲁⲛ
ⲣⲟⲩϣⲱⲡⲉ ⲉⲃⲟⲗ
ⲁⲗϫⲓ ⲛ̄ⲛⲉⲉⲓⲱⲁϫⲉ ⲉⲣⲟⲥ ϩⲛ̄ⲟⲗϩ
ⲧⲉ ⲙⲛ̄ⲟⲩⲥⲧⲱⲧ ⲁⲩⲱ ⲁⲥⲧⲁϩⲟ ⲙ̄
ⲙ̄ⲟⲟⲩ ⲉⲣⲁⲧⲟⲩ ⲙⲛ̄ϩⲉⲛⲁⲣⲭⲱⲛ
ϫⲉⲉⲃⲟⲗ ⲙ̄ⲙⲟⲥ ⲙ̄ⲡⲉⲗⲁⲁⲩ ⲉⲓ ⲉ
ⲃⲟⲗ ⲁⲗⲗⲁ ⲁⲛⲟⲕ ⲛ̄ⲧⲉⲣⲓⲉⲓ ⲁⲉⲓ
ⲟⲩⲱⲛ ⲉⲧⲉϩⲓⲏ ⲁⲉⲓⲧⲥⲁⲃⲟⲟⲩ ⲉ
ⲧⲇⲓⲁⲃⲁⲥⲓⲥ ⲉⲧⲉⲩⲛⲁϫⲱⲃⲉ ⲙ̄ⲙ
ⲛϭⲓⲛ̄ⲥⲱⲧ ⲡ ⲙⲛ̄ⲙ̄ⲙⲟⲛⲟⲭⲟⲥ

Although many of these odd Gnostic texts seem disturbing, they contribute interesting insights into the first few crucial centuries of our common era, with its developing and competing religious philosophies.

Gnosticism and Christianity do have a few things in common, especially a belief in a struggle of good against evil and the ultimate triumph of the spiritual world. How much influence the two groups had on each other is something that scholars continue to sort out. In the end, however, the biggest difference is that Christianity sees all creation as good, the result of a loving and just God. While we can misuse the things of creation, creation itself exists for our benefit.

Revelations

The ancient copying and translation of texts into other ancient languages, for example, from Greek into Coptic, might be responsible for some of the distortion and variation found in copies of the same books.

The Book of Mormon

America has served as the cradle for all kinds of interesting religious movements, and one of the fastest growing of these home-grown institutions is the Church of Jesus Christ of Latter-day Saints, also known as the *Mormons*.

Mormons believe that in 1827, an angel revealed some ancient golden inscribed plates to their prophet, Joseph Smith. These plates, written in a strange language, were buried in a stone box on a hillside in New York state. Smith claimed that he was able to translate these plates, and the end result was the *Book of Mormon*.

American Jesus

The *Book of Mormon* calls itself "an additional testimony of Jesus Christ." In addition to giving new details for stories found in the Bible, it gives a kind of ancient history of the New World. Among other things, Jesus comes to visit the Americas after his Crucifixion and spreads his message.

A belief in the *Book of Mormon* requires a belief in the prophetic abilities of Joseph Smith. Over 10 million Mormons worldwide find the book authoritative and inspirational.

Illuminations

The Mormons claim that a number of witnesses examined the golden plates. But the angel who revealed them later took the plates back, so they're not around to be examined today.

Pearls from Egypt

Apart from the *Book of Mormon,* Joseph Smith also claimed to have translated something called the *Book of Abraham* from an Egyptian document obtained in 1835 from a traveling exhibit featuring a couple of mummies and other Egyptian artifacts. This ancient manuscript was said to be written in Abraham's own handwriting! The *Book of Abraham* is included in a set of Mormon scriptures called *A Pearl of Great Price.*

The original *Book of Abraham* papyrus was thought to have been destroyed in the Chicago fire of 1871, but was rediscovered in New York's Metropolitan Museum of Art in 1966. When presented to professional Egyptologists, they declared the papyrus to be a common Egyptian funerary text. While this evidence may appear damning to the credibility of Joseph Smith, few of his followers doubt his abilities, and some claim that the portion of the document that he translated is still missing.

Revelations

Evangelizing, or spreading the word to the uninitiated, is an important part of the Mormon tradition. When a pair of nice young Mormon missionaries comes knocking on your door, at least offer them a snack. Separated from their families for up to two years and often stationed far from home, they are likely to appreciate a friendly face.

Jesus Goes to India, and Other Fascinating Fakes

In addition to these somewhat controversial books, which many people believe to be valid expressions of their faith, there are a number of just plain bogus texts that attempt to pass themselves off as genuine. There has been a wide assortment of these over the years.

In 1887, a Russian journalist named Nicolas Notovitch claimed that Tibetan monks showed him a manuscript revealing many of the adventures of Jesus during his so-called missing years. According to *The Unknown Life of Jesus Christ,* published in English in 1894, Jesus traveled to India when he was thirteen and studied with Brahmans and Buddhists before preaching in Persia and elsewhere. Unfortunately for Mr. Notovitch, somebody investigated the details of the story of how he came across the manuscript, and very little checked out.

The Good Friday Papers

There have been a few questionable documents that purport to be related to the Crucifixion of Jesus. One is an alleged death warrant written in Hebrew, which was said to have been found on a copper plate discovered in Naples, Italy.

There were supposedly 12 copies of the text distributed to the 12 tribes of Israel. The story has many holes, however, including the fact that the 12 tribes were no longer intact at the alleged time of its writing.

In another dubious discovery, a man named Rev. W. D. Mahan claims to have found, in the Vatican archives, a report about Jesus from Pontius Pilate to the Roman emperor Tiberius. The circumstances surrounding this particular gem are likewise dubious, and the Vatican claims no knowledge of such a manuscript.

VISIT
BEAUTIFUL
JERICHO!!

People and Places

Dr. Levi H. Dowling (1844–1911) had his own special way of obtaining spiritual revelation. By meditating in the early morning hours in his Los Angeles home, Dowling brought forth the *Aquarian Gospel of Jesus* (originally published in 1911), a book still in print today.

Paul's European Vacation, and More

The list of fabulous fakes goes on. The New Testament Book of Acts usually contains 28 chapters, unless you believe in the remarkable twenty-ninth chapter, said to have been obtained from a Greek manuscript in Constantinople. It tells of Paul's journeys to Spain and Britain. We can only hope that he went during the sunny months.

A very early likely fake goes way back to the sixth century A.D., and copies of it have been floating around for some time. It's called the Letter from Heaven, and was said to have been written by Jesus himself and found under a stone at the base of the cross. The message basically says to go to church and don't work on Sunday.

Illuminations

It is important to consider the motives of those who knowingly promote false scriptures. While fame and profit might play a role, it's possible that some are self-deluded or believe that a bit of dishonesty is acceptable if it will ultimately help to win souls.

In 1927, Luigi Moccia claimed to have discovered something called the Gospel of Josephus, and he even had the manuscript to prove it! Upon closer examination, the book proved to be a hoax, which even included modern Greek punctuation.

One Good-Looking Guy!

Since about the thirteenth century, an alleged eyewitness description of Jesus has been making the rounds. In this document, which is of questionable authenticity, Jesus is described as having wavy brown hair, which he wears parted in the middle. He has nice skin, a beard, gray eyes, and good posture. Sound familiar? Regardless of its origin or accuracy, the description made a lasting impression on medieval artists, who incorporated it into countless religious paintings.

The title page of Dr. Levi H. Dowling's Aquarian Gospel of Jesus the Christ.

THE AQUARIAN GOSPEL
of
JESUS THE CHRIST

The Philosophic and Practical Basis of the Religion of the Aquarian Age of the World

AND OF

THE CHURCH UNIVERSAL

TRANSCRIBED FROM THE BOOK OF GOD'S REMEMBRANCES, KNOWN AS THE AKASHIC RECORDS,

BY

LEVI

WITH

INTRODUCTION

BY

EVA S. DOWLING, A. Ph. D.

SEVENTH EDITION

LONDON:

L. N. FOWLER AND COMPANY

PUBLISHED AND FOR SALE BY

E. S. DOWLING

Los Angeles, California

1922

Lost Books of the Bible

The preceding documents are undoubtedly hoaxes, but it is easy to see the temptation to produce them. There are in fact known to be a number of lost works that would be priceless if they could be discovered. The Bible itself refers to a number of books whose names are now unfamiliar or even completely unknown.

In 1 and 2 Chronicles, we have references, for example, to the Books of the Kings of Judah and Israel, the Acts of Samuel the Seer, and the Acts of Nathan the Prophet. Although there are no books by those names included in the Bible, it's likely that they refer to Biblical books known by other names, such as 1 and 2 Kings and 1 and 2 Samuel.

The Good Fight

Other books, however, are truly lost. The Biblical book of Numbers (21:14), for instance, contains one or more poems from something called the Book of the Wars of YHVH. Although a copy of this book has never been found, some scholars have suggested that it might have been a compilation of poems and songs from the time of the Israelite conquest of the Promised Land.

Words of Wisdom

This excerpt from the Book of the Wars of YHVH provides some geographical information about boundaries:

> "Wherefore is it said in the Book of the Wars of the Lord, Waheb in Suphah, and the valleys of the Arnon, and the slope of the valleys that extends to the seat of Ar, and leans to the border of Moab."
>
> —Cited in Numbers 21:14

Jashar Who?

Something called the Book of Jashar is mentioned twice in the Old Testament. When Joshua is fighting the Ammorites and commands the sun to stand still, we find the following:

> "Sun, stand thou still at Gibeon, and thou Moon in the valley of Ai'jalon." And the sun stood still, and the moon stayed, until the nation took vengeance on their enemies. Is this not written in the Book of Jashar? (Joshua 10:12–13)

In an introduction to David's mournful poem concerning the deaths of his best friend Jonathan and King Saul, we find this reference:

> And David lamented with this lamentation over Saul and Jonathan his son, and he said it should be taught to the people of Judah; behold, it is written in the Book of Jashar. (2 Samuel 1:17–18)

Like the Book of the Wars of YHVH, the Book of Jashar might also have been a collection of songs and poems.

Revelations

Not surprisingly, a "Book of Jashar" has been rediscovered more than once, under dubious authorship and circumstances. One version was reputedly discovered in Persia in the eighth century A.D. by an English church official named Alcuin, who then translated the work. According to Alcuin, the book was written in early Hebrew characters on a scroll. Unfortunately, an alleged photograph of the original translation is written in the English of King James and appears in a printed format over 600 years before the invention of the printing press. Oops.

Jesus Without the Frills

You may recall that in Chapter 1, I mentioned some of the discussions about who wrote what part of the Bible. Some scholars argue that traces of several authors can be detected in the Old Testament.

In the New Testament, there are strong similarities between the Gospels of Matthew, Mark, and Luke which suggest that one may have been borrowing from the other. Mark is often promoted as an older source to which Matthew and Luke might have had access when they wrote their contributions.

The Gospel of Q

Yet there are some who suggest that there was an additional source from which all three borrowed, which scholars have named "Q," of which there are no known copies. The name "Q" comes from the German word *Quelle,* which means "source."

Some of the advocates for the existence of Q argue that it contained a simple story of Jesus without the addition of any of the supernatural bits. It is a story, they say, of a roving Jewish sage whose primary following was mostly in Galilee. There's no virgin birth, no death and resurrection, none of the other mystical things dear to the hearts of Christian followers. In short, he was just a man whose teachings outlived him.

Do-It-Yourself Gospels

While there are scholarly arguments to be made for the existence of Q, some of the Q believers have much in common with the members of the Jesus Seminar. They seem to have no problem tearing down and bending traditional theology if it happens to get in their way. At least one scholar has even written a reconstructed text of the hypothetical Q!

Critics of the Q hypothesis are not shy about pointing out the flaws in the theory. For starters, the fact remains that an ancient copy of the book has yet to be discovered, if it even exists at all. Furthermore, there are other theories that might explain the similarities in the Gospels without resorting to Q.

On the other hand, if such an ancient manuscript does come to light, we'll all be interested in taking a (close) look at it. But even without it, there is little doubt that the message of Jesus will persist.

Illuminations

The Gospel of Luke mentions the existence of other narratives about Jesus: "Inasmuch as many have undertaken to compile a narrative of the things which have been accomplished among us, just as they were delivered to us by those who from the beginning were eyewitnesses and ministers of the word, it seemed good to me also ... to write an orderly account for you." (Luke 1:1–3)

The Least You Need to Know

- Although a basic core of books appears in all forms of the Bible, several, such as the Apocrypha, are not accepted in all versions.
- Apart from the mainstream Biblical books, many peculiar "Gospels" and other works were rejected for inclusion in the Bible.
- Mormons have their own sacred writings, which they accept as divine truth.
- There are a number of bogus Biblical books and documents, while some writings that are mentioned in the Bible have never been found.

Chapter 18

Reading Between the Lines

In This Chapter

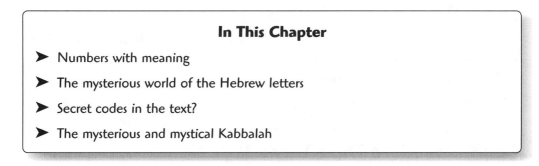

- Numbers with meaning
- The mysterious world of the Hebrew letters
- Secret codes in the text?
- The mysterious and mystical Kabbalah

As if the stories in the Bible weren't interesting enough, there are layers of meaning immersed in the numbers, letters, and words found in the text. In this chapter, we're going to take a brief look at some of these interesting factors. In doing so, we'll be reading a bit between the lines. What we'll find might prove fascinating, provocative, or maybe even disappointing. You decide.

Mysterious Numbers

Anyone who spends any time with the Bible will soon begin to take notice of numbers. Many reappear over and over again, and one can't help wondering if there might be something more behind them. Let's take a look at just a small sampling of them.

Illuminations

One of the greatest number mysteries is the secret 72-letter name of God. The forbidden name is said to be able to unleash great powers, and only a few Kabbalah masters apparently knew it, or know it today. (See later in this chapter for more on the Kabbalah.)

One and One Alone

- One God.

Two Make a Pair

- Two of each kind of animal on Noah's Ark (a biological necessity).
- Two tablets of law on which the Ten Commandments were written.
- Two angels at the Resurrection.

Three Is Not a Crowd

- Three sections of the Hebrew Bible: Torah, Prophets, and Writings.
- Three patriarchs: Abraham, Isaac, and Jacob.
- Jonah spent three days inside a fish.
- For Christians, the Trinity represents three aspects of God in one.
- Jesus rose from the dead on the third day.

Four: One More Than Three

- Four rivers flowing out of Eden.
- Four matriarchs: Sarah, Rebekah, Rachel, and Leah.
- Four Gospels.
- Four horsemen of the apocalypse.

Five: Gimme Five!

- Five books of the Torah.
- Jesus fed 5,000 people with five loaves of bread.

Six: Pay Attention

- Six days of creation.
- 666: The mark of the apocalyptic beast.

Seven: A Complete Number

- God rested on the seventh day after six days of Creation.
- The seventh day of the week is the Sabbath day.
- There were seven good years and seven famine years in Joseph's dream in Genesis.
- On the seventh day of marching, seven priests blowing seven trumpets circle around Jericho seven times, and the walls come tumbling down.
- Jesus taught that one should forgive seventy times seven times.

Logos

The fourth book in the Bible is called Numbers because it talks about a census of the twelve tribes of Israel that occurs at the beginning of the book. Its name in Hebrew, however, is **Ba-Midbar,** which means "in the wilderness"—where most of the action in the book takes place.

Eight: One More Than Seven

- Eight human survivors of the great flood.
- Eight days of Passover.

Illuminations

In some cultures, the number 13 is considered jinxed. Some link this to the number of people at The Last Supper: Jesus and his 12 disciples. The thirteenth man was Judas, who betrayed Jesus. Some people avoid this number like the plague, and many hotels won't even acknowledge a thirteenth floor. (Guess what? It's the one labeled 14!) Such a fear is known as triskaidekaphobia.

Ten: What Happened to Nine?

- Ten plagues in the Exodus story.
- Ten Commandments.
- Ten northern tribes of Israel.

Twelve Form a Club

- Twelve tribes of Israel.
- Twelve "minor prophets" in the Old Testament.
- Twelve disciples of Jesus.

Forty: A Long Time

- Forty days and forty nights of rain during the great flood.
- Moses spent forty days on Mount Sinai.

- Forty years of wandering the wilderness by the Israelites.
- Jesus spent 40 days wandering in the desert.
- Forty days between the Resurrection of Jesus and his ascension into heaven.

The repeated use of these numbers is notable. Seven in particular seems to be significant, often indicating completeness. Forty tends to connote a lengthy bit of time, and the numbers 50 and 70 appear here and there as well. Are all of the numbers in the Bible to be taken literally? A lot of the big ones seem to be rounded off to the nearest zero. On the other hand, if you are a Biblical literalist, then the question doesn't even need to be asked.

Revelations

The biggest number in the Old Testament is found in Genesis (24:60) when Rebekah's family blessed her with the wish that she might be the mother of "thousands of millions." In the New Testament, the Book of Revelations (9:16) mentions an army "twice ten thousand times ten thousand."

What's in a Number?

Logos

Gematria is the study of the numerical equivalents and relationships found in words.

The 22 letters of the Hebrew alphabet not only served to write words, but also had numerical values as well. The first letter, *aleph,* for example, was the numerical equivalent of the number one, followed by *bet* for two, and so forth.

At the tenth letter, *yod,* the numbers begin to represent units of 10, and then 100s. Five Hebrew letters have special shapes when they occur at the end of words, and these, too, can have numerical values in the hundreds.

With these numbers assigned to letters, it is possible to make all kinds of discoveries and connections by determining the numerical value of a given word or phrase, and comparing that to other words and phrases with similar values. This kind of research is known as *gematria*.

Your Words Are Numbered

Numerous interesting and sometimes provocative relationships can be demonstrated via gematria. Let's apply a little gematria, for example, to the Hebrew word for year, *shanah.* With a numerical equivalent of 355, it is equal to the 355 days found in the Jewish lunar calendar.

The numeric equivalent for one of the names for God, *Elohim,* is 86, which is the same number produced from the Hebrew word for nature. The gematria for the Hebrew words for both "life" and "wisdom" are identical, as are the words for "lion" and "strength."

The Hebrew word for child has a number of 44, the sums of the words for father (3) and mother (41). Include God in the equation by adding one, and you get 45, the numeric equivalent for the name of Adam, the first man, and humans in general.

The first letter of the Hebrew alphabet, *aleph,* has the numerical equivalent of one, but the physical shape of the letter can also be envisioned as composed of three letters: two yods and a diagonal vav, whose numerical equivalent is 26, the same number as that produced by the letters in the personal name of God, YHVH. Thus, the one God is represented in this one letter.

Words of Wisdom

"Scientists speak of matter being formed via the arrangement of molecules. Mystics go a step further. Letters are powers of their own. Their rearrangement gives us insight into the relationship between seemingly different words and concepts ... for words that share the same numerical total have a kinship comparable to seemingly unrelated items that share hydrogen, oxygen, or other basic elements."

—Rabbi Benjamin Blech, *The Secrets of Hebrew Words* (1991)

Who's Counting?

There are a number of ways of manipulating numerical letters to find various relationships. Apart from the traditional equivalents, the letters can be counted straight through so that after the tenth letter, the next is equal to 11. The numbers can also be squared, the sum of the entire word can be squared, the numerical values for the names of each of the letters in the word can be included, and so on.

VISIT
BEAUTIFUL
JERICHO!!

People and Places

In an early non-Biblical example of gematria, the Assyrian King Sargon II (reigned 721–705 B.C.) was said to have ordered the building of the wall around the city of Khorsabad according to dimensions determined by the numeric equivalents in his own name.

The letters of the Hebrew alphabet with their basic numeric equivalents.

Hebrew Letters	Numerical Value
א	1
ב	2
ג	3
ד	4
ה	5
ו	6
ז	7
ח	8
ט	9
י	10
כ	20
ל	30
מ	40
נ	50
ס	60
ע	70
פ	80
צ	90
ק	100
ר	200
ש	300
ת	400

Wonderful Insights

The relationship of Hebrew letters to each other can produce some lovely and often provocative connections between letters and verses. Here's just a sample of some of the more poetic insights. The Hebrew word *Israel,* for starters, contains the first initials of the names of the three Jewish patriarchs and the four matriarchs: Abraham, Isaac, Jacob, Sarah, Rebecca, Rachel, and Leah.

The smallest written letter in the Hebrew alphabet is yod, and the largest is lamed. The Hebrew name for Israel begins with yod and ends with lamed, thus seemingly reflecting the passage at Genesis 12:2, "Yet the smallest in number will be blessed beyond any other, and I will make of thee a great nation, and I will bless thee and make thy name great." Thus, from humble beginnings to a great nation.

The word for truth in Hebrew, *emet,* is written with three letters beginning with aleph, the first letter of the alphabet, followed by mem, the middlemost, and ending in tav, the last. One might then argue that the word itself expresses the notion of the entire truth.

Mystery Codes

Several years ago, Czech Rabbi Michael Weissmandel was reading a book by a fourteenth-century rabbi and found a reference to secret coded messages that could be found in the Bible. Checking it out for himself, he found that there was something to it. Here and there in the Hebrew text of the Torah, messages could be found by reading letters that were spaced at an equal distance from each other. These are known as *equidistant letter sequences,* or *ELS.*

One classic example is that of the word *Torah,* which can be found spelled out with a spacing of 50 letters in the first few verses of Genesis and Exodus, beginning with the first occurrence of the first letter in the word. In the beginning of Leviticus, the sacred name of God can similarly be found every eighth letter. Elsewhere, it can be found written backward.

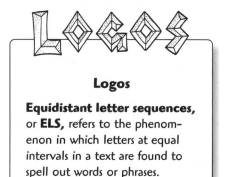

Logos

Equidistant letter sequences, or **ELS,** refers to the phenomenon in which letters at equal intervals in a text are found to spell out words or phrases.

Search for Meaning

Rabbi Weissmandel published some of this research in 1958, but it wasn't until 1988 that Biblical ELS really got some attention. At that time, Israeli mathematicians Eliyahu Rips, Doron Witzmun, and Yoav Rosenberg submitted an article to the prominent *Journal of the Royal Statistical Society,* which described the phenomenon as it occurs in the book of Genesis.

A similar article was published in the very prestigious mathematical journal *Statistical Science* in 1994. The researchers demonstrated that within the 78,064 Hebrew letters in Genesis, 300 pairs of related words could be found encoded in close proximity, for example, hammer and anvil.

Another search found the Hebrew names of 23 different trees encoded in the second chapter of Genesis. More striking, though, was a test that involved finding the names of 66 prominent rabbis and the dates of their birth encoded in the text. This is really quite remarkable, because the individuals involved weren't even born when Genesis was written.

The opening verses of Genesis showing the equally spaced letters that spell out the Hebrew word Torah. Don't forget that the text reads from right to left!

TORAH תורה ←

בראשית ברא אלהים את השמים ואת הארץ והארץ

היתה תהו ובהו וחשך על־פני תהום ורוח אלהים מרחפת

על־פני המים ויאמר אלהים יהי אור ויהי־אור וירא

אלהים את־האור כי־טוב ויבדל אלהים בין האור ובין

החשך ויקרא אלהים לאור יום ולחשך קרא לילה ויהי־

ערב ויהי־בקר יום אחד

Words of Wisdom

"Our referees were baffled: their prior beliefs made them think the Book of Genesis could not possibly contain meaningful references to modern-day individuals, yet when the authors carried out additional analyses and checks the effect persisted. The paper is thus offered to *Statistical Science* readers as a challenging puzzle."

—Robert Kass, editor of *Statistical Science* (August 1994)

Code Mania!

The puzzle of the mysterious codes was growing. Could they be proof of intelligent design and purpose in the Bible? Tradition says that God dictated every word to Moses, so was the truth of that finally being proven by the marvels of modern mathematics and computers? Are the Bible codes really nonrandom, beyond any possibility of chance occurrence?

In 1997, American journalist Michael Drosnin published a book titled *The Bible Code,* which grabbed public attention. In it, he describes the ELS phenomenon and the results of some of his own research. His most provocative claim was that he was able to predict the impending assassination of Israeli Prime Minister Yitzhak Rabin. He had even tried to warn Rabin, but was ignored. Rabin was assassinated at a rally in Tel Aviv in 1995.

Drosin and many other ELS researchers have uncovered all kinds of interesting things in the Bible, including information about World War II, the Holocaust, Nazi Germany, the assassinations of the Kennedys and Anwar Sadat, and even the sinking of the *Titanic*. More recent events include Nixon's resignation, Bill Clinton's election, the Gulf War, the AIDS epidemic, and the Oklahoma City bombing. If it can foresee all these things, then the Bible must indeed be a powerful document!

The Bucket of Cold Water

Doesn't that all sound mysterious and great? Before you get too excited, though, here comes the downside: The whole phenomenon is an illusion. Not surprisingly, the critics jumped all over the Bible codes, and for pretty good reason.

Criticism has come from all sides, including those who are religious, those who definitely are not, and those who appear to be completely impartial. Yes, statisticians have recognized ELS as a phenomenon, that is, things can be read in the Bible in such a manner, but what is the cause? Alas, it doesn't seem to be what they say!

Losing the Challenge

In the June 9, 1997, issue of *Newsweek,* Michael Drosnin was quoted as offering the following challenge: "When my critics find a message about the assassination of a prime minister encrypted in *Moby Dick*, I'll believe them."

The challenge was met when Australian mathematician Brendan M. McKay used similar computer methods on the text of Hermann Melville's classic work and therein found encrypted assassination information regarding Indira Ghandi, Leo Trotsky, John F. Kennedy, Abraham Lincoln, Princess Diana, and Yitzhak Rabin, some in considerable detail. ELS appears to be a random phenomenon that can be made to work with nearly any text of reasonable length.

Illuminations

Some might argue that the Bible approves of code-breaking activities. Proverbs 25:2 states: "It is the glory of God to conceal things, but the glory of kings to search things out."

Easier Than You Think

If it was easy to do in English with *Moby,* it's a lot easier to do in Hebrew. Traditional Hebrew doesn't include vowels, so the code-meisters are using only the consonants. With such a framework, you can find a lot more "messages," because the same combination of consonants can be read in a number of ways. And then the code-searchers look forward, backward, diagonally, and so forth to find any hidden combination. Some of the messages include words whose letters are separated by as many as 4,472 letters.

And then there's the fact that the people touting the Bible codes are working from modern printed transcriptions of the Bible, which they assume are authentic transcripts of the original. Not so. There are many different, often subtle, variations found in different ancient versions of the Bible. There are also different spellings for the same word! ELS is absolutely dependent upon letter order, so a difference of one letter can change a lot!

Seek and You Shall Find

It seems that many of these code exercises are foregone conclusions. One picks what one is looking for and then finds it in the Bible using ELS. The information rarely appears unless you have already decided what to look for, so the system's ability to predict things is dubious at best. As a test, some investigators looked for ELS codes that were derogatory toward God, and they found them. References to Jesus, too, can be found where he is both praised and condemned.

Revelations

You can now buy computer software programs to search the Bible for codes. There's a good chance that you'll find your name, and your favorite color as well.

The public, and even some scientists, can be quite gullible when it comes to odd phenomena such as the Bible codes. Here are a few reasons for that:

- Mathematics, and especially statistics, can be baffling. It's a mysterious world of numbers and equations that many people learned to hate, yet respect, while they were still in school.
- Mathematics and statistics are often seen as completely objective. Wrong. If you use the wrong data or procedure, misinterpret the results, or do not understand all of the possible variables, you could make some huge errors in your conclusions. As the old saying goes, "garbage in, garbage out."
- People are often impressed with academic degrees. The Ph.D., which is the ultimate research degree in many fields, doesn't impart infallibility on its holder. Many such well-educated people are not immune to gullibility. (I know a few who are real suckers!)

➤ The fact that the ELS phenomenon was published in worthy scientific journals bestowed a certain amount of legitimacy on the effort. The articles that appear in these journals have to be approved by a panel before they are printed. The journals, though, are at liberty to describe a phenomena without necessarily explaining or endorsing it.

In short, the Bible codes are a provocative but misleading phenomenon. Although seductive, it's perhaps better if one's faith, or lack thereof, is based on something more solid than mathematical gimmickry.

Illuminations

The letters of the Greek alphabet also had numerical equivalents. Gematria has been applied to various Greek words, and the text of the New Testament has been used in Bible code searches as well.

Where Few Understand

Aside from the modern use of computers for games such as ELS, the Bible has long generated a variety of serious and thoughtful mystical traditions among its believers. Among Jews, there is the *Kabbalah,* a generally difficult-to-understand body of esoteric knowledge accessible only through intense study and contemplation.

Logos

Kabbalah is the name for the Jewish mystical tradition. Its primary written work is called the **Zohar.**

The study of Kabbalah is thought to allow one to trancend the mere written word and peer at the mystical secrets and wonders which dwell beneath the surface of the Biblical text. For a reward, the student might uncover hidden knowledge about heaven, God, and other things of another realm.

The principle written Kabbalistic tome is called the *Zohar,* and it attempts to unlock the hidden wisdom contained within the Bible. Its proper study is intended to result in an awareness of the union of the soul of humans and the soul of God, and a lot more specific knowledge about the past, present, and future. The *Zohar* is not intended for casual reading, and is best studied under someone who has been well-initiated. In fact, it is traditionally not studied until a person reaches the age of 40!

As you can see, there's more to the Bible than just the printed page. The few samples discussed in this chapter merely scratched the surface. You can be assured that those hungering for further knowledge and insight into God's word will continue to squeeze, in whatever ways they can devise, every last drop of meaning from the text.

The Least You Need to Know

- Many numbers are found in the Bible, and they often have symbolic meaning.
- Using the numerology of Hebrew letters, it is possible to construct interesting relationships between similar words and phrases.
- The ELS phenomenon finds modern messages in patterns of letters in the Bible. Though superficially impressive, it is a statistical effect, and not a miraculous one.
- Followers of Jewish mystical traditions attempt to unlock the mysteries of God and the human soul, as do believers of all faiths.

Chapter 19

Extraordinary Artifacts

In This Chapter

- Holy mementos
- Souvenirs from the Crucifixion
- The Shroud of Turin: burial shroud of Jesus?
- The search for the Holy Grail

Artifacts have long been of interest to many readers of the Bible. In this book, we've already discussed archaeological discoveries and the fascination with such objects as Noah's Ark and the Ark of the Covenant. In this chapter, we'll look at some very special artifacts indeed—physical things directly related to Jesus or to his most esteemed followers. Some of these artifacts, or *relics*, as they are called, are very controversial, as you will see.

Very Special Objects

In Christian religion, a relic is an object thought to be directly related to a Biblical individual or a saint of the Roman Catholic or Orthodox churches. Relics take many forms, from actual pieces of saintly individuals' bodies to things that have merely come into contact with other relics. There is a classification system for these kinds of artifacts:

- First-class relics are bodies of saints or pieces thereof, including blood, hair, or even ashes.
- Second-class relics are objects that belonged to a saint or were closely associated with their lives or deaths.
- Third-class relics are objects that have been placed in contact with first- or second-class relics, thus rendering them special to the keeper.

Logos

A **relic** is an item associated with a Biblical individual or one of the saints. It can consist of an actual body part, an object related to the saint's life or death, or something that has come into direct contact with those items.

Although most first- and second-class relics are kept in houses of worship where they can be visited and venerated, third-class relics are quite common. Many are in the form of swatches of cloth or cards bearing a picture of the relevant saint.

A Piece of History

For those who are not believers in the Roman Catholic or Orthodox faiths, this interest in relics might seem bizarre. But many believers hold the relics in high regard, venerating them as very personal symbols of the holy saints and their goodness.

It is a way of having a physical encounter, of sorts, with a piece of history. In some cases the relics are related directly to Jesus himself. Miracles of many sorts are often said to occur to those who visit or come into contact with the relics.

The Search for Relics

The search for relics began relatively early on in the history of Christianity. The emperor Constantine made Christianity the official religion of the Roman Empire, and his mother, Helena, visited the Holy Land in A.D. 313, seeking sites and objects relating to the Bible.

Pilgrims following in her wake were also interested in visiting such sites and collecting a few souvenirs. It was during the Crusades, however, beginning in the eleventh century A.D., that a large number of relics from the Holy Land began to make their way into Europe.

The relics were highly prized, of course, and in high demand. The result was that along with the authentic came the fake. It is said that greedy entrepreneurs even raided the Christian burial catacombs beneath Rome to retrieve whole bodies. No doubt some of them were early martyrs, but many were not.

Revelations

Many of the Protestant religious reformers were heavily critical of churches that kept relics and accused such churches as promoting "bone worship" or idolatry. The notion of venerating either saints or relics was considered unacceptable, and most Protestant churches today are involved in neither.

Bits and Pieces

Some genuine relics, though, were divided and shared, and consequently it is not unusual to find several pieces of the same saint or other kinds of relics in widely separated locations. Relics are frequently stored in beautifully crafted containers called reliquaries, often designed around the individual object.

Relics can take many different forms. A church in Germany claims to have the "swaddling clothes" of the baby Jesus, and another in Italy has boards said to be from the baby's cradle. St. Peter, the disciple chosen by Jesus to lead the church, is especially venerated. Chains that were used to imprison him are found in Rome, and a cathedral in Spain has one of his sandals.

Aging Well

A number of human relics are still looking good after all these years, including a number of bodies that remain amazingly well-preserved year after year, sometimes for centuries. Bodies or parts of bodies that display this phenomena are referred to as *incorrupt,* and do not appear to be engaged in the normal process of decay.

An altar in St. Peter's Cathedral in Rome, for example, preserves the incorrupt body of Pope St. Pius. Apart from complete bodies, there are examples of incorrupt hearts, amputated hands, and even a tongue, all of which appear remarkably well-preserved. Some of the incorrupt bodies are on display and can be viewed today.

Sacred Bones

The bones of the actual followers and disciples of Jesus are highly cherished. Occasionally there is some controversy. For example, there appear to be several different heads of John the Baptist. One of his index fingers can be found in Finestere, France. The head of the apostle Thomas can be found in Ortona, Italy, and that of Andrew in Patras, Greece.

Many relics of the original apostles can be found in Italy, which is not surprising given that region's role in the early church. A good portion of the mortal remains of the Apostles James, Peter, Bartholomew, Phillip, Simon, and Jude are preserved in Rome or the Vatican.

A few bone relics seep residues. The body of St. Walburga, housed in a church in Eichstatt, Bavaria, annually seeps oil between October 12 and February 25. Elsewhere, vials of dried saints' blood

VISIT
BEAUTIFUL
JERICHO!!

People and Places

The body of St. Bernadette (1844–1879) of Lourdes fame was still looking good 30 years after her death. When some well-meaning nuns gave her a good cleaning in 1909, she lost some of her life-like appearance, and a bit of restoration was done with wax.

liquefy on a given date or under special circumstances. Skeptics claim that it isn't blood at all, but some red substance that reacts chemically to shaking or slight changes in temperature. Tell that to the believers!

Artifacts from the Crucifixion

Bits and pieces of objects related to the Crucifixion of Jesus are highly prized. Several churches in Europe claim to have nails from the Crucifixion, and there are a number of claims to pieces of the crown of thorns that was placed on Jesus' head. Fragments of the vinegar-filled sponge offered to Jesus on the cross are also to be found here and there. The loin cloth said to have been worn by Jesus on the cross is in a church in Bavaria.

Illuminations

In a strange footnote to history, Hitler was allegedly interested in finding and collecting powerful Biblical artifacts, supposedly because they might play a role in curious Nazi occult practices.

Perhaps the most powerfully symbolic of the Crucifixion relics are pieces of the cross itself. Skeptics have long scoffed that there are enough pieces of the so-called True Cross in Europe to build a boat (or a church, or whatever).

This old saw is often repeated, so one enterprising investigator set out to prove otherwise. In 1870, G. Rouhault de Fleury announced that he had calculated the volume of wood that would have constituted the cross. He had then gone about and measured every known fragment of the True Cross in Europe.

The results? The total amount of wood alleged to have come from the true cross accounts for less than a third of its estimated total volume, thus effectively countering the scoffers.

The Shroud of Turin

The most controversial of all the religious artifacts related to the story of Jesus is the Shroud of Turin. The Shroud is a piece of linen cloth, 14½ feet long by 3½ feet wide. The cloth bears a strange image of a man with the marks of a crucifixion, complete with blood stains at the wrist and feet.

The Shroud shows both the back and front of the man, as if a body were first laid down on it, and the cloth was then folded over on top of it. Blood stains found around the head are suggestive of a crown of thorns, and the back of the image appears to have been flogged. A traumatic wound can be seen on his right side. The man is estimated to be about six feet tall, with long hair and a beard.

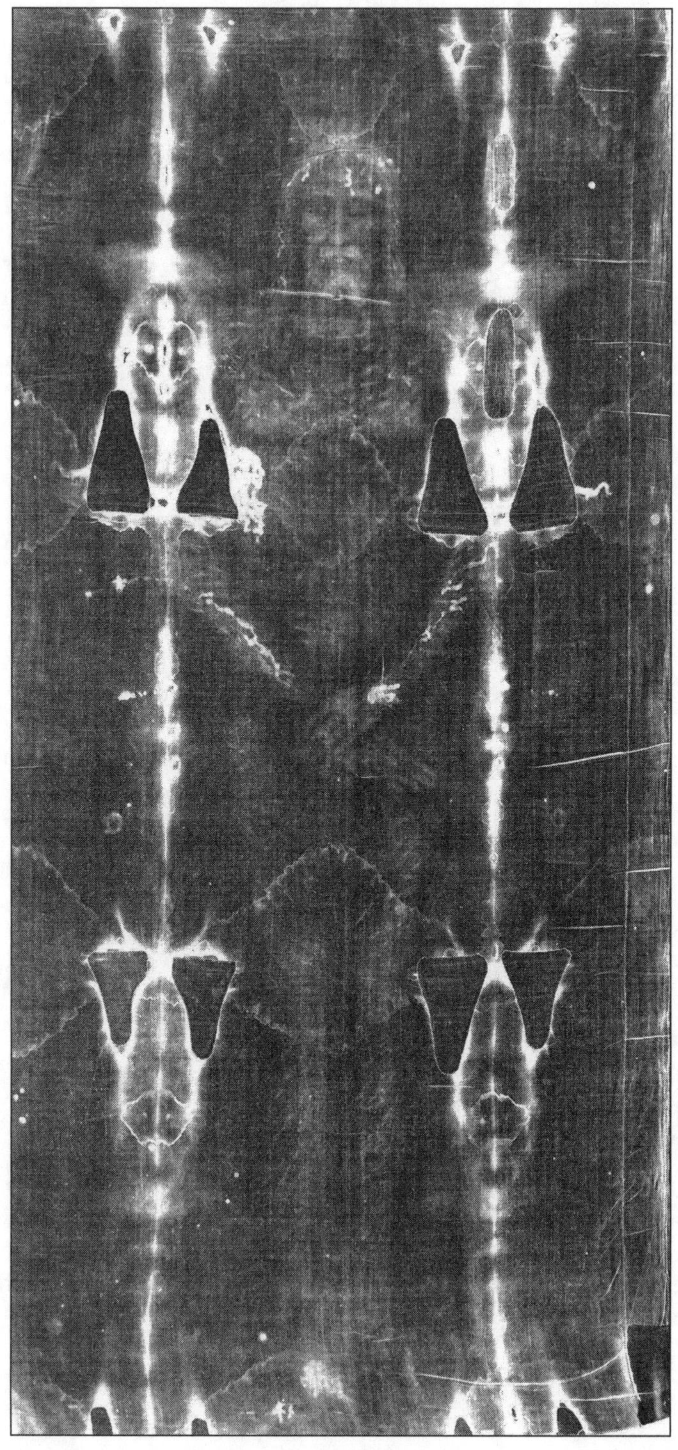

The Shroud of Turin.

(Photo courtesy of Barrie M. Schwortz)

Words of Wisdom

"And he [Joseph of Arimathea] bought a linen shroud, and taking him [Jesus] down, wrapped him in the linen shroud, and laid him in a tomb ..."

—Mark 15:46

The amazing image appears almost like a photographic negative—so much so that when it was first officially photographed in 1898, the result was startling. The photographic negative revealed an incredibly life-like positive image. To many believers, this is the actual burial shroud of Jesus, and the face on the Shroud is that of the Son of God himself.

The Shroud has an interesting history. It first appeared publicly in a church in Lirey, France, in 1357 and was eventually transferred to Turin, Italy, where it remains today. Speculation has suggested that the Shroud had originally been retrieved by Crusaders from Constantinople or the Holy Land.

Examining the Shroud

In 1978, an international team of experts was given permission to examine the Shroud in detail. Some came away convinced it was an extremely clever medieval forgery produced by some unknown methods. Others were convinced that this was indeed a very special relic. Whether real or fake, over the years there has been so much interest in the Shroud that a name has been coined for its study: *sindonology*.

Logos

Sindonology is the study of the Shroud of Turin.

Advocates will say that the details on the Shroud match closely that of Scripture and the known effects of crucifixion and torture on the human anatomy. There is no evidence of brush strokes indicative of painting, and if it were somehow painted, it would require a very long brush indeed, as the image is best seen from several feet away.

The pollen of several dozen plants known from the Holy Land is said to have been recovered from the Shroud. And a couple of Shroud advocates have argued that, with special photographic techniques, traces of first-century Roman coins can be detected over the image's eyes. Others are not convinced.

The image on the Shroud is puzzling. Believers in the Shroud's authenticity suggest that it was produced by a blinding light occurring during the Resurrection, perhaps in combination with body residues and/or anointing substances used in preparing the body. Despite many experiments, some of which present interesting possibilities, the results remain inconclusive.

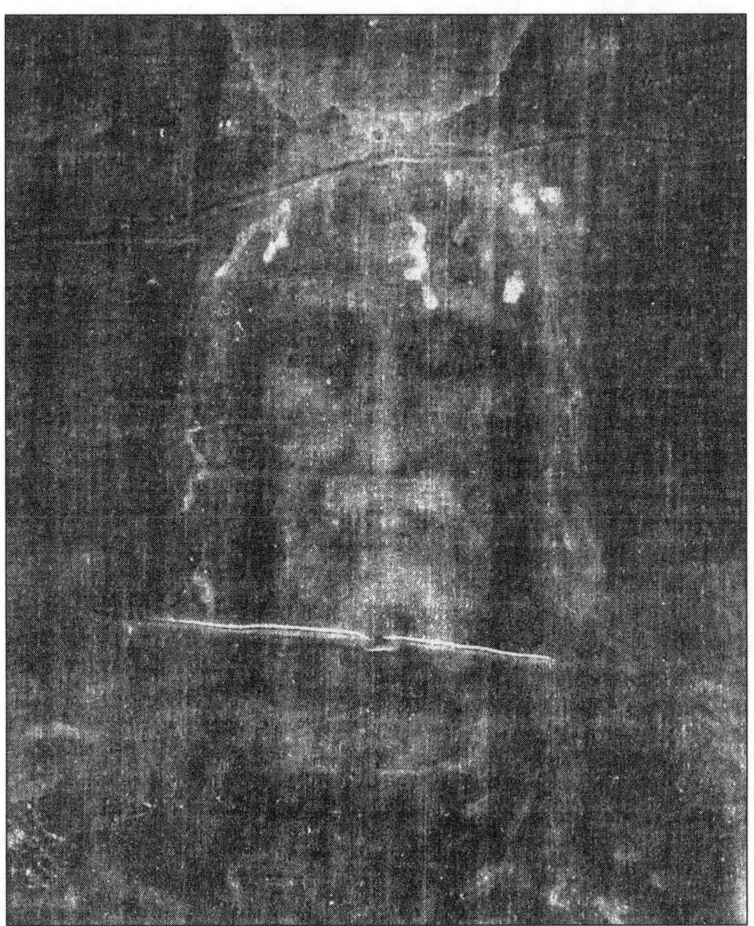

A close-up of the Shroud of Turin. Is this the face of Jesus?

(Photo courtesy of Barrie M. Schwortz)

Clever Monks!

One theory has argued that twelfth-century monks produced the image using a crude *camera obscura* and a quartz crystal. This scenario requires that a corpse be hung for several days in the sun in front of a cloth that had been covered in silver nitrate, thus forming a kind of photographic film, which was then processed to fix the image. The corpse would then be flipped upside down for the opposite shot.

Although such a method might possibly work, it would require a great deal of technical know-how in the fields of chemistry and optics that doesn't seem to have been generally available at the time.

Illuminations

Even if it was possible to prove that the Shroud had its origins in the Middle East during the first century A.D., how would it be possible to prove that it belonged to Jesus?

Rub It In!

Others have suggested that the Shroud was produced by creating a drawing using colored carbon powders mixed with a binder. The image would be transferred onto the cloth by rubbing and then heating. Other experiments have attempted to produce images by placing cloth over three-dimensional images and applying pigments. None match the quality of the original.

A recent theory argues that the famous Renaissance scientist and inventor Leonardo da Vinci was the creator of the Shroud. Da Vinci, it is claimed, had invented a crude camera which enabled him to produce the photograph-like image. As incredibly clever as he was, however, it seems very unlikely that he had anything to do with it. For one thing, the Shroud apparently was known to exist and was exhibited nearly a hundred years before da Vinci's birth in 1452!

Revelations

Just because something *can* be done in some way or another doesn't mean it *was* done that way. Archaeologists, for example, have experimented with how the large stone blocks of the Egyptian pyramids were moved. Although several methods seem to work, there is no guarantee that any one of these ideas is the one that the Egyptians actually used.

Giving It a Date

One of the most compelling tests that could be performed on the Shroud, scientifically speaking, was to use radiocarbon dating in order to determine its age. This was actually done in 1988. Shroud samples were given to three separate laboratories in Oxford, Geneva, and Tucson. The results came as a shock to many Shroud advocates: The samples dated from between A.D. 1260 and 1390.

The radiocarbon dates would seemingly put an end to the Shroud speculation, but not so. Some Shroud defenders argue that the linen has been contaminated, either when it was exposed to fire in 1532 or as a result of modern micro-organic growth on its surface.

And there are complaints that the samples taken were from a part of the Shroud that had been subject to all kinds of handling and other abuse over the years. Furthermore, the samples might have contained material from later repairs made to the Shroud. In any case, they say such factors may have contributed to a much younger date than the true age of the Shroud.

A Close Call

The Shroud almost went up in smoke late at night on April 11, 1997, when a major fire broke out in the Turin Cathedral. Firemen raced to rescue the precious object, smashing its case of bulletproof glass with a sledge hammer and then with their bare hands.

The Shroud was saved and the firemen became heroes. In 1998, the Shroud received a new case that weighs three tons. The case is temperature-controlled and filled with inert gas. The Shroud itself is protected with special thick UV protective bulletproof glass.

Whatever the Shroud might be or however it might have been made, its full story remains a worthy mystery. Given its controversial nature and the enthusiastic intensity of its supporters, the story of the Shroud will no doubt continue to unfold in interesting ways for years to come. For believers, however, it isn't a piece of cloth that is ultimately important, but the Resurrection of Jesus.

Illuminations

Even if an ancient date were proven for the Shroud, skeptics could argue that the Shroud was an ancient forgery or even a medieval forgery created on ancient cloth.

VISIT
BEAUTIFUL
JERICHO!!

People and Places

The Shroud of Turin will be on public display for eight weeks in the year 2000. Visitors can take a look at it in the Turin Cathedral from August 26 until October 22. This will be only its fifth exhibition since 1898.

The Spear of Destiny

The Gospel of John (19:32–34) tells the story of how the legs of those being crucified with Jesus were broken in order to hasten their death. This was not done to Jesus, as it was noted that he was already dead:

> So the soldiers came and broke the legs of the first, and of the other who had been crucified with him; but when they came to Jesus and saw that he was already dead, they did not break his legs. But one of the soldiers pierced his side with a spear, and at once there came out blood and water.

There is nothing in the New Testament that directly names this Roman soldier, but an apocryphal work called the Gospel of Nicodemus identifies him as "Longinus." The spear with which Jesus was stuck is called the Holy Lance, the Lance of Longinus, and sometimes the Spear of Destiny.

One can imagine what a prize such a relic would be if it could be found. But alas, objects claimed to be the lance can be found in Austria, Rome, Krakow, and Hatay (Antioch), Turkey. It might be one of them, or none of them!

Logos

The **Holy Grail** is the cup from which Jesus drank during the Last Supper. In common parlance, the Holy Grail has come to signify an ultimate, elusive goal.

People and Places

Joseph of Arimathea was a wealthy Jew who requested the body of Jesus from Pontius Pilate after the Crucifixion. The body was placed in Joseph's own expensive rock-cut tomb. No more is heard about this man in the Bible, although there are apocryphal books that elaborate on his story.

The Holy Grail

Perhaps the most famous and most elusive Biblical artifact from the New Testament is the *Holy Grail*. The Holy Grail is the cup from which Jesus drank wine during the Last Supper. This act, with its accompanying words, initiated one of the most sacred rituals of Christianity. So what happened to this noteworthy object?

The Bible doesn't give any clues, and in fact, it's possible that Jesus' companions didn't especially value it. Whatever the case, apart from its mention in the Last Supper story, it is never heard from again. There are, however, other stories in the form of legends that give the Grail quite a career. Among them is one that says the Grail served to catch blood flowing from the body of Jesus after the Crucifixion.

Tales of the Grail

The most common story tells how the Grail was obtained by Joseph of Arimathea, a wealthy Jew who gave away his own tomb to be used for the body of Jesus. In one version, Jesus actually appeared to him and personally gave him the Grail.

In order to escape persecution, the story goes, Joseph took the cup with him on a long journey, ending up in Glastonbury, Scotland. There, a shrine for the sacred artifact was built, and some say that although the shrine no longer stands, the Grail is buried nearby.

Crusader Booty

Another legend has a group of Crusaders, the Knights Templar, digging under the Temple Mount in Jerusalem and finding the hidden Grail underneath. The Grail was then taken back to Europe, and some say it is concealed in a pillar in the medieval Rosslyn Chapel in Scotland, or beneath the chapel's floor.

The Grail also has its place in medieval lore in such tales as the adventures of Perceval. The knight Perceval visits a castle, sees the Grail, and is irresistibly drawn to it, but to revisit it he first experiences a series of trials and adventures.

The Grail, too, is featured in some of the wonderful stories of King Arthur. On one occasion, when the Knights are seated around their famous Round Table, the Grail appears hovering overhead and inspires them to go in search of it.

Visit
Beautiful
Jericho!!

People and Places

The Knights Templar were a group of European knights who united during the Crusades to protect pilgrims and sacred sites in the Holy Land. In the process, they accumulated great wealth, to the point where they became a potential political threat, resulting in their persecution in the early fourteenth century. A good number fled to Scotland, and some say they took the Holy Grail with them!

Walking Among Us?

There is an interesting idea that the Holy Grail is not a cup at all, but an expression relating to a bloodline. Those who promote this idea believe that Jesus was married to one of his followers, Mary Magdalene, and the two had children.

They believe that it is these direct descendants of Jesus who were sought and protected by the likes of the Knights Templar. There is no evidence in the New Testament that Jesus was married or a father, but so much is unknown about the personal details of Jesus' life that such speculation can't be either proven or disproven.

Revelations

The so-called Holy Grail is the cup mentioned in the following verses from the Gospel of Matthew (26:27–28):

> And he took a cup, and when he had given thanks he gave it to them, saying, "Drink of it, all of you; for this is my blood of the covenant, which is poured out for many for the forgiveness of sins."

Icons: Images of Concentration

Any visitor to a Roman Catholic or Orthodox church will be impressed by the amazing variety of art depicting Jesus, his mother Mary, and many of the saints. In Orthodox churches, beautifully painted images on boards, known as icons, are common.

These artistic representations of holy people, like relics, serve as a focus of veneration. Like pictures of one's family carried in a wallet, they act as a kind of remembrance. Icons can often be found in private homes, and their use has been criticized by outsiders for the usual reason—that they can be misused as idols.

A Coptic icon from Egypt featuring St. Mark.

(Courtesy of the author)

A few rare icons are reported to have mysterious properties, such as the ability to weep tears. Some statues, usually of Mary and other saints, are also said to cry, bleed, or even move. These are the kinds of miracles that appeal to the faithful and, like all miracles, raise the skeptical eyebrows of doubters.

Like many of the mysteries related to the Bible, relics are often perplexing to the skeptic or scientist. There is no way, for example, to determine if a fragment of wood is really from the True Cross, although it would be possible to eliminate it as a candidate if it was of the wrong date or inappropriate tree species.

The most we can say is that these relics, real or not, have had a powerful effect on believers for centuries, and will probably continue to do so for centuries to come. And why not? People want to be close to the sacred.

The Least You Need to Know

- Over the centuries, believers have collected relics as mementos of extraordinary individuals.
- Some relics are said to have mysterious properties.
- Although scientific studies tend to cast doubt on the Shroud of Turin as Jesus' burial cloth, it continues to command the fascination of many believers.
- The famous Holy Grail continues to remain elusive.
- Icons are artistic representations of holy people that, like relics, serve as a focus of veneration for believers.

Part 7

The Strange and the Supernatural

God isn't the only supernatural being found in the Bible. Angels and devils likewise inhabit the ethereal realms and occasionally influence and interact with us mortals. The Bible is also home to a number of human beings who were physically extraordinary in various ways. In this part, we're going to examine some of these heavenly, hellish, and unusual personages.

Some of them are to be found in Revelation, the last and perhaps the most curious book in the Bible. It purports to describe a scenario for the end of time. It's a strange, complicated, and controversial book which has received extra attention with the turn of the so-called new millennium. And it gets some attention here, too, as a bona fide Biblical mystery.

Finally, we'll take a look at how the Bible has shaped the huge variety of human beliefs up to the present day. And if this book has piqued your interest, I'll give you a few tips on how to pursue the subject further.

Chapter 20

Angels and Devils

In This Chapter

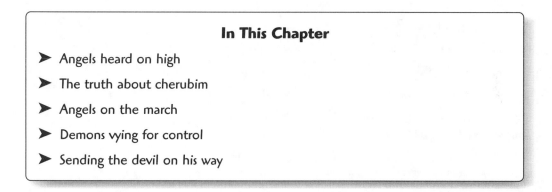

- Angels heard on high
- The truth about cherubim
- Angels on the march
- Demons vying for control
- Sending the devil on his way

Angels and devils play an important role in the Bible-based religions. Both show up in Genesis, the very first book of the Bible, and their sporadic appearances elsewhere in the Scriptures are generally unforgettable. In this chapter, we'll take a look at some of these otherworldly entities and try to get a glimpse of what they're about.

Employees of the Lord

Let's start with the good guys! When we think of angels in our modern day, we tend to picture a floating human in glowing white robes with big white wings to help it stay aloft. But, surprisingly, much of our imagery and knowledge of angels does not come from the Bible.

Instead, the majority of our ideas about angels comes from apocryphal works or the poetic and artistic imagination of scholars who have studied angels over the last two millennia or so. What they all have in common is that angels are depicted as spiritual beings who worship and serve God and occasionally interact with us mortals on earth.

An Angel Hierarchy

There has long been an interest in how these heavenly beings are organized and what their relationship might be to God, humans, and each other. In order to clarify things, a fellow named pseudo-Dionysius (ca. A.D. 500), a theologian and mystic, came up with a list of nine ranks, or *choirs* (seems they like to sing and make music!), of angels, in order of their perceived importance and closeness to God.

The names were taken from Scripture, though the rankings and details of their function were pretty much from his own imagination and the embellishments of earlier writers. Here's the list:

- Seraphim
- Cherubim
- Thrones
- Dominions
- Virtues
- Powers
- Principalities
- Archangels
- Angels

Illuminations

Angels of one sort or another are mentioned in the Bible over 270 times!

Very Close to God

The seraphim seem to guard the very throne of God. With such an important position, one might think they'd be mentioned all over the Bible. *Au contraire*. These beings with their immensely high status appear but once, in the Book of Isaiah. Therein, the prophet Isaiah is having a vision of God in heaven:

> I saw the Lord sitting upon a throne, high and lifted up .... Above him stood the seraphim; each had six wings: with two he covered his face, and with two he covered his feet, and with two he flew. And one called to another and said: "Holy, holy, holy is the Lord of hosts; the whole earth is full of His glory." (6:1–3)

Isaiah, being in the presence of God, felt unworthy to speak to the Lord. One of the seraphim took care of that problem:

> Then flew one of the seraphim to me, having in his hand a burning coal which he had taken with tongs from the altar. And he touched my mouth and said: "Behold, this has touched your lips; your guilt is taken away, and your sin forgiven." (6:6–7)

Formidable Cherubs

When you hear the word "cherub," you probably think of some fat-faced little baby flying around with wings, or maybe a good-looking child of some sort. Match that thought with the frightening description from a vision of Ezekiel. These four cherubim emerged from a cloud flashing fire:

> ... they had the form of men, but each had four faces, and each of them had four wings. Their legs were straight, and the soles of their feet were like the sole of a calf's foot; and they sparkled like burnished bronze. Under their wings on their four sides they had human hands. And the four had their faces and their wings thus: their wings touched one another; they went every one straight forward, without turning as they went. As for the likeness of their faces, each had the face of a man in front; the four had the face of a lion on the right side, the four had the face of an ox on the left side, and the four had the face of an eagle at the back. (Ezekie1 1:5–10)

Logos

The word **angel** is derived from the Greek word *angelos,* which means "messenger." An angel refers to any of several kinds of heavenly beings that serve God in heaven.

Illuminations

In a couple of places in the Old Testament, God is depicted as riding upon a flying cherub. Check out Psalms 18:10 and 2 Samuel 22:11.

These are formidable creatures, and like the seraphim, they are apparently adept at singing God's praises:

> And the glory of the Lord went up from the cherubim .... And the sound of the wings of the cherubim was heard as far as the outer court, like the voice of God Almighty when he speaks. (Ezekiel 10:4–5)

We first meet the cherubim early on in the Bible. They're stationed at the Garden of Eden after Adam and Eve got kicked out. The angels guarded the east sector of the Garden with a flaming sword in order to bar the way to the Tree of Life that got the first couple in trouble in the first place.

Images of cherubim also played an important role in the Holy Temple and its furniture. The Ark of the Covenant, you may recall, featured a pair of winged cherubs on its lid, which served as a kind of throne for God. Installed in the Holy of Holies in the Temple in Jerusalem, the ark was flanked by two huge gilded winged cherubim made of olive wood. Other parts of the Temple featured cherubim as motifs.

Logos

Although angels are often referred to as **seraphim** and **cherubim,** these Hebrew words are in the plural. An individual angel would be a **seraph** or a **cherub.**

The Heavenly Choir

The angels classified as Thrones are described in the intense visions of Ezekiel as gleaming wheels with eyes in their rims. Dominions are supervisors, the Virtues are the ones who guard earthlings and work miracles, and the Powers fight evil forces such as demons.

Principalities protect religious leaders as well as earthly cities and countries. Archangels are the messengers. The regular angels are at the bottom of the order, do as they're told, and probably are assigned to the more mundane affairs dealing with humans.

Keep in mind that this whole hierarchy of nine choirs does not appear as such in the Bible. It is the result of human minds scouring the Scriptures in an attempt to ferret out the subtleties of heavenly existence.

Words of Wisdom

"Do not neglect to show hospitality to strangers, for thereby some have entertained angels unawares."

—Hebrews 13:2

Angels on the Job

The word "angel" is itself derived from the Greek word for messenger, and indeed, that is the role many angels have played in the Bible. Three angels deliver the news to 90-year-old Sarah that she and Abraham are going to have a son. Sarah thought this was so funny that she laughed. Her son would be named Isaac, which means "laughter." In the troubling story in Genesis where Abraham is about to sacrifice Isaac, an angel mercifully interrupts the proceedings.

It was an angel named Gabriel who informed Zechariah, the future father of John the Baptist, that his elderly wife would give birth. Because of his incredulity, Zechariah was struck mute until the day John was circumcised and named. Gabriel also notified the Virgin Mary that she had been selected to give birth to Jesus, and he let her fiancé Joseph know things were okay.

An artist's vision of a beautiful angel.

(Illustration by Gustave Doré)

In the much retold Christmas tale, "shepherds watching their flocks by night" are terrified when an angel appears and tells them of the birth of Jesus nearby. The angel is then joined by some of his magnificent colleagues:

> And suddenly there was with the angel a multitude of the heavenly host praising God and saying, "Glory to God in the highest, and on earth peace, good will toward men." (Luke 2:13–14; KJV)

Illuminations

Only two angels are directly named in the Bible: Gabriel and Michael. Others such as Raphael are found in the Apocrypha and pseudepigraphic literature.

Tough Guys

Angels can be tough. A pair of them fought off and blinded the unruly mob in Sodom, and one wrestled all night with Jacob in Genesis. The Angel of Death slew the first-born children of the Egyptians in Exodus and 185,000 Assyrian soldiers outside of Jerusalem. In Acts 12:23, an "angel of the Lord" killed the arrogant Jewish king Herod Agrippa.

Illuminations

For an excellent review of the subject of angels, Biblical or otherwise, take at look at *The Complete Idiot's Guide to Angels* (1999) by Jay Stevenson.

Mighty armies of angels seem to have engaged in both spiritual and physical battle. Psalms 68:17 refers to the army of the Lord:

> With mighty chariotry, twice ten thousand, thousands upon thousands, the Lord came from Sinai into the holy place.

Joshua, leader of the Israelites during the Conquest, met "the commander of the army of the Lord." (Joshua 5:14) The commander appeared as a man with a drawn sword.

Plenty to Do

There appear to be a goodly number of angels with many tasks. Jesus himself refers to more than "twelve legions of angels," (Matthew 26:53) and elsewhere in the New Testament, their numbers are called "innumerable." (Hebrews 12:22) The Book of Revelation (5:11) indicates "myriads of myriads and thousands of thousands."

Many believe that angels not only exist, but are active today. Some people believe that everyone is assigned an individual guardian angel who can step in with assistance from time to time. Let's hope so. Who couldn't use the extra help and attention once in a while? And if you actually see one, you've had an *angelophany*.

Logos

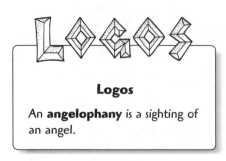

An **angelophany** is a sighting of an angel.

Angels in the Gene Pool?

Did angels visit earth and mate with humans? These curious and controversial verses of Genesis 6:1–4 are thought by some to suggest it:

> When men began to multiply on the face of the ground, and daughters were born to them, the sons of God saw that the daughters of men were fair; and they took to wife such of them as they

> chose .... The Nephilim were on the earth in those days, and also afterward, when the sons of God came in to the daughters of men, and they bore children to them. These were the mighty men that were of old, the men of renown.

Whoever these sons of God were, the Nephilim were apparently the giant-sized offspring of these matings. Their extra-large descendants must have survived the great flood, because they are later sighted in the land of Canaan when Moses and company are approaching the Promised Land.

Words of Wisdom

"Some Bible students insist that angels do not sing. This seems inconceivable. Angels possess the ultimate capacity to offer praise, and their music from time immemorial has been the primary vehicle of praise to our all-glorious God."

—Billy Graham, *Angels: God's Secret Agents* (1975)

Troublemakers

If God is good but there is evil in the world, there must also be some kind of evil forces at work. The Bible describes some of these bad influences, but like angels, much of the popular conception we have today about these forces, personified as demons, evolved over time.

Demons are typically perceived as fallen angels who, given free will, chose to disobey God and were tossed from his company. Given a bit of free rein, they are capable of lots of mischief.

Mortal humans, likewise given the freedom to choose between good and evil, can fall prey to the temptations of "the dark side." In Christian theology, the teachings, death, and resurrection of Jesus were meant to address and ultimately save people from their sinful nature.

VISIT
BEAUTIFUL
JERICHO!!

People and Places

The Nephilim were a race of giants that the Bible suggests was produced by the mating of angels and female humans.

Head of the Demons

The chief of the demons is most commonly referred to as the Devil, Lucifer, or Satan. The latter name in Hebrew actually means "accuser" or "adversary." He makes his first appearance in the Bible as the snake who successfully tempts Adam and Eve in the Garden of Eden.

Revelations

The New Testament tells us that even Jesus was subjected to Satan's attempts at temptation. A prime example is found in Matthew 4:1–11. After his baptism, Jesus spent 40 days fasting in the wilderness. The devil tempted him to turn stones into food, tried to talk him into jumping off a building, and offered great kingdoms if Jesus would worship him. Needless to say, Jesus did not succumb, and afterward, "angels came and ministered to him."

Words of Wisdom

"I think if the devil doesn't exist, but man has created him, he has created him in his own image and likeness."

—Feodor Dostoevsky, *The Brothers Karamazov* (1880)

Ever since they were banished from Eden, there has been a perpetual battle of the human spirit between the goodness of God and the secular temptations of the world. God's wrath against evil is shown in such stories in Genesis as Noah and the flood and the destruction of Sodom and Gomorrah.

Later on, the Israelites were given specific rules by God and were told that to disobey these rules was to do wrong, and a lot of wrongdoing would occur. When things weren't going well, some of the Israelites were quite capable of lapsing into pagan worship while the devil clapped on the sidelines.

Satan plays quite a role in the New Testament, where he is directly involved in many peoples' lives, and his role in the scheme of things is well acknowledged. When demons interfere directly with people, they often tempt them into bad behavior, and in a worst-case scenario, they enter someone's body and take over.

The Hot House

The red skin, pointed tail, and pitchfork of the popular portrayals of the devil and demons are not found in the Bible. The imaginative minds of Medieval theologians and artists filled in a lot of the details in an attempt to describe these entities and their domains.

Hell, a place prepared for the devil and his followers, has likewise been a subject of contemplative speculation. The Bible describes it as a fiery place where the wicked will be condemned for eternity, upon death and/or immediately following divine judgment. As described in the Bible, it is not a pleasant place. Those who find themselves there will suffer unspeakable physical pain and suffering, mental and emotional anguish, and spiritual separation from God.

Evil Among Us

Just as there are many who believe in angels today, there are many who likewise believe in the devil and demons. Evil has often been routinely explained as the devil at work, often through people such as Hitler, Stalin, or other purveyors of pain, death, and destruction.

Thus, the struggle continues between good and evil. Many a Sunday pastor will lecture on the subject of free will, which allows people to choose either good, as represented by God and Jesus, or evil, represented by the Devil.

Call the Exorcist!

The New Testament tells tales of demonic possession, in which the spirit of a demon seemingly takes over and controls the affected individual. There are some who believe that such possessions have never ceased to take place.

Are you possessed? Here are just a few of the possible symptoms:

- An aversion to Christianity
- A foul blasphemous mouth
- Supernatural knowledge
- Odd contortions
- Levitation
- Speaking incomprehensible babble
- Appearing and disappearing wounds
- Ability to produce weird objects or substances out of various body orifices

VISIT
BEAUTIFUL
JERICHO!!

People and Places

The Hebrew word for "hell" is *Gehenna.* The name is derived from an actual place, the Valley of Hinnom, which runs outside the Old City walls of Jerusalem. It apparently was once used as a site for pagan worship, including human sacrifice. Today, there's not much to see, but it does get hot in the summer.

For a good re-creation of the whole possession scene, watch the now-classic film *The Exorcist,* which graphically displays the symptoms, along with attempts by priests to drive the demons away.

Revelations

One of the most troubling stories in the Bible is that of Job, in which God, when challenged by Satan, allows him to test Job's faith in the most harsh of manners. Job's faith in God prevails and he is ultimately rewarded, but it is a most enigmatic and uncomfortable tale. Read all about it in the Old Testament Book of Job.

Jesus Does the Driving

The Gospels describe many incidents of Jesus driving demons out of possessed individuals. An extraordinary story is reported in Matthew 8:28–32:

Illuminations

Jesus was accused of himself being associated with the devil when he exorcised a blind and speechless man of demons. The accusing Pharisees got an impressive earful in response, including being called "a brood of vipers." (Matthew 12:22–37)

And when he [Jesus] came to the other side, to the country of the Gadarenes, two demoniacs met him, coming out of the tombs, so fierce that no one could pass that way. And behold, they cried out, "What have you to do with us, O Son of God? Have you come here to torment us before the time?" Now a herd of many swine was feeding at some distance from them. And the demons begged him, "If you cast us out, send us away into the herd of swine." And he said to them, "Go." So they came out and went into the swine; and behold, the whole herd rushed down the steep bank into the sea, and perished in the waters.

Some researchers have suggested that certain medical or psychological conditions may have been misdiagnosed in the past as demonic possession. Epilepsy or cerebral palsy, for example, can produce erratic physical movements that, sadly, might have been interpreted as the work of the devil.

The symptoms of mental conditions such as schizophrenia, with its often bizarre effects upon the personality, were also likely cause for alarm and otherworldly explanations. Tourette's Syndrome can produce an unintended foul mouth. Unfortunately, the cures for such supposed possessions were often harsh, if not deadly.

Jesus exorcising a demon and healing a man.

(Illustration by Gustave Doré)

Illuminations

If you maintain a fundamental belief in the accuracy and truth of the Bible, then you must believe that angels and demons are at work in the world today.

The Devil's Fan Clubs

Worshipping the devil can get you in trouble. Consider what happened to those considered to be witches in Salem, Massachusetts, in the year 1692. Several young girls claimed to be under the spell of local witches, and after a series of trials based mostly on hearsay, 19 people were hanged.

Today, in the United States and free societies elsewhere, there is actually a Church of Satan, along with various groups practicing witchcraft, now without fear of official retaliation.

In the end, the Bible tells us that God and goodness will ultimately prevail over evil. Satan and his associates will be eternally damned and put away for all time. You can read more about this pleasant idea in Chapter 22, "Revelation: The End?"

The Least You Need to Know

- Both angels and demons play a big role in the Bible.
- Angels serve God in many ways. Some of them are messengers and warriors, and all engage in praise.
- Satan and demons are usually perceived as "fallen angels" who tempt people to act against the will of God.
- Jesus was known to exorcise demons, and believers look forward to the day when God will stop evil for good.

Chapter 21

Some Strange Characters

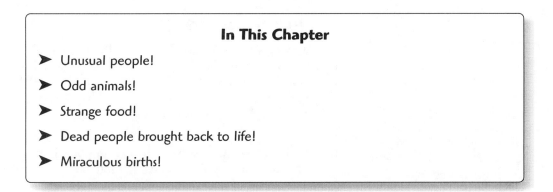

In This Chapter

- Unusual people!
- Odd animals!
- Strange food!
- Dead people brought back to life!
- Miraculous births!

So far we've covered a lot of mysterious territory in this book. But it's only a fraction of the many wonders the Bible has to offer. In this chapter, we'll look at a variety of people, animals, and circumstances that are truly out of the ordinary.

Living a Very, Very Long Time!

The first couple books of the Bible mention several people who are said to have lived an extraordinarily long time. The book of Genesis contains genealogical information that is quite impressive. Take a look at these life spans:

- **Adam**—930 years
- **Seth**—912 years
- **Enosh**—905 years
- **Kenan**—910 years

- ➤ **Jared**—962 years
- ➤ **Methusaleh**—969 years (the record holder!)
- ➤ **Noah**—950 years

And those are just the old-timers! Mahalalel reached 895 years, and Lamech lived a mere 777. After Noah, God seems to have decided to limit the human life span to 120 years, as indicated in Genesis (6:3):

> Then the Lord said, "My spirit shall not abide in man for ever, for he is flesh, but his days shall be a hundred and twenty years."

Moses lived to be 120, but in one of the Psalms (90:10) an even shorter life span is mentioned: "The years of our life are threescore and ten"—that is, 70.

Words of Wisdom

According to Job 12:12, the long-lived folk in the Bible may have become wiser as they got older: "Wisdom is with the aged, and understanding in length of days."

Visit
Beautiful
Jericho!!

People and Places

The Guinness Book of World Records lists the oldest verifiable age known as that of Jeanne Calmet (1875–1997), a French woman who lived to be 122 years old.

Happy Birthday

Average life spans have fluctuated dramatically through the ages and continue to do so, depending upon one's living conditions. In 1998, males in the United States could expect to live to be about 73.9, and females to 79.4. Compare this to 46.3 and 48.3 respectively in 1900!

So how does one deal with the big numbers found in the Bible? Saying they are just figurative expressions for "a ripe old age" doesn't work—they seem to be very specific. At least one apologist has suggested that prior to Noah's flood, the earth had a different atmosphere that was conducive to longer life.

Not Dying at All

There are two people in the Bible who are said not to have died at all. In Genesis 5:24, we learn that after 365 years …

> Enoch walked with God; and he was not, for God took him.

The reasons why he was so special are not given. The other individual who did not die was Elijah, who ascended into heaven in a fiery chariot. (2 Kings 2:11–12)

Land of the Giants

The Bible mentions a number of people who were extra-big—giants, in fact. As we saw in Chapter 20, "Angels and Devils," the Book of Genesis mentions the giant Nephilim, who were apparently the offspring of human women and angels.

Also, several territories mentioned in the Bible seemed to be full of huge people. The name for one such territory, *Rephaim,* means "giants." And remember that the spies who investigated the Promised Land returned with reports of giants:

> The land ... is a land that devours its inhabitants; and all the people that we saw in it are men of great stature. And there we saw the Nephilim (the sons of Anak, who come from the Nephilim); and we seemed to ourselves like grasshoppers, and so we seemed to them. (Numbers 13:32–33)

Jumbo Warrior

The most famous Biblical giant is the Philistine warrior Goliath, who was said to be "six cubits and a span," or approximately 9½ feet tall. Heavily armed and with a magnificent suit of armor, he struck fear into the hearts of his opponents. In the famous story, Goliath challenges the Israelites to send someone out to fight him.

Visit
Beautiful
Jericho!!

People and Places

Og, the king of Bashan, was so big he had an iron bed about 13½ feet long by 6 feet wide.

Apart from having a huge body, Goliath had a big mouth. Here are some of his fightin' words, as recorded in 1 Samuel 17:

> "I defy the ranks of Israel this day; give me a man, that we may fight together."
>
> "Am I a dog, that you come to me with sticks?"
>
> "Come to me, and I will give your flesh to the birds of the air and to the beasts of the field."

Only David, a scrawny shepherd boy, took him up on the challenge. Finding armor and weapons too heavy, David took a sling, nailed Goliath with a rock, and then cut his head off with the giant's own sword. It was a fine example of bravery.

You Big Philistine

Those Philistines sure could grow them big! In a battle at the Philistine city of Gath, the Israelites encountered some more large folk, and one with some extra equipment:

> And there was again war at Gath, where there was a man of great stature, who had six fingers on each hand, and six toes on each foot, twenty-four in number; and he also was descended from the giants. (1 Chronicles 20:6)

He also taunted the Israelites and lost.

Illuminations

The Guinness Book of World Records lists the tallest man as Robert Wadlow, an American who stood 8'11" tall!

Animal Acts

There are a good number of stories in the Bible involving animals. Many different kinds are mentioned, and they were often involved in miracles. Insects played a role in the plagues of the Exodus, and Jesus caused fish to be caught and to multiply.

Quails were sent as food to the Israelites in the wilderness, and God kept lions from eating the prophet Daniel. And that's only the beginning! Here are a few of the more unusual animal stories.

The Talking Donkey

During the Exodus, when the Israelites were traveling from Egypt into new territory, they would encounter various peoples who weren't always pleased to see the huge number of newcomers. In one case, the elders of Moab and Midian paid a professional soothsayer named Balaam to put a curse on the Israelites.

Balaam set out on his donkey to place the curse, but an angel appeared, blocking his path. Only the donkey could see the angel, and the animal began to behave uncooperatively. Balaam beat the donkey and was quite startled when God miraculously caused the animal to talk back: "What have I done to you, that you have struck me these three times?"

Balaam, whom one might think would be utterly startled, answers that he feels like a fool, and the donkey continues to berate him:

> "Am I not your donkey, upon which you have ridden all your life long to this day? Was I ever accustomed to do so to you?"

Balaam admitted that was true—the loyal donkey had never beaten him. The angel then made himself visible and chastised the man; ultimately, Balaam blessed the Israelites, much to the consternation of those who hired him. The story of Balaam can be found in Numbers 22 to 24.

Just Get a Toupee

There are many uncomfortable stories in the Bible, and the following one probably rates near the top. I have also found it to be one of the lesser-known incidents. The story involves the prophet Elisha, who apparently had a thin skin and a harsh temper.

> He [Elisha] went up from there to Bethel; and while he was going up on the way, some small boys came out of the city and jeered at him, saying, "Go up, you baldhead! Go up, you baldhead!" And he turned around, and when he saw them, he cursed them in the name of the Lord. And two she-bears came out of the woods and tore forty-two of the boys. (2 Kings 2:23–24)

It's not clear if the boys were mauled or outright killed. Either way, it's hard to justify that one. It has been suggested that insulting a prophet was tantamount to mocking God himself, but it still seems like a bit of an overreaction.

Revelations

Apart from the story of bald-headed Elisha, there are a few other tales of animal attacks in the Bible. There were the insect plagues in Exodus, and God sent hornets to drive away the Amorites in Joshua 24:12. Samson was attacked by a lion (Judges 14:5), and Paul was bitten by a snake while on the island of Malta (Acts 28:3).

Jonah and the Big Fish

Like most people, I prefer eating fish to being eaten by them. The story of Jonah tells the dramatic story of how a man survives such an ordeal, and even lives for a few days inside a giant sea creature.

Jonah was chosen by God for the incredibly intimidating task of preaching repentance to the mighty Assyrian city of Nineveh. Jonah didn't want the job, so he got on a ship and tried to leave town. God caused a big storm at sea, and the sailors drew lots to see who was causing the bad luck.

Jonah lost, and when the crew confronted him, he admitted that things were not good between him and God. At his own suggestion, he was tossed overboard to calm the sea. Luckily, he didn't drown, although he might have wished he had, when he was swallowed up by a big fish:

> And the Lord appointed a great fish to swallow up Jonah; and Jonah was in the belly of the fish three days and three nights. (Jonah 1:17)

Illuminations

Weird creatures still lurk beneath the seas. In 1977, a Japanese fishing vessel pulled up the rotting carcass of an unidentifiable giant flippered animal. It was photographed and then tossed back into the ocean. Some say it was the remains of a huge basking shark, while others are by no means so sure.

Back on the Beach

Jonah spent a lot of time praying in that big fish, and finally, when he was sufficiently chastised, he was puked up onto a beach. Jonah then went on to fulfil his missionary trip to Nineveh, which, amazingly, succeeded. (Read the whole story in the Book of Jonah.)

Now, you might say, what's the likelihood of being swallowed by a giant fish and then surviving inside? You'd at least need air, and it would stink pretty bad in there. There are a couple of old sea stories of people having been swallowed by certain species of whales, giving them indigestion, and then being vomited back out. It might stretch credulity a bit, but strange things do happen on occasion!

Jonah washed up on the beach after the big fish lost his lunch.

(Illustration by Gustave Doré)

More Big Fish

Jonah's big fish isn't the only one in the Bible. Genesis 1:21 mentions the creation of "great sea monsters." One of them is called the Leviathan, and he is described in terrifying detail in Job 41. Here's just a sample:

> No one is so fierce that he dares to stir him up .... Who can penetrate his double coat of mail? ... Round about his teeth is terror. His back is made of rows of shields, shut up closely as with a seal .... Out of his nostrils comes forth smoke, as from a boiling pot and burning rushes .... Though the sword reaches him, it does not avail; nor the spear, the dart, or the javelin .... Behind him he leaves a shining wake .... Upon the earth there is not his like, a creature without fear.

It has been suggested that the description of this mighty beast is that of a crocodile, a creature that is quite worthy of awe and fear. On the other hand, perhaps some other symbolic or actual creature is being described. Another monster of the sea is mentioned by name, a dragon named Rahab, but there is no detailed description.

Revelations

Only a fraction of the vast expanse of the world's oceans has been thoroughly explored. New species of sealife continue to be discovered, and creatures thought to have been extinct for millions of years are occasionally rediscovered in the oceans' depths. Many scientists, for example, believe in the existence of the elusive giant squid, a specimen of which has yet to be captured.

Another Great Beast

Another mysterious creature is also described in Job 40:15–24. This fellow is called *Behemoth,* who "eats grass like an ox" and lives in rivers "under the lotus plants ... in the covert of the reeds and in the marsh." This sturdy beast's "bones are tubes of bronze, his limbs like bars of iron." It seems like none other than the hippopotamus is being described. Like the crocodile, the hippo is a fierce and dangerous creature that spends much of its time in the water.

Biblical Plant Life

One of the most important plants related to the Bible isn't particularly mysterious, but its prominence calls for a few words of explanation. The plant is called the bulrush, or more commonly, papyrus. It grows in fresh water, especially along the Nile. A basket made from this plant protected baby Moses. (Exodus 2:3)

Apart from the fact that it is mentioned here and there in Biblical stories, the papyrus plant was used to produce the paper upon which many of the earliest known bits of literature were written, including books of the Bible. Egypt produced much of the paper for the ancient world, and at one time maintained a library in Alexandria with upward of half a million scrolls.

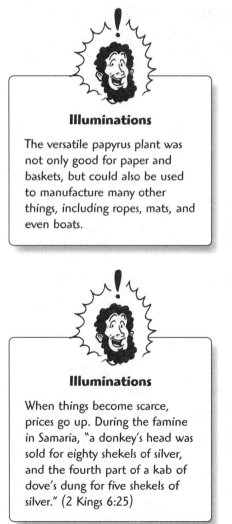

What's for Dinner?

We've already talked about the mysterious food called manna that God miraculously provided for the wandering Israelites (see Chapter 8, "Laying Down the Law"). Elsewhere in the Bible, we have a few curious examples of unusual meals. John the Baptist was known to subsist on locusts and wild honey, and Samson ate honey out of a dead lion. Moses had the Israelites' golden calf turned into powder and mixed with water, and then made the idol worshipers drink it!

Illuminations

The versatile papyrus plant was not only good for paper and baskets, but could also be used to manufacture many other things, including ropes, mats, and even boats.

Who's for Lunch?

Fortunately, there isn't a lot of cannibalism in the Bible. In fact, it's only mentioned twice. During a famine in Samaria, things were tough. An angry woman explained to the king how she had been double-crossed:

> "This woman said to me, 'Give up your son so we may eat him today, and tomorrow we'll eat my son.' So we cooked my son and ate him. The next day I said to her, 'Give up your son so we may eat him'; but she had hidden him." (2 Kings 6:28–29, NIV)

The Babylonian siege of Jerusalem likewise caused some desperate action, as noted in Lamentations 4:10: "The hands of compassionate women have boiled their own children; they became their food …."

Illuminations

When things become scarce, prices go up. During the famine in Samaria, "a donkey's head was sold for eighty shekels of silver, and the fourth part of a kab of dove's dung for five shekels of silver." (2 Kings 6:25)

Revelations

Although cannibalism is not very common in the world, it has occurred in desperate situations. In some cultures, human meat is referred to as "long pig" or "man-corn," and sometimes the cannibalism is symbolic, or is an attempt to acquire the power of the consumed.

A Bunch of Long-Hairs

Among the more unusual groups of people in the Bible were the Nazarites. These individuals took vows of holiness to God, or their parents made vows for them. The Nazarites were to avoid doing three things if they wanted to retain their status (as described in Numbers 6:1–21):

- Partaking of the "fruit of the vine" (including grapes, wine, grape juice, and raisins) or partaking of intoxicants.
- Touching dead people.
- Cutting their hair: "He shall let the locks of hair of his head grow long."

The most famous Nazarite was Samson (Judges 13–16), whose long hair seemed to be the source of his mighty strength. Here are some of the wild things Samson accomplished in his life:

- He killed a lion with his bare hands.
- He killed 30 men in the city of Ashkelon to get their nice clothes and pay back a bet.
- He caught 300 foxes, tied their tails together, and let them loose with torches to burn down the Philistines' fields and trees.
- He killed 1,000 warriors with the jawbone of a donkey.
- He uprooted the city gates of Gaza and carried them off.

Illuminations

For a fine film, watch the 1949 Cecil B. DeMille classic, *Samsom and Delilah,* starring Victor Mature. Especially exciting is the lion-wrestling scene.

Meet My Friend Delilah

The Philistines were, of course, interested in knowing what was the secret of Samson's power, and they used a woman named Delilah to woo him as his girlfriend. After Samson gave up his secret to her, he woke up one morning with his hair gone. The Philistines poked out his eyes and threw him in jail. While he languished in prison … his hair was growing back.

The Philistines were so happy to have subdued Samson that they decided to have a big celebration. They brought Samson out and tied him between two pillars holding up the party house. With all of the Philistine officials there and 3,000 people on the roof, the teasing must have been ruthless.

Bringing Down the House

Pleading with God for strength, Samson got an answer to his prayers, and he was able to press against the pillars, causing the building to collapse. Samson was killed, along with a whole lot of others. According to the story, "… the dead whom he slew at his death were more than those whom he had slain during his life." That's a lot of people!

Samson bringing down the house.

(Illustration by Gustave Doré)

Back to Life

While there's quite a bit of death and destruction in the Bible, there are also some miraculous returns from the grave. It doesn't happen very often, but when it does, it's certainly worthy of notice!

- On two different occasions, the prophet Elijah raised young men from the dead.
- A dead man came back to life when his body touched the bones of the prophet Elisha.
- Jesus raised two young people from the dead, as well as his good friend Lazarus.
- The disciples Peter and Paul each raised one deceased individual.
- Jesus, of course, himself rose from the dead.

VISIT
BEAUTIFUL
JERICHO!!

People and Places

Absalom, a son of David, cut his beautiful long hair once a year, when it got too heavy. He met a very weird death. While riding a donkey under an oak tree, his hair got caught in the branches and he was left hanging. It was not long before his enemies appeared and killed him. (2 Samuel 18:9–15)

And in one very special case, a whole bunch of dead people got up and went visiting. The Gospel of Matthew (27:51–53) tells the scary story of what happened at the moment of Jesus' death:

> ... the earth shook and the rocks were split; the tombs also were opened, and many bodies of the saints who had fallen asleep were raised, and coming out of the tombs after his resurrection they went into the holy city and appeared to many.

Babies on Board!

To balance out all the death we've been talking about, let's look at a little life. There are a number of miraculous births to be found in the Bible, some of which we've already encountered here and there. Here's a list:

- Although 90 and 100 years old respectively, Abraham and the previously barren Sarah were able to produce a child, Isaac. After the death of Sarah, Abraham fathered numerous other children.

Words of Wisdom

"Miracles are God's signature, appended to His masterpiece of creation; not because they ought to be needed, but because they are needed."

—Ronald A. Knox, *Miracles*, 1928

- Isaac's wife Rebekah was unable to conceive, but her husband's prayers resulted in the birth of twin boys, Jacob and Esau. Rachel, the wife of Jacob, likewise was able to produce two sons, Joseph and Benjamin.
- Divine intervention was involved in the births of Samson and Samuel.
- John the Baptist was born to two elderly parents who had been unsuccessful in producing children.
- Mary gave birth to Jesus by way of the Holy Spirit, while still a virgin.

A description, or even a mere list, of the interesting people and events in the Bible could go on and on. Whether the Bible is taken at face value or read as literature, the stories continue to amaze and provoke wonder.

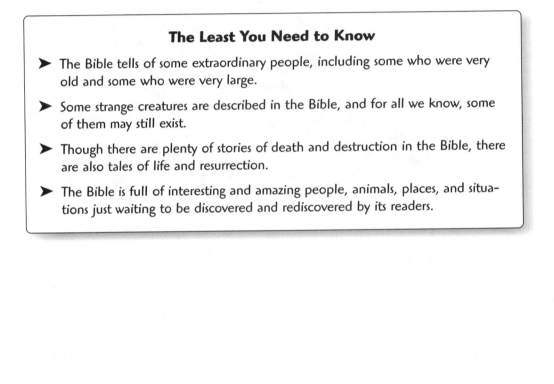

The Least You Need to Know

- The Bible tells of some extraordinary people, including some who were very old and some who were very large.
- Some strange creatures are described in the Bible, and for all we know, some of them may still exist.
- Though there are plenty of stories of death and destruction in the Bible, there are also tales of life and resurrection.
- The Bible is full of interesting and amazing people, animals, places, and situations just waiting to be discovered and rediscovered by its readers.

Chapter 22

Revelation: The End?

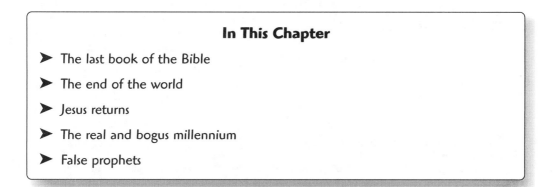

In This Chapter

- The last book of the Bible
- The end of the world
- Jesus returns
- The real and bogus millennium
- False prophets

While archaeologists such as myself tend to dwell in the past in order to discover what has already occurred, there are a lot of other people who are interested in events that are yet to come. Apart from sharing history and wisdom, there are some who say that the Bible has laid out a map of the future.

And we're not talking about what's going to be on the menu at the school cafeteria tomorrow. No, we're talking about the end of time as we know it, and some of the details aren't very pretty. In this chapter, we're going to examine a few of these futuristic ideas, and then you can come to your own conclusions.

Prophetic Writings

A good portion of the Old Testament consists of books referred to as the Prophets. Many of these books consist of warnings and predictions about what will happen to those who didn't or won't follow God, and passages that refer to the coming of the Messiah.

To Christians, the belief in Jesus as the Messiah is confirmed by some of the writings of the Prophets that they believe Jesus fulfilled. Still other prophecies in these books refer to what are often called "end times."

In the New Testament, Jesus promises to return, and in its final book we find a controversial vision of the future that has inspired, confused, and terrified believers for centuries. This last book, called Revelation, is believed by many to give a picture of the end of time, often referred to as the *apocalypse*.

Logos

The word **apocalypse** is derived from Greek and means the revealing of hidden things. It has taken on a broader meaning over the years and now refers to the events leading to the end of the world.

Time for an Apocalypse?

The notion of an end time or apocalypse was not new with the Book of Revelation. In much of Jewish history, there has been a yearning for some sort of spiritual resolution to the world's woes, a time when good will ultimately triumph over evil.

In the case of the Jews, the Babylonians' destruction of Jerusalem and the Holy Temple in 586 B.C. was a catalyst for such thinking. The abuses of the Hellenistic rulers and the tragic experiences with the Romans, including another destruction of the Temple, likewise stimulated hope for deliverance by God.

When Good Will Triumph

The Old Testament books of Isaiah and Ezekiel poetically describe a longed-for Messiah who will come and save the day, and the Book of Daniel provides a visionary look at the end times. Apart from the Bible, there are also many other apocryphal or pseudepigraphic works dealing with the apocalypse.

Dramatic examples can be found in the Dead Sea Scrolls. The Essenes (if that's who the Scrolls people were), under Roman domination like everyone else, were mightily opposed to the Jewish mainstream based in Jerusalem. They looked for their overthrow as part of a battle between the "Sons of Light" and the "Sons of Darkness," in which the Sons of Light ultimately win, of course.

They probably expected that the much-anticipated battle would be fought against the oppressive Romans. Unfortunately for the scrolls' authors, the real outcome wasn't happy. The Romans seem to have destroyed the Essene community at Qumran in A.D. 68, followed by Jerusalem two years later.

Revelation: The Scary Book

The Book of Revelation appears at the end of the New Testament, which is a good place for it. Just as Genesis describes the creation of the world, Revelation describes its ending. The book is also known as the Apocalpyse of John.

Illuminations

The Greek Orthodox Church does not include the Book of Revelation in their editions of the Bible.

For centuries, people generally assumed that it was written by John, a disciple of Jesus and the supposed author of the Fourth Gospel (although many scholars today think the author was someone else). When compared to the Gospel of John, though, the style and substance of Revelation is quite different.

The Book of Revelation is controversial. Since it was written, many have questioned its coherency and authority as a book worthy of inclusion in the Bible. The assumption that it was written by John the disciple gave it some credibility, and despite some serious doubts, it made its way into the accepted canon of New Testament books by the end of the fourth century A.D.

Martin Luther, the religious reformer who translated the Bible into German, found the book's symbolic imagery to be ambiguous to the point of confusing the average reader. The history of its interpretation seems to indicate that he was correct.

A Confusing Vision

So what's in the book of Revelation? Basically, it's a vision presented by an angel to John while he was exiled on the Greek island of Patmos. It appears to have been written around the year A.D. 95, and was directed to seven early Christian congregations in Asia Minor.

It describes a woefully sinful earth that will be harshly punished for a few years, followed by a great battle that the heavenly forces win. Jesus returns and reigns for 1,000 years. Satan is released one more time and is forever vanquished. It's also judgment time.

Visit
Beautiful
Jericho!!

Words of Wisdom

Apart from the gruesome apocalypse rhetoric, the Book of Revelation also presents some poetic verses, such as this much-beloved invitation from Jesus:

> "Behold, I stand at the door and knock; if any one hears my voice and opens the door, I will come in to him and eat with him, and he with me." (Revelation 3:20)

The average reader will likely be increasingly confused beginning around chapter 4. Here's a sample from chapter 6:

> Now I saw when the Lamb opened one of the seven seals, and I heard one of the four living creatures say, as with a voice of thunder, "Come!" And I saw, and behold, a white horse, and its rider had a bow; and a crown was given to him, and he went out conquering and to conquer .... When he opened the third seal, I heard the third living creature say, "Come!" And I saw, and behold, a black horse, and its rider had a balance in his hand; and I heard what seemed to be a voice in the midst of the four living creatures saying, "A quart of wheat for a denarius, and three quarts of barley for a denarius; but do not harm oil and wine!" (Revelation 6:1–6)

Logos

Eschatology is the study of the end time, its literature, and the signs of its unfolding.

Waiting for the End

The allegorical language in much of the book can be interpreted in a number of different ways, and so it has been, for centuries! Jesus said he was coming back, and his disciples must have thought it would be in their lifetimes. Thereafter, the waiting has continued.

Generation after generation, from Roman times to the present, has interpreted the events of its times to fit with scenarios derived from Revelation. The twentieth century has been especially fruitful for apocalyptic speculation. Two brutal World Wars and the conflicts in the Middle East have provided excellent inspiration.

Revelations

Many scholars see apocalyptic literature as being heavily influenced by the Persian religion of Zoroastrianism. Zoroaster was a Persian prophet who lived in the seventh century B.C. and preached a dualistic view of the world in which there was a conflict between good and evil. Good would triumph in the end. It was the Persians, you may recall, who ruled the Near East after the Babylonians were conquered, and it is possible that some of their ideas influenced the Hebrew prophets.

Signs of the Times

Revelation talks about seven seals, seven trumpets, and seven bowls, or judgments. There will be seven years of *Tribulation,* meaning bad, bad times, with devastating and unprecedented earthquakes, plagues, and violence. Eventually, much of the earth will be destroyed, and a good bit of the human population will be killed.

One of the horsemen of the Apocalypse, as described in the Book of Revelation—and he looks like he means business!

(Illustration by Gustave Doré)

Revelation is not the only book that describes such horrible times. The Gospels of Matthew, Mark, and John all contain references to such an apocalyptic scenario. Here's a sample:

> And you will hear of wars and rumors of war; see that you are not alarmed; for this must take place, but the end is not yet. For nation will rise against nation, and kingdom against kingdom, and there will be

Logos

The **Tribulation** refers to a seven-year period of human and environmental catastrophes, followed by the return of Jesus.

> famines and earthquakes in various places ... and many false prophets will arise and lead many astray .... But he who endures to the end will be saved. (Matthew 24:6–13)

The Antichrist

Sometime during the first three and a half years of the seven-year period of Tribulation we find the appearance of an individual often called the "Antichrist." The Antichrist is essentially an agent of Satan, whose personal charisma and political genius result in worldwide popularity. During this period the Temple in Jerusalem is rebuilt, and things appear to be good.

Illuminations

Some Christians at the time of the American Revolution suggested that the hated Stamp Act, which required a tax and stamp on commerce, was the Mark of the Beast. In modern times, the advent of Social Security numbers, supermarket bar codes, and ATM machines have provided fuel for apocalyptic prognosticators.

But then, during the last three and a half years of the Tribulation, the Antichrist shows his true nature and turns evil. A world government is established, headed by the Antichrist, whose capital is in Babylon. The Antichrist, assisted by a false prophet, will be worshipped as a god. A single currency will be established, and a special mark on one's body will be necessary to engage in commerce. Everyone is to be marked ...

> ... on the right hand or the forehead, so that no one can buy or sell unless he has the mark, that is, the name of the beast or the number of its name. This calls for wisdom: Let him who has understanding reckon the number of the beast [the Antichrist], for it is a human number, its number is six hundred and sixty-six. (Revelation 13:16–18)

Some Promising Candidates

If the Book of Revelation has been consistently reinterpreted to apply to the given times at hand, we can expect that every generation will have its suspected Antichrist. Here are just a few of the candidates who have made it to the list over time:

- **Roman emperors.** Particularly the dastardly Caligula and Nero, who presided over the persecution of Christians.
- **Napoleon Bonaparte.** A little man with great ambitions.
- **The Pope.** Whichever one happens to be in office when the impending end times are predicted.

- **Adolf Hitler.** Bad to the bone. Ditto for Josef Stalin.
- **Henry Kissinger.** Curious man with a thick accent.
- **Ronald Wilson Reagan.** All three of his names consist of six letters: 666!
- **John F. Kennedy.** The recipient of 666 votes at the 1956 Democratic Convention.
- **Mikhail Gorbachev.** A suspicious peacemaker with a strange mark on his head.
- **Sadaam Hussein.** The leader of Iraq, where the ancient city of Babylon was located.
- **Bill Gates.** It's a control thing.

Here are a few others: David Rockefeller, former U.S. president Jimmy Carter, assassinated Egyptian president Anwar Sadat, Protestant religious reformer Martin Luther, televangelist Pat Robertson, Iranian fundamentalist leader Ayatollah Khomeini, and King Juan Carlos of Spain.

Using Hebrew numerology, it is possible to derive the number 666 from a version of the name of the lunatic Roman emperor Nero. This is also possible with Henry Kissinger.

Logos

In the Book of Revelation, the **Antichrist** is Satan's agent on earth who will seduce the world into evil.

Armageddon: The Last Battle

A final earthly battle involving the western armies of the Antichrist against an eastern army will be resolved when heavenly forces appear. This great battle is to take place at Armageddon, a plain in modern-day northwestern Israel. But Jesus saves the day, sets up his divine kingdom in Jerusalem, administers justice, and puts Satan in his deserved place.

People and Places

Armageddon is the place mentioned in Revelation 16:16 as the scene of the final battle. The name is derived from the Hebrew name *Har Megiddo,* or mountain of Megiddo. An ancient Canaanite city called Megiddo was located there, and several important battles did take place there in ancient times.

Rapture!

So if all of these horrible things are going to happen, what about all of the faithful Christians? Will God put them through the suffering of the Tribulation? Not according to some folks, who believe that they're going to be spared the worst. In what has been called the "Rapture," the true believers in Jesus will be brought into heaven while they are still alive.

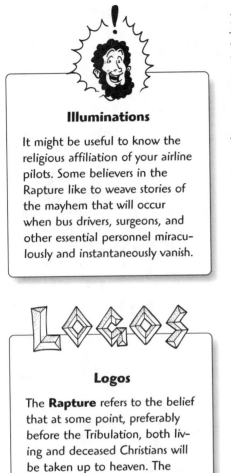

Around the same time, the dead who believed in Jesus will also ascend physically into heaven, and everyone going up will have transformed bodies. At what point will this happen? The believers in the Rapture are hoping that it will occur just before things get ugly, and not during or after.

Illuminations

It might be useful to know the religious affiliation of your airline pilots. Some believers in the Rapture like to weave stories of the mayhem that will occur when bus drivers, surgeons, and other essential personnel miraculously and instantaneously vanish.

According to Paul

Rapture is not in the Bible, nor is such an event mentioned in Revelation. The belief in the Rapture is principally derived from one of the letters of Paul to a Christian congregation in Thessalonica. In the letter, Paul refers to this ascension into heaven:

> For the Lord himself will descend from heaven with a cry of command, with the archangel's call, and with the sound of the trumpet of God. And the dead in Christ will rise first; then we who are alive, who are left, shall be caught up together with them in the clouds to meet the Lord in the air; and so we shall always be with the Lord. (1 Thessalonians 4:16–17)

Logos

The **Rapture** refers to the belief that at some point, preferably before the Tribulation, both living and deceased Christians will be taken up to heaven. The term "rapture" does not appear in the Bible; it is derived from the Latin word for "caught up."

A Long Time to Wait

A lot of people can't wait for all of this to happen, especially if they believe in the Rapture and that it will take them before all of the bad stuff begins! People have been waiting for almost 2,000 years now, and maybe they'll be waiting another 2,000. The Bible makes one thing about the issue of timing clear: You don't know when it will be!

Consider these words of Jesus to his inquiring apostles: "It is not for you to know times or seasons which the Father has fixed by his own authority." (Acts 1:7) And in Matthew 24:42–44, Jesus is equally unforthcoming. He does say, however, that you'd better be ready:

> "Watch therefore, for you do not know on what day your Lord is coming. But know this, that if the householder had known in what part of the night the thief was coming, he would have watched and would not have let his house be broken into. Therefore you also must be ready; for the Son of man is coming at an hour you do not expect."

This sort of advice hasn't kept the speculation down, and apocalypse students are constantly scrutinizing the latest news for tell-tale signs of the grand finale!

Millennial Fever

There is a certain fascination with the number 1,000 and its multiples. It's nice and round and is fun to see coming, kind of like when the odometer in your car turns over to a new big number! The Bible mentions the number here and there, and it has, in some people, sparked a fascination, if not a fixation, with millennia. Referring to God, Psalms 90:4 states ...

> For a thousand years in thy sight are but yesterday when it is past, or as a watch in the night.

This theme is repeated in 2 Peter 3:8:

> But do not ignore this one fact, beloved, that with the Lord one day is a thousand years, and a thousand years as one day.

Illuminations

Adolph Hitler used millennial imagery from the Bible in building his own Nazi ideology, in which the notion of a thousand-year Reich (or political rule) was promoted.

Y2K

Around the year 999, some people had millennial expectations for the return of Jesus. He didn't arrive. The hopes for the year 2000 have also been dashed. However, there is something special about the year 2000 that the year 1000 didn't have.

There are some who believe that the earth will have a 6,000-year life span from its creation until the coming of the 1,000-year reign of Christ. Some of this is tied in to the young earth chronology of Archbishop Ussher, which states that the earth was created in 4004 B.C. (see Chapter 4, "The Creation Controversy"). If you're following this chronology, the 6,000 years expired just a few years ago.

The 6,000 years also parallels the six days of creation, followed by a seventh (seven being a number of fulfillment), which is the long-awaited millennium. Thus, 2000 stands out as extra-special to those who put their bets on the apocalypse happening soon.

Revelations

Of great concern to government authorities, especially those in Israel, are the efforts of individuals or groups to "hasten" the coming of the apocalypse and thereby the coming, or the return, of the Messiah. These efforts include rebuilding the Temple in Jerusalem (see Chapter 12, "City at the Center of the World").

Come and Gone

As we saw in Chapter 13, "A Miraculous Life," the calendar used universally today was developed in A.D. 525, when a monk reformed the calendar then in use. The new calendar began its annual count from what was considered the most significant event in human history, the birth of Jesus. So the "zero" point was the birth of Jesus, and the count continues to this day.

This is all nice and convenient, except that there is strong evidence Jesus was born four to seven years earlier than year zero. In the real world, this doesn't particularly matter, since the calendar still serves just fine in providing us with a useful framework for orienting time.

But if you are someone who, for apocalyptic or other reasons, is overly concerned with the coming of the new millennium, or the year 2000, this might be especially important to you. If Jesus was born four years prior to year zero, the big millennial thing happened a few years before the year 2000 on our calendar.

Add to that the fact that even if the counting was correct, the new millennium doesn't really start until January 1, 2001! The year 2000 is the last year of the twentieth century, not the first year of the twenty-first. So add this to the earlier year for the birth of Jesus, and the "new millennium" passed you by way back in 1997, if not earlier.

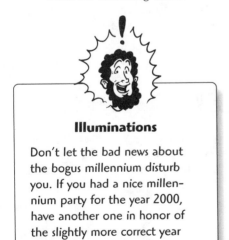

Illuminations

Don't let the bad news about the bogus millennium disturb you. If you had a nice millennium party for the year 2000, have another one in honor of the slightly more correct year 2001.

False Prophets

Several religious groups have been founded on the strength of predictions about the arrival of the apocalypse. Unfortunately, it's darned embarrassing when someone makes a big prediction about the end time, gives a deadline, and then nothing happens. This has happened repeatedly.

The typical response seems to be an admission of some human error that led to a miscalculation by a few years or perhaps a decade; this excuse gets the "prophet" temporarily off the hook and keeps the momentum of the organization going for a while. Too many false alarms, however, and you're going to lose your followers, as has been known to happen!

Some prophets continue to be popular even when their predictions don't quite pan out. Both Nostradamus and Edgar Cayce have come and gone, but people bring them up over and over again, thus revealing a human fascination with knowing the future.

Nostradamus: The Ambiguous Prophet

The famous French "prophet" Michel de Nostredame (1503–1566) was a physician who enjoyed peering into a bowl and foretelling the future. His prophecies were typically in the form of four-line verses, and he came up with a good many over a period of several years. In some ways they are reminiscent of Revelation in the sense that they are rarely specific and can be interpreted in a number of different ways.

There is one important difference, however. Although the credibility of the Book of Revelation can only be proved when its events unfold and Jesus arrives (because it doesn't give any specific dates using our calendar), Nostradamus made at least one prediction with a date: July 1999:

> In the year 1999, and seven months, from the sky will come the great King of Terror. He will bring to life the great King of the Mongols. Before and after, Mars reigns happily. (Century X:72)

July 1999 has come and gone, and maybe it's just me, but I haven't noticed a great King of Terror, or even the King of the Mongols—have you?

Edgar Cayce: The Sleeping Prophet

Edgar Cayce (1877–1945) was known as the "sleeping prophet" because he would drop into a trance and talk about many different things. He, too, provided some interesting scenarios with specific dates that didn't quite pan out. The lost continent of Atlantis, for example, was supposed to rise out of the ocean in the 1960s. It didn't happen.

Revelations

Humans have probably been interested in predicting the future from the get-go. Knowing when the best time might be to hunt, go to war, invest, or stay away from this or that is, if nothing else, a valuable survival skill. Astrologers and practitioners of divination were prominent in the Near East. Even today, it's still popular. Look at all of those people reading horoscopes and such in the newspapers!

VISIT
BEAUTIFUL
JERICHO!!

People and Places

The name **Koresh** is the Hebrew for the Persian king Cyrus, who freed the Jews from Babylon and sent them home to rebuild their Temple in Jerusalem.

Tragedy at Waco

Sadly, some self-styled prophets aren't content to let their prophesied apocalypses pass by quietly. One tragic recent case was that of self-proclaimed prophet and messiah Vernon Howell, a.k.a. David Koresh, who claimed he saw a vision of angels in Jerusalem. He started his own religious group, known as the Branch Davidians, and preached that the end was at hand.

In a great standoff with government troops, Koresh and more than 80 of his followers, including children, were burned to death in their compound in Waco, Texas. Koresh had his own mixed-up version of history and theology, but some experts have suggested that the tragedy at Waco might have been avoided if the officials involved in negotiations with Koresh had been Biblically knowledgeable. The symbolic and apocalyptic phraseology he used sounded like sheer babble to the uninformed.

Profits for Prophets

Walk into any Christian bookstore, and you'll probably find a big rack of volumes dealing with "prophetic literature." Dozens of these sorts of books have come and gone with the times. As the date for each set of predictions passes without result, room is left for the next crop.

There is also a boom in "apocalyptic fiction," which presents dramatic stories involving the Tribulation, the Antichrist, and other scenarios and characters from the Book of Revelation. There is also a market for television prophecy, whereby the signs of the times can be analyzed and presented as they continue to evolve.

The Final Judgment, as envisioned by Gustave Doré.

Jesus himself said that no one knows when he's coming back. So it would make sense that if you're a loyal follower, you'll simply continue your steadfast belief and live a good and responsible life, and you won't have too much to worry about.

God, Jesus, and/or the Messiah will appear in their own good time, and if you're ready, there you'll be. Nearly every generation reinterprets the Book of Revelation according to the negative events of its own time. Expect it to continue.

The Least You Need to Know

- The Book of Revelation has sparked controversy and confusion ever since it was written.
- Revelation provides a scenario for the end of time featuring death, mayhem, and the return of Jesus.
- Revelation has been repeatedly reinterpreted to fit various times and conditions.
- Because of a mix-up when the calendar was revised, the year 2000 is not the real millennium, which has already come and gone. Even so, doomsday predictions continue.

Chapter 23

What Does It All Mean?

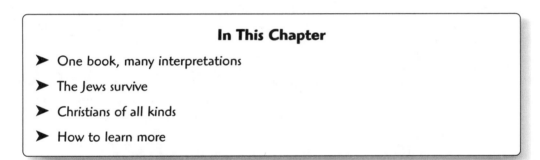

In This Chapter

- One book, many interpretations
- The Jews survive
- Christians of all kinds
- How to learn more

If you've read all the way through this book, you've been exposed to a lot of information about the Bible and its mysteries. In this chapter, I'd like to tie up a few loose ends. For one thing, I'd like to emphasize that despite the tremendous importance of the Bible, there are thousands of ways of looking at it.

In this chapter, we'll take a quick look at how the Bible-based religions developed their diversity and what the situation is like today. And then I'll leave you with a few of my own predictions for the future and a couple of tips about how you can learn more about the Bible and its study.

Changing Times

Let's start with a bit of post-Biblical Jewish and Christian history. When we looked at the story of Jesus, we saw that by his time there was already a fair amount of religious diversity among the Jews in Palestine. There were Pharisees, Sadducees, Essenes, political radicals, and probably a few other groups we don't know much about. Jesus came along and added yet another perspective.

With the final destruction in A.D. 70 of the Jewish center of worship, the Temple of Jerusalem, a new kind of Judaism would emerge. It continued to flourish without a central focus for worship and spread to many parts of the world as Jews fled oppression or otherwise settled in other lands.

Jesus Would Not Have Approved

It's a sad fact of history that religious intolerance has been both experienced and practiced by many followers of the Bible. Crusades, inquisitions, and other questionable acts were not uncommon. And it's not necessary to recite the long list of atrocities perpetrated against Jews, Christians, and others in the last two millennia.

The discrimination, trials, expulsions, and executions could, and in fact do, fill many books. The great human catastrophe known as the Holocaust, in which six million Jews and a good many Christians were murdered during the twentieth-century Nazi regime, is but one example.

Since 1945, when the extent of the Holocaust became apparent, many Jewish groups have vowed that such a thing should never happen again. "Never again" is a popular motto and, surprisingly, there are critics who complain that they are sick of hearing about it all. In response, Jewish historian and Holocaust survivor Elie Wiesel commented:

> "One Jew was put to death in Jerusalem two thousand years ago and the non-Jewish world has not ceased to speak of this death. Do we Jews not have the right, the duty, to keep alive the memory of the six million dead?"

A Dream Comes True, for Some

During the nineteenth century, a political movement known as *Zionism* gained popularity. Its goal was to create a Jewish state somewhere in the world where Jews could live freely without fear of persecution. The sentimental favorite was Palestine, the Promised Land, conquered in ancient times by the ancestors of the Jewish people, as described in the Bible.

Jewish emigration to Palestine began in earnest in the late nineteenth century and continued steadily into the twentieth. Many of the local inhabitants of modern Palestine, who were primarily Arab and Muslim, weren't pleased with what they saw as a foreign invasion. The end result of a very complicated and difficult political process was the establishment of the State of Israel on May 14, 1948.

Logos

Zionism is the political movement advocating the establishment and perpetuation of a homeland for the Jewish people.

The Past Becomes the Present

Wars broke out as soon as the Jewish state of Israel was established. A large number of Palestinian Arabs, both Muslims and Christians, felt they were being either physically displaced or otherwise made unwelcome in the new country, which was formed without the approval of all the people affected.

Thus, Israel's Arab neighbors attempted to destroy the new country; but after several major conflicts, Israel continues to survive intact today as a refuge for Jews from around the world. (For more details on this incredibly complex issue, see *The Complete Idiot's Guide to Middle East Conflict* by Mitchell G. Bard [1999].)

Illuminations

Some Jews and Christians see the establishment of the state of Israel as being a miracle of God or a Biblical prophecy fulfilled. Some groups consider it a major step in the scenario that will result in the coming of the Messiah or the return of Jesus.

The Battles Continue

Although peace treaties have been signed with Israel's neighbors Egypt and Jordan, the battle continues still. It is a conflict that is 3,000 years old, dating back to the conquest of the Promised Land. A central issue is a 1946 United Nations resolution that originally divided the territory of Palestine into Arab and Jewish states.

In 1967, large territories that had been under Arab control were occupied by the Israelis, displacing a number of Arabs, who became known as the Palestinians. Today, portions of the disputed territories are gradually being returned to the Arabs. Yet some Jewish groups still want the full measure of ancient territory described in the Bible, no matter who lives there now. Thus, the Biblical past continues to influence the present.

VISIT
BEAUTIFUL
JERICHO!!

People and Places

In a flashback to ancient Biblical animosity, the modern Iraqi leader Saddam Hussein enjoys publicly comparing himself to the ancient Babylonian king Nebuchadnezzar II. Nebuchadnezzar was responsible for destroying the Israelite city of Jerusalem in 586 B.C. and leading the Jews into captivity. Hussein wishes the same for the modern State of Israel.

Judaism Today

Judaism thrives in Israel today and in many other countries, with the largest population outside of Israel located in the United States. The majority of American Jews identify themselves as members of Reform or Conservative congregations, as opposed to the more traditional Orthodox.

The Reform and Conservative movements were the result of attempts to adapt and adjust Jewish worship and practice to more modern times. Whatever the mode of worship, though, the modern survival of the Jewish people after centuries of adversity is an amazing thing. (To learn more, check out *The Complete Idiot's Guide to Jewish History and Culture* [1999] or *The Complete Idiot's Guide to Understanding Judaism* [1999], both by Benjamin Blech.)

Revelations

In May 1991, in what was called "Operation Solomon," the Israeli government airlifted 14,000 Jews out of Ethiopia to a new home in Israel. The entire operation took only 48 hours!

How About Those Christians?

Pick up a telephone directory from any large American city and turn to the Yellow Pages. Now look at the listings under churches. What do you see? I'm betting it's a lengthy array of names and places. In the Tacoma, Washington, phone book, for example, one can find the following:

- Anglicans, Brethren, Seventh-day Adventists
- Assemblies of God, Bible Missionary churches
- Disciples of Christ, Churches of God in Christ, the United Church of Christ
- Covenant churches, Foursquare Gospel churches, Full Gospel churches
- Lutherans, Methodists, Episcopalians
- Nazarenes, Presbyterians, Roman Catholics

And that's just a sample.

Just among the group of Christian believers known as Baptists, you have the choice of attending a variety of congregations. They include the following:

- American Baptists, Baptist Bible Fellowships
- Conservative Baptists, General Conference Baptists
- Independents, Missionaries
- Baptist National Convention of America
- Reformed Baptists, Regular Baptists, Southern Baptists

You'll also find quite a diverse selection of congregations listed under the other major Protestant headings.

Illuminations

There are a growing number of "Messianic" Christian congregations which attempt to integrate Jewish and Christian traditions and practices. Some members are Jews who have accepted Jesus, while others are Christians who emphasize the Jewish roots of their own religion.

In the Beginning

Where did all of these different Christian groups come from? An explanation would take at least a book the size of this one, if not several, so I'll give you just a few highlights.

The original Christian church was established in the Roman Empire. In the early days, as you might recall, there were a variety of theological ideas floating around, particularly about the nature of Jesus.

In A.D. 313, Christianity became legal in the Roman Empire. The Council of Nicaea in A.D. 325, and other similar conferences, laid the foundation for agreement on many basic Christian principles. The center of the Church was established at Rome with the Pope as its spiritual leader. The religion quickly spread.

The Big Split

There were still significant differences in belief, however, and power and politics proved to be huge factors. In 1054, several of the churches in the eastern portion of the old Roman Empire split off from Rome and today are referred to as Eastern Orthodox churches. Each has its own patriarch, or spiritual leader, analogous to the Roman Catholic Pope.

Logos

Protestant churches are those that were formed in protest of the teachings, practices, and power of the Roman Catholic Church.

People and Places

Martin Luther was a German theologian who was a major figure in the Reformation. Luther was a monk until he was excommunicated from the Roman Catholic Church in 1521. His teachings and writings have had a tremendous effect upon the Christian Church, and a Protestant denomination, the Lutheran Church, is named after him in many countries. (Oddly, the Lutherans are known as Evangelicals in Germany.)

Meanwhile, most of western Europe fell under the domain of the Roman Catholic Church. In the 1500s, critics of the beliefs and practices of the Church began a movement known as the Reformation. The result was the formation of a number of *Protestant* churches, which separated from the overwhelming power of Rome.

Reformation leaders such as Martin Luther (1483–1546) and John Calvin (1509–1564) inspired churches that include the Lutheran, Presbyterian, and Methodist, which continue to thrive today.

Another major split with the Roman Catholic Church occurred in 1534, when English King Henry VIII refused to take orders from the Pope and set up the Church of England, also known as the Anglican Church. While the Anglican Church was following in the Protestant spirit, its members do not consider themselves Protestants, and even today it continues to be closer to the Catholic churches than to the Protestant in many important issues of doctrine and styles of worship.

The Christian Church continued to change as European colonization of the Americas opened up new prospects for the Christian religion. The New World hosted religious groups escaping persecution in Europe, or just looking for a place to do their thing.

With the establishment of the United States, a country guaranteeing religious freedom, new groups were formed, old ones split, and the end result is the dizzying variety we find today. Meanwhile, the Roman Catholic Church is still alive and well, and there is scarcely a place on this planet to which one religious group or another hasn't sent a missionary to spread the Word.

Revelations

Whereas the tendency for religious groups is to split, an interesting exception occurred in 1988. Three separate branches of the Lutheran Church—the American Lutheran Church, the Lutheran Church in America, and the Associated Evangelical Lutheran Churches—combined to form a single body, the Evangelical Lutheran Church in America. Still other groups of Lutherans remain outside of this body.

What's the Big Mystery?

What's the source of all of this Jewish and Christian variety? At their core, they're using the same book, the Bible, yet obviously they don't all agree on how to interpret it, as history demonstrates. And to me, this emphasizes one of the greatest mysteries of the Bible: What does it all mean?

Although the Bible is used as a spiritual handbook by many, the various interpretations can be so far afield that one often wishes God had left more detailed instructions and unambiguous directions.

Let's Get Ecumenical

In this modern age, it's interesting and hopeful to see a number of groups trying to find common ground rather than perpetuate divisiveness. Many Jews, Christians, and other groups, within and among themselves, are attempting to engage in meaningful dialogue.

Some Christian groups, long at odds with each other, participate in what is known as the *ecumenical* movement. Their aim is to find understanding and unity with each other so they can all get along and maybe even learn to appreciate one another, despite their seemingly irreconcilable differences.

Logos

The **ecumenical movement,** or **ecumenism,** involves dialogue between different religious groups in order to find common ground and understanding.

Words of Wisdom

"There are many theological questions which can be asked—even interesting ones, for which the truest answer this side of the grave is, 'I don't know.'"

—James A. Pike, *Beyond Anxiety* (1953)

So Who's Right?

If everyone thinks they've got the spin on God, Jesus, and religion in general, who's correct? A black-and-white perspective would say it can only be one of them, and the others are wrong in one way or another. On the other hand, could it have been God's intention for religion to be practiced and explored in different ways by different people?

This is yet another question to ponder, debate, and leave unanswered until the time comes when you meet your Maker and get the straight scoop. And while you're at it, ask God about the location of Noah's Ark, the authenticity of the Shroud of Turin, and all the other fascinating questions you've discovered in this book!

What's Next?

As has been the case during the last couple of millennia or so, the Bible will doubtless have a major impact in the centuries to come. Here are a few of my predictions for what's ahead:

- The Bible will continue to be translated and retranslated in languages both old and new.
- New archaeological discoveries and continued studies of the text will produce more insights into the Bible.
- A good many of the Bible's mysteries will remain unresolved.
- Bible-based religions will continue to evolve in many different ways.

How to Learn More

I hope you have enjoyed this book and its fascinating topic. I know that in writing it I've developed a deeper appreciation for the Bible and its numerous interesting facets. No matter whether you are an earnest believer or a hard-nosed skeptic, there is much to be gained by studying it. Following is a list of things you can do to further an interest in the Bible and its mysteries. (See Appendixes B, "Biblos," and C, "Scrollwork: Resources for Further Exploration," for more details.)

- Read some of the books on the subject. (Thank you for buying this one.)
- Attend different religious congregations and see how they differ.
- Take a class at a local church, synagogue, or college.
- Learn Hebrew, Aramaic, or Greek so you can read and study the Bible in the original languages.
- Keep an eye out for programs dealing with Biblical history and archaeology on educational television channels.
- Participate as a volunteer on an archaeological dig in Israel.
- Support Biblical research and archaeology with your money, assistance, or good wishes.
- Get on out there. Visit the Holy Land. There's nothing like seeing the real thing!
- Read the Bible and discover some of the mysteries for yourself!

Illuminations

In the old days, traveling preachers used to go from town to town spreading their Christian message. Today, the wonders of modern technology have allowed untold millions to be exposed to these teachings via radio, television, and now the Internet. If you like what you hear, there's more. If you don't, you can always change the channel!

See You Later

The best way I can think of to conclude this final chapter of our book on the Bible's mysteries is with a quote from that esteemed genius of the twentieth century, Albert Einstein. He addressed the subject of the mysterious in the October 1930 issue of *The Forum:*

> The most beautiful thing we can experience is the mysterious. It is the source of all true art and science. He to whom this emotion is a stranger, who can no longer pause to wonder and stand rapt in awe, is as good as dead: His eyes are closed.

The Least You Need to Know

- A number of different sects and divisions developed out of the original Christian Church in Rome.
- Religion has been the source of much persecution over the centuries, as well as much good.
- Some of the old conflicts in the Bible continue to be replayed in the modern world.
- Modern Christianity is an incredibly diverse religion with many hundreds of different viewpoints and practices.
- The Bible and its mysteries remains one of the most rich and fascinating subjects you will find anywhere.

Logos

A.D. *Anno Domini,* "the year of our Lord." The number of years since the birth of Jesus.

agnostics Those who acknowledge the possibility that God might exist, but aren't sure.

angel Any of several kinds of heavenly beings who serve God in heaven.

angelophany A sighting of an angel.

antediluvian The world before the Deluge.

Antichrist In the Book of Revelation, the Antichrist is Satan's agent on earth who will seduce the world into evil.

Apocalypse The events leading to the end of the world. From the Greek word meaning "revelation."

apocrypha Additional books found in some Bibles that aren't universally accepted.

apologetics The defense of one's beliefs.

apologists The practitioners of apologetics.

Ark of the Covenant A wooden box constructed under God's orders which contained the tablets of the law given to Moses, along with a couple of other important objects.

Arkologists Those who are interested in locating the remains of Noah's Ark.

atheists Individuals who don't believe God exists.

B.C. "Before Christ." Refers to the number of years before the birth of Jesus.

B.C.E. "Before the Common Era." The religiously neutral term referring to the same time period as B.C.

B.P. "Before Present." The number of years prior to the present. Essentially it means "years ago."

Bible A collection of books held sacred, particularly by Jews and Christians. The word "Bible" is derived from the Greek word *biblos,* which means "book."

bris A Jewish circumcision ceremony.

bulla (plural **bullae**) A clay seal bearing a stamp with an individual's name, typically used to seal documents.

C.E. "Common Era." The religiously neutral equivalent of A.D., the number of years since the birth of Jesus.

canonization The process by which potential parts of a book, or a group of books, are accepted or rejected on the basis of their appropriate merits.

Christ As derived from the Greek word *christos,* Christ means "Messiah."

Christians Followers of Jesus and his teachings.

codex A group of flat pages that are typically bound or assembled in book form.

creationists Those who believe that God created the earth as described in the Book of Genesis.

deists Those who believe in the general concept of the existence of God.

Deluge The great flood recorded in the book of Genesis.

ecumenism Engaging in dialogue between different religious groups in order to find common ground and understanding.

equidistant letter sequences (ELS) The phenomenon in which letters at equal intervals in a text are found to spell out words or phrases.

eschatology The study of the end of time, its literature, and the signs of its unfolding.

exegesis The process of analyzing the Biblical text.

gematria The study of numerical equivalents and relationships.

geniza A temporary repository for sacred Jewish documents until they can be properly buried or otherwise disposed of.

Gospel Greek for "good news," a Gospel is one of the four books of the New Testament—Matthew, Mark, Luke, and John—that described the life and teachings of Jesus.

Hebrew Bible The books of the Bible originally written mostly in Hebrew and known to Christians as the Old Testament.

Holy Grail The cup from which Jesus drank during the Last Supper. Some say it was also used to catch his blood after the Crucifixion.

infidel A pejorative term for someone who doesn't hold the same religious beliefs as you do.

Kabbalah The name for the Jewish mystical tradition and texts associated with it.

kashrut Rules relating to Jewish dietary laws.

kosher Clean or fit according to Jewish law. It applies especially to food, but refers to other things as well.

manna A kind of food that miraculously appeared on the desert ground in the morning to feed the wandering Hebrew people.

maximalists Those who believe in the general historical accuracy of the Bible.

Messiah An awaited savior sent by God to deliver his people from oppression and to restore the world. Christians believe that this Messiah is Jesus.

minimalists Those who argue that there is little compelling evidence that many of the events described in the Bible actually happened.

monotheism The belief in one God.

New Testament The Christian addition to the Hebrew Bible/Old Testament relating to the life and teachings of Jesus of Nazareth.

Old Testament A Christian term for the Hebrew Bible.

Original Sin The concept that humans have inherited the sinful nature of Adam and Eve.

Palestine A geographical term for the region in the vicinity of the modern state of Israel.

Passover A Jewish festival commemorating the Exodus story.

Penteteuch A Greek term referring to the first five books of the Hebrew Bible/Old Testament.

Pesach Same as Passover.

Pharaoh The ruler of ancient Egypt.

polytheism The belief in many gods.

proselytize To actively promote one's religious viewpoint with the aim of converting others.

Protestant churches Churches that were formed in protest of the teachings, practices, and power of the Roman Catholic Church; a follower of such views is called a Protestant.

pseudepigrapha Books which were supposedly written by notable people of the Bible.

Rapture An event in the end times when both living and deceased Christians will be taken to heaven.

relic An item associated with a Biblical individual or one of the saints. It can consist of an actual body part, an object related to the saint's life or death, or something that has come in direct contact with such parts or objects.

Rosary A set of Roman Catholic prayers performed as a kind of meditation. The prayers are typically counted off with a set of strung beads.

saint Ordinary Christian believers (as in "the communion of saints"), or used more specifically, a special status accorded to those who have led an exemplary and honorable Christian life.

scientific creationists Believers in God who look at the findings of science to demonstrate and confirm their belief in Biblical creation.

scroll A rolled-up manuscript which is unrolled for reading.

sindonology The study of the Shroud of Turin.

Tanach The Hebrew name for the Hebrew Bible, or Old Testament.

tell (or **tel**) A mound made up of the accumulated debris of human occupation.

tetragrammaton The four Hebrew letters, YHVH, which represent the personal name of God.

Torah The first five books of the Old Testament, sometimes referred to by its Greek name, the Penteteuch.

Tribulation As described in the Book of Revelation, a seven-year period of human and environmental catastrophe followed by the return of Jesus.

Yeshua The name "Jesus" in Hebrew.

Zionism The political movement advocating the establishment and perpetuation of a homeland for the Jewish people.

Zohar The primary written work of the Kabbalah.

Biblos

Looking to read some more? There are tens of thousands of books dealing with the Bible. For starters, check out some of these great tomes.

Achtemeier, Paul J., ed. *Harper's Bible Dictionary*. San Francisco: Harper and Row, 1985.

Aharoni, Yohanan, and Michael Avi-Yonah. *The Macmillan Bible Atlas*. New York: Macmillan, 1977.

Barnstone, Willis, ed. *The Other Bible*. San Francisco: Harper, 1984.

Bell, Jim, and Stan Campbell. *The Complete Idiot's Guide to the Bible*. New York: Alpha Books, 1999.

Beskow, Per. *Strange Tales About Jesus*. Fortress: Philadelphia, 1983.

Bickel, Bruce, and Stan Jantz. *Bruce and Stan's Guide to the End of the World*. Eugene: Harvest House, 1999.

Blech, Benjamin. *The Secret of Hebrew Words*. London: Aronson, 1991.

——. *The Complete Idiot's Guide to Jewish History and Culture*. New York: Alpha Books, 1999.

——. *The Complete Idiot's Guide to Understanding Judaism*. New York: Alpha Books, 1999.

Buttrick, George A., ed. *The Interpreter's Dictionary of the Bible*. Nashville: Abingdon, 1962.

Danker, Frederick W. *Multipurpose Tools for Bible Study*. Minneapolis: Augsburg Fortress, 1993.

Dart, John. *The Jesus of Heresy and History*. San Francisco: Harper and Row, 1988.

Deuel, Leo. *Testaments of Time*. New York: Alfred Knopf, 1965.

Doré, Gustave. *The Doré Bible Gallery*. Chicago: Clarke and Co., 1888.

Faid, Robert W. *A Scientific Approach to Biblical Mysteries*. Green Forest: New Leaf, 1993.

——-. *A Scientific Approach to More Biblical Mysteries*. Green Forest: New Leaf, 1994.

Finegan, Jack. *The Archeology of the New Testament: The Life of Jesus and the Beginning of the Early Church*. Princeton: Princeton University Press, 1992.

Friedman, David N., et al. *Anchor Bible Dictionary*. New York: Doubleday, 1992.

Gould, Stephen Jay. *Questioning the Millennium*. New York: Harmony Books, 1997.

Hanson, K. C., and Douglas E. Oakman. *Palestine in the Time of Jesus: Social Structures and Social Conflicts*. Philadelphia: Fortress, 1998.

Kee, Howard Clark, et al. *The Cambridge Companion to the Bible*. Cambridge: Cambridge University Press, 1997.

Mazar, Amihai. *Archaeology of the Land of the Bible, 10000–586 B.C.E.* New York: Doubleday, 1990.

McDonald, William J., et al. *New Catholic Encyclopedia*. New York: McGraw-Hill, 1967.

Metzger, Bruce M., and Michael D. Coogan, eds. *The Oxford Companion to the Bible*. Oxford: Oxford University Press, 1993.

Plaut, W. Gunther, ed. *The Torah: A Modern Commentary*. New York: UAHC, 1981.

Price, J. Randall. *In Search of Temple Treasures*. Eugene: Harvest House, 1994.

——-. *The Stones Cry Out*. Eugene: Harvest House, 1997.

Pritchard, James B. *Ancient Near Eastern Texts Relating to the Old Testament*. Princeton: Princeton University Press, 1969.

Reader's Digest. *After Jesus: The Triumph of Christianity.* Pleasantville: Reader's Digest, 1997.

——. *The Bible Through the Ages.* Pleasantville: Reader's Digest, 1992.

——. *Mysteries of the Bible: The Enduring Questions of the Scriptures.* Pleasantville: Reader's Digest, 1996.

Richards, Larry. *Every Miracle and Wonder in the Bible.* Nashville: Thomas Nelson, 1998.

Roth, Cecil. *Encyclopedia Judaica.* New York: Macmillan, 1971–1972.

Ryan, Donald P. *The Complete Idiot's Guide to Lost Civilizations.* New York: Alpha Books, 1999.

Shanks, Hershel. *Jerusalem: An Archaeological Biography.* New York: Random House, 1995.

——. *The Mystery and Meaning of the Dead Sea Scrolls.* New York: Random House, 1998.

Shanks, Hershel, ed. *Understanding the Dead Sea Scrolls.* New York: Random House, 1992.

Stern, Ephraim. *The New Encyclopedia of Archaeological Excavations in the Holy Land.* Westwood, New Jersey: Prentice Hall, 1993.

Stevenson, Jay. *The Complete Idiot's Guide to Angels.* New York: Alpha Books, 1999.

Walsh, Michael ed. *Butler's Lives of the Saints.* San Francisco: Harper, 1991.

Wilson, Ian. *The Blood and the Shroud: New Evidence That the World's Most Sacred Relic Is Real.* New York: Simon & Schuster, 1998.

Scrollwork: Resources for Further Exploration

Following are some other resources, besides books, that can help you pursue an interest in Biblical mysteries. These include specialty magazines and Web sites, along with a few other items of interest.

A word of caution about the Internet sites: Web sites come and go in the anarchistic world of the Information Highway. Sometimes they change addresses or disappear altogether. The Web site addresses in this appendix were current as of early January 2000. Needless to say, I am not responsible for their content, except, of course, for my own material on my own site.

Magazines

Archaeology Magazine is published by the Archaeological Institute of America. It provides well-illustrated articles and news on archaeological sites and subjects worldwide, including occasional topics of Biblical interest.

Archaeology
Subscription Service
P.O. Box 469025
Escondido, CA 92046-9659 USA
877-275-9782
www.archaeology.org/main.html

Bible Review offers illustrated feature articles on all aspects of the Bible, including controversial subjects.

Bible Review
c/o Biblical Archaeology Society
4710 41st Street NW
Washington, D.C. 20016
1-800-221-4644
www.bib-arch.org/br2.html

Biblical Archaeology Review is one of the most dynamic magazines that deal with Biblical archaeology and history. Along with the latest news and great articles by important scholars, it regularly contains sassy commentary on a variety of controversial issues and occasionally takes an activist stance.

Biblical Archaeology Review
c/o Biblical Archaeology Society
4710 41st Street NW
Washington, D.C. 20016
1-800-221-4644
www.bib-arch.org/bar2.html

Christian History magazine offers all sorts of interesting information about the life and times of Jesus and his followers through the ages.

Christian History
Subscription Service
P.O. Box 37055
Boone, IA 50037
www.christianity.net/christianhistory/current/

Near Eastern Archaeology (formerly *Biblical Archaeologist*) is produced by the American Schools of Oriental Research. As the title suggests, it deals with the Near East, the land of the Bible.

Near Eastern Archaeology
Membership/Subscriber Services
P.O. Box 15399
Atlanta, GA 30333-0399
www.asor.org/BA/BAHP.html

Opportunities to Participate

Many people dream of being an archaeologist and bringing the ancient past to light in some exciting locale. Although making a living doing such a thing calls for some real professional credentials, it's actually possible to get a piece of the action as an amateur. And if you're fascinated with the Bible, you're in luck!

Numerous excavations in Israel solicit volunteers to participate in real digs each summer. The volunteers range from young adults to people well into their retirement years, who work under the supervision of experienced archaeologists. Some excavations require dozens of volunteers, so if you're willing to pay your own expenses and work hard, you may be in for the experience of a lifetime!

- The January/February issue of *Biblical Archaeology Review* usually publishes a list of excavations seeking volunteers in Israel and sometimes Jordan. (See the magazine information given earlier.)
- The Archaeological Institute of America produces an annual Archaeological Fieldwork Opportunities Bulletin that is available for purchase. It lists field schools for training and volunteer opportunities. Order your copy from:

  AIA Order Department
  Kendall/Hunt Publishing Co.
  4050 Westmark Dr.
  Dubuque, IA 11000
  1-800-228-0810 or 319-589-1000
  www.archaeological.org/Publications/AFOB/afob.html
- The University of California, Los Angeles, maintains a Web site that lists Archaeological Fieldwork Opportunities. Check it out at www.sscnet.ucla.edu/ioa/afs/testpit.html

Learning the Languages

Would you like to be able to read the Bible in its original languages? You might try learning a little Hebrew or Greek. Both languages are still spoken today but in modern forms that differ somewhat from ancient times.

Hebrew is regularly used in the liturgy of Jewish congregations and ancient Greek can be found in use in Greek Orthodox churches. Many synagogues teach Hebrew in classes for children and adults. Courses in ancient Greek are typically taught at universities as part of their Classics or Ancient History curricula.

If you want to try to learn on your own, you might consider these volumes:

Hudson, D. F. *Teach Yourself New Testament Greek*. New York: David McKay, 1979.

Kelley, Page H. *Biblical Hebrew: An Introductory Grammar*. Grand Rapids: Eerdmans, 1992.

Simon, Ethelyn, et al. *The First Hebrew Primer* (3rd ed.). Albany: EKS, 1992.

Whittaker, Molly. *New Testament Greek: An Introduction*. London: S.C.M., 1980.

The Web

Here's a nice sample of Internet sites. Half the fun of the Web is the surfing, so use these as a starting point for the further exploration of Biblical mysteries.

General Sites

- **Bible 101 Biblical Studies Unit.** www.bible101.org/main.html
- **Catholic Encyclopedia.** www.newadvent.org/cathen/
- **Christianity On Line.** www.christianity.net/
- **Jewish/Roman World of Jesus.** niner.uncc.edu/~jdtabor/index.html
- **Judaism and Jewish Resources.** shamash.org/trb/judaism.html
- **Lambert Dolphin's Web Link.** www.best.com/~dolphin/URLres.shtml
- **Resource Pages for Biblical Studies.** www.hivolda.no/asf/kkf/rel-stud.html

Organizations and Institutions

- **American Schools of Oriental Research.** www.asor.org
- **Biblical Archaeology Society.** www.bib-arch.org/
- **British School of Archaeology in Jerusalem.** britac3.britac.ac.uk/institutes/jerus/index.html
- **Israel Exploration Society.** www.hum.huji.ac.il/ies
- **Israel Museum.** www.imj.org.il/
- **Vatican Museums.** www.roma2000.it/zmusvat.html

Biblical Archaeology

- **Christian Answers to Biblical Archaeology Questions.** www.christiananswers.net/archaeology/home.html
- **Dig the Bible, by Digger Doyle.** www.digbible.org/
- **Karen Meyer's Biblical archaeology page.** www.lpl.arizona.edu/~kmeyers/archaeol/bib_arch.html

Documents and Manuscripts

- **Ancient Biblical Manuscripts Center.** www.abmc.org
- **Apocrypha.** home.fireplug.net/~rshand/streams/scripts/enoch.html wesley.nnc.edu/noncanon.htm
- **Biblical Hebrew Resource Page.** www.reslight.addr.com/biblehebrew.html
- **Hellenistic Greek Language.** www.entmp.org/HGrk/
- **Nag Hammadi Library.** www.webcom.com/gnosis/naghamm/nhl.html
- **Orion Center for the Study of the Dead Sea Scrolls.** orion.mscc.huji.ac.il
- **Shrine of the Book.** www.imj.org.il/shrine/

Special Topics

- **Angels.** saints.catholic.org/angels.html
- **Ark of the Covenant.** happy.net.ut.ee/~chris/ark.html
- **Apocalypse.** www.pbs.org/wgbh/pages/frontline/shows/apocalypse/
- **Creationism.** books.nap.edu/html/creationism/mall.turnpike.net/C/cs/index.htm; suhep.phy.syr.edu/courses/modules/ORIGINS/origins.html; www.icr.org/
- **Holy Grail.** www.the-spa.com/kirk.burkins/GRAIL.htm; www.geocities.com/Athens/Delphi/3636/indexe.htm
- **Jerusalem.** www.jerusalem.muni.il/
- **Mary appearances.** members.aol.com/bjw1106/marian.htm
- **Noah's Ark.** arksearch.com/
- **Relics.** www.geocities.com/Athens/Olympus/9587/relics.html
- **Saints.** saints.catholic.org/index.shtml
- **Shroud of Turin.** www.shroud.org/
- **The Temple in Jerusalem.** www.temple.org.il/
- **The Tabernacle.** happy.net.ut.ee/~chris/holy1.html

The author's own Web site can be found at www.plu.edu/~ryandp/.

Index

Symbols

A

H

I

J

K

L

M

N

Q

R

S

T

U

V

W–X

Y–Z